MRS. ELLIOT'S HOUSEWIFE.

CONTAINING

PRACTICAL RECEIPTS IN COOKERY

BY

MRS. SARAH A. ELLIOTT.

OXFORD, N. C.

To do good, and to communicate, forget not.—HEB. xiii. 16.

Published by Left of Brain Books

Copyright © 2021 Left of Brain Books

ISBN 978-1-396-31916-7

First Edition

Table of Contents

THIS, MY FIRST OFFERING TO THE PUBLIC,

Is respectfully inscribed

TO THE PHILANTHROPIST,

GEORGE PEABODY,

IN GRATITUDE FOR HIS AID TO THE WOMEN OF THE SOUTH, AND FOR MENTAL AND MORAL IMPROVEMENT.

ENGLAND ERECTS SCULPTURED STONE TO ENDURE FOR AGES, BUT THE GOOD SEED SOWN IN THE HEARTS OF AMERICAN YOUTHS WILL ERECT A MONUMENT, "IN THE RANK OF GRACIOUS AFFECTION," TO STAND FOR ALL TIME TO COME.

SARAH A. ELLIOTT.

OXFORD, GRANVILLE COUNTY, NORTH CAROLINA.
Sept. 20th, 1869.

PREFACE.

Although one may not aspire to exert a wide influence like such women as Hannah More, Harriet Newell, or Isabella Graham, it is still true that there is an influence in woman, always pervading and powerful, and the importance of exerting it in every sphere of life should be deeply impressed upon her mind. The change of times in the South indicates to woman there a solemn duty. In the discharge of it she must look to God, to sustain her. Her influence at home and abroad over her *own sex*, and through the various circles of human life, makes it a duty to call into action the power of the mind, and lay every resource under contribution. Woman exerts a vast influence upon society as well as in the ordinary scenes of life, and to her is intrusted a moral power that hardly knows a limit. The mother exerts an influence that years will never dislodge, though the child may be far removed from her. The wife can exert it over her husband for good; to her the instruction of children, the regulation of the domestic, and the entire management of the household are committed, and her dominion should be in her family circle. Feeling the extent of that influence, that ought to be written on every female heart, I have prepared a work, original in its ideas and novel in this progressive age.

I have not aimed at great attainments in science or literature, but with a view of accomplishing some good in the household, I offer these receipts for cooking. When the care of all that appertains to the interest of him woman vows to love, honor, and obey, is committed to her charge, she will not find that anything adds more to the consummation of his perfect and complete happiness, than a well regulated, systematic management of his household affairs.

Two years ago I heard an address delivered by Dr. Leroy M. Lee, whose talent is too well known to require an elaborate encomium from my pen. Upon a friendship formed in early years (that difference in church doctrine has never lessened) I requested the following selection, to give it circulation in the "Housewife." "Our young ladies need a chemistry, that understands the merit of soap, knows how to make it, and *loves* to use it; that, appreciating good bread as a cardinal virtue of personal comfort and family happiness, studies the hidden qualities and mysterious workings of yeast, the art of *kneading*, and of first and second rising, and of baking; and preserves quiet, and promotes good humor, by daily deliverances of rolls, biscuit, and bread, and veritable hot cakes, that rest on their plates as graceful and light as foam on the sea; that extracts stains and stings from the heart; that disintegrates the 'rocks of offense' in domestic life; that displaces the 'stones of stumbling' from the manners and characters of the household; that analyzes the contents of the family purse and consults the thermometer of prudence for the temperature of home economy; that gathers and groups the elements and affinities of the family into a compound of order, harmony, and love; that distills from sorrow and trouble a precious perfume and balm for wounded spirits; that crystallizes the tears of the household into precious jewels of grace and loveliness; and transmutes the family circle into a crystal palace, peerless in beauty, graceful in its proportions, and glorious in its furnishings for personal comfort and social happiness. Such I desire my feeble effort to teach; and when with this she can add painting with artistic taste and skill, and with artless coloring, upon the sacred substance of her own soul, portraits of Faith, Hope, and Charity; pictorial representations of the power 'of the world to come,' as a power in her own heart, and, especially, in the world of her own life; landscape views of heavenly life in the home circle, its tranquil pleasures, its diligence in sowing good seed in gentle and stony hearts, its joyous harvest songs, its silver fringed clouds, and its ever-shining light, streaming down on hill and valley, forest and fountain, from the Great Father of Lights through the Sun of righteousness and peace embroidering her heart and home life with soft, delicate, and many colored threads of patient toil and loving care; filling up the texture of daily life with flowers of beauty in words of kindness and deeds of love; making even common duties to take the form and order of holy employments; and working into all the habits of the household, and of her own thoughts, feelings, and actions, the order, regularity and beauty of 'wrought needlework of scarlet and fine linen;' clothing herself with 'the garment of salvation,' and wearing on all occasions, as the most precious and priceless of all garniture, the white robes of purity and peace, gemmed and crowned with 'the ornament of a meek and quiet spirit;' and music, child of the skies, light, life, and love vocalized music, whether scientific or natural, vocal or instrumental, secular or sacred, anyhow, anywhere, always a power and always in place, when the heart's in tune—the soul singing is 'the soul of song;' music, a charm and a power, of which God gave the use, but of which too often and too generally the devil has the control and application; music, not a fashionable accomplishment of fashionable hours for fashion's sake, but an embellishment of personal character, a graceful expression of the otherwise inexpressible sentiments and feelings of the soul, as, in its gladness and hope, it stretches up to catch and reëcho the descending strains of the singing angels, making heaven and earth vocal with their jubilee song of Glory to God in the highest, peace on earth and good will to man.

"Music, sweet music, while working and at rest; in the pantry, in the chamber, in the parlor; over the *cradle of infancy*, and by the couch of the dying; in the closet of secret prayer; in the devotions of family worship, in the assemblies of God's people on the holy day in the holy place, singing not, in the absurd notion, as a part of worship, but as worship itself; singing out of and up to the realized sense of personal religious life, whose source is heaven, and whose inspiration is love; 'singing with grace' and 'making melody in the heart unto the Lord,' fulfilling, in experience and expression, the prescript of the Apostles, 'Let the word of Christ dwell in you richly in all wisdom teaching and admonishing one another in psalms and hymns and spiritual songs; singing with grace in your hearts to the Lord,'—a kind of music this, not as fashionable as it deserves to be, but yet ennobling and transforming, first learned amidst earthly toils and cares, and then, and forever to be sung as the new song of heaven. With these deportment, comprising not, as its sum total of character and object, the easy mannerisms of polite and fashionable society, but the gentle outflowings, in home life and daily duty, of true womanly excellence, in personal goodness and social usefulness; a character, self-reliant, and sustained, not by pride of wealth and station, or the gay trappings of costly adorning, but by the power of an inward life of grace and truth, seen in gentleness and purity of conduct, and in modesty, simplicity, and *economy of apparel*; and *felt* in earnest efforts to multiply home comforts, and lessen household expenses; a dignity of honor and honesty that declines all acquaintance with *'bills of the store'* and loves 'Pay as you go' or refuses to go at all; and that is brave-hearted enough not to 'eat the bread of idleness' nor to waste the energies of the intellectual and moral nature in the reading of novels, and the pursuit of the deceptive and pernicious frivolities of a life of pleasure; in short, a deportment involving a grade of character resting on goodness, governed by duty, and guided by *religion*, that refines the feelings and gives the charms of grace and *dignity* to the conduct; and that realizes in personal experience and social approval the full measure of the inspired sentiment and assurance, 'Favor is deceitful and beauty is vain; but a woman that feareth the Lord, she shall be praised.' Yes, praised by all who have sense enough to discern and appreciate true excellence of character; and to discriminate between the substantial virtues of the queen bee in the orderly management of the home hive. With such instructions, may not the result be a vision of brightness and beauty bursting upon the mind, and growing with ever expanding glory before the imagination; our land blooming with the freshness and fragrance of a garden; homes of peace and plenty multiplying on every hand; busy hands and happy hearts filling all the places of life with contentment and joy; the sad past be forgotten, and Time and Providence healing the wounds and effacing their scars. The living present is the good time to come; come with its heart full of love, and its hands full of blessings; and the future is, to faith and hope, as gorgeous as a saint's vision of the holy city, descending from God out of heaven.

"In that good time coming, and to be hastened by the busy hands and blessed agency of educated and holy women, daughters of the South, ye who heed these instructions, will occupy a prominent and honorable position of labor and love. May it happily be exclaimed, 'many daughters have done virtuously; but thou excellest them *all.*'"

WEIGHTS AND MEASURES.

About twenty drops of any thin liquid will fill a common size teaspoon.
Four tablespoonfuls, or half a gill, will fill a common wine-glass.
Four wine-glasses will fill a half pint, a common tumbler, or a large, coffee cup.
A quart black bottle holds in reality about a pint and a half.
Ten hen eggs weigh one pound before they are broken.
A tablespoonful of salt is generally about one ounce.
One pound of butter is one quart.
One pound of flour is one quart.
One pound of loaf sugar is one quart.
One pound and two ounces of Indian meal are one quart.
One pound and two ounces of brown sugar is one quart.
One pound and one ounce of powdered sugar are one quart.

PRELIMINARY.

FIRST DIRECTION.

The first direction I offer is to have every convenience in your kitchen your means will allow, to prepare each meal expeditiously. If you use a stove, see that your wood is cut the right length, so the door will shut tight, and kept near at hand; have your holders in place to remove the covers; put on your tea-kettle filled with water, and as the fire burns, that will heat and be in readiness to scald your pans. Have a shelf on the right hand of the stove and a table near it; have nails or pegs on the edge of the shelf to hang towels, wash-rags, and mops on, and a dish with soap on the shelf. Have a standing rule that there must be soap kept in it, and the articles for use hung up immediately after being used, to avoid a search when in haste to take up the meals or prevent overcooking. Have a drawer in the table in which to keep the knives and forks, cake-turners, and spoons which you require in cooking, and on the table a piece of sheet iron or tin to set the hot pans or stove-covers on. If you have no closet in your kitchen, have a large tin safe or a cupboard to keep your cooking utensils in, and have them always cleaned after being used, and put in their respective places—iron ware on lower shelves, pans and moulds on the upper. You will find not only economy of time by attending to these rules, but a great saving in their use. Nothing is more calculated to ruffle the temper than having to wait for an article to be cleaned we are in a hurry to use, particularly if unexpected company requires an addition to the meal. Have a standing order for water to be always in the kettle during cooking hours, for there is constant need of it, not only for proper cleanliness, but to add to soups or other boiled dishes. In addition to the utensils usually sent with a stove, have a porcelain kettle for custards, preserving and pickling oysters, a porcelain saucepan for boiling rice, milk, and little delicacies for the sick, tin and earthen pans for puddings, and shallow plates for pies. If there is no steamer to fit the top of the dinner-pot, have one made of tin, to cook your Irish potatoes in, and one to fit the large tin boiler, with a fish slice in it to boil rock-fish or sheep's-head.

The same rules apply to a range, but those who are not so fortunate as to have either stove or range, will have to be guided by different ones, in the open fire-place, with the Dutch oven to bake in, spider to fry in, broiling irons to broil on, and a crane in the chimney to hang pots and kettles on. In our good old days, how well I remember seeing a large ham, from the well-filled smoke-house, nicely washed and put in a large dinner-pot of cold water, and hung on the crane, to be swung back over a hot hickory fire, cracking and burning to prepare coals for the numerous dishes to be cooked on the wide hearth in front; and when the ham was partly done, cabbages quartered and dumplings of corn meal made up with the "pot liquor" were thrown in to have the rich flavor of the ham imparted to them; then smaller pots on the crane, with soup of some kind, corn or bouillon beef, vegetables of every variety as they were to be cooked, and before this hot fire a turkey and pig hung up to be roasted (or placed in a tin kitchen made for that purpose); Dutch ovens filled with chicken and oyster pies, baking in large pans; spiders with chickens frying and ducks baking; fish boiling and fish stewing; and at the same time a rich English plum-pudding boiling, to take its place at the head of dessert, prepared the day before, of orange, lemon, citron, and cocoa-nut puddings, jellies, trifles, syllabubs, blancmange, ice-cream, and fruits to tempt the palate of invited guests; and though stoves and ranges are more convenient, yet they can never equal the good old fire-place, when managed by one of our well skilled Southern cooks.

PROVIDING FOR THE TABLE.

Providing for the table should be guided by the means that you can honestly command. Within the reach of all there is a style in which the millionaire's wife in her gilded walls cannot surpass the wife of the peasant in her humble dome. It is, that the prominent feature of her table should be cleanliness, with a tasteful arrangement of the dishes bearing the savory meats to tempt the appetite.

The snow-white cover, damask or home-made (or the clean white table with those unable to enjoy the luxuries of life), speaks the character of the housewife. With her pure white china or ware, polished from hot water and soap, her castors bright and well-filled, her knives and forks shining, the napkin folded tastily in the crystal goblet and the salt-cellar with fine sifted salt by each plate, the nicely printed butter with bright spoons lying by, her husband is not afraid to urge a friend to partake of his frugal meal. "Knowing her household is clothed with scarlet," he is sure the repast will be made sweet by the influence of her smile, when recommending the dishes as his favorites, and the absence of all apologies.

A Place for Everything and Everything in Place.

Housekeepers in the country villages or through the South, have not the many conveniences city ladies enjoy, therefore they are entitled to more credit for their skill. This work is prepared for the rising generation in the Southern States, but the receipts given for cooking will tempt the most fastidious taste. They are the result of twenty years experience, not only from presiding over a household, but as a superintendent of fairs and feasts for church and charitable purposes during that time. I acknowledge my indebtedness to Mrs. Randolph of Virginia and Miss Leslie of Pennsylvania for many useful recipes in preparing for my table and feasts, and some few selections from their admirable works could not be resisted, to add to my practical experience. My first instructions are given to the kitchen. My second comprises the dining-room, pantry, smoke-house, daily-room and others. With the dining-room well arranged, white walls free from webs and specks, carpets swept, or floor nicely scoured, the snow-white table spread for a repast, will give zest to a meal, be it ever so frugal, that unwashed windows and a careless air of a room can never invite. The old-fashioned cupboard and sideboard have given place to pantries attached to the dining-room that are very convenient. Shelves put up on the wall, with glass doors in front, for china and glass; net wire-work doors for cold food and drawers underneath for table linen and other articles for use; with a table or wide shelf in one corner to place cup pan, soap dish and brush on, and hooks above to hang cup towel, mop, and wash-cloth. On the lower shelf, with glass front, arrange dishes for breakfast and tea, the tea-pot with strainer on the spout, coffee-pot and hot water kettle, basket for silver, and box for knives, with a waiter for salt-cellars and butter save-alls. Next shelf, goblets, castors, and dinner dishes; and extra glass and dishes on the upper. If you have no dairy-room or tin safe to keep your milk in, place it on lower shelf with wire front. These arrangements will enable you to spread or clear off a table with dispatch. Always have your knives cleaned when breakfast dishes are being washed, castors inspected and well filled. Keep a piece of silver soap or whiting near at hand, with woolen cloth to polish the stand and remove any green spot the vinegar may have made. On opposite corner have a hook for the broom and duster, and large boxes made with lids to keep meal, flour, and sugar, secured by a lock. I once visited a systematic farmer, near my home, who had a place for everything, and, by the influence of a good wife, everything was in place. The dairy-room was under a shady tree with a pump close at hand; under the roof, back and front, a ventilator, with the milk pans hanging near; an upper shelf for jars of butter, and lower cross shelves, with sliding doors in each end, made deep and tight to hold water for the milk pans to be placed in. A simple trough conveyed the water from the pump to the deep shelf, and three times a day the opposite sliding door was raised, when cool water was pumped in, to let the other flow in a reservoir for the cows. After they drank, the stop was taken out of the bung at the side, water ran off, stop replaced, and when their thirst was again to be quenched, all was fresh and no stagnant water to produce disease. These hints, with the modern improvements, may appear stale, yet remember all parts of our vast country have not the improvements at hand and must be guided by simple rules. In a straight line with the dairy-room was the smoke-house, with two doors, one strong to secure it by night and the other latticed to admit the air, particularly *when curing bacon.* It was made rat-proof by brick-work around the sills between the sleepers, before the floor was laid; in the centre a brick oven, arched over the top (with sides open) to prevent an accidental blaze heating the meat while being smoked from hickory chips; on the side a narrow room for sausages and tom thumbs to be cured, getting a portion of the smoke through an aperture in the partition, and large jars of souse meat, tied up on the shelves. Next was an ash-house with a beam extended out in front, a large iron hook on it under the extended roof, with a copper kettle hanging, and that was used by twenty persons to take the ashes from the great house and cabins, and deposited in its place immediately after using it. Then the soap-house, with barrels around for the grease from cabins and kitchen, and soft soap, with the measure by the barrel, and dipper to fill the measure, and shelves arranged around with white and brown bars of hard soap, a knife to cut them, and give to each servant, on their washing day, to encourage cleanliness and work systematically. Next was the wash-room, with its huge boilers, and every convenience, joining the nice kitchen, with everything at hand to make the work light, and prepare meals seldom excelled. Near a tasteful flower-garden, under the shade of a broad oak-tree, was the hospital for the sick, to be carefully attended to by a trained nurse, everything having an air of comfort and cleanliness. To their memory I recount this as a guide for systematic management, not forgetting the well-stored cellar with potatoes in one end, lard and pickled meats in the other. The sweet potatoes were taken from the ground by hand and placed in large tubs, the tubs placed in a wagon and backed up to the door, and then taken out, one by one, and corded as we do wood, with occasionally a layer of dry straw between. They were packed wall high on the sides and one end, with an open space for a small stove, that fire was kindled in from bark, during a very severe freeze, and from that room from one September to the next, could nice sound sweet potatoes be taken, simply because they were handled carefully, not bruised, and a *little* pains taken to preserve them. In fact, I have ate old potatoes cooked for Christmas from that cellar fifteen months from the time they were dug. The part for meat in hogsheads and lard had nice shelves for jars, all marked with the initials of his name, and when they were filled with butter or lard to send to their merchant, there was no delay in selecting them from others, that had been sent from another source, or to retain the jars until the butter was retailed to customers in a small village. Wood, cut by measure, and kindling, were packed in one room for the wife's special use, with the sawhorse and saw, axe, hatchet, and iron mallet near the door. Through the well-swept yard (with pump *between* house and kitchen, nicely paved around with brick) it was pleasant to walk and see the sheep and hogs when driven from the pasture, each go in their respective stall under the low shelter erected for them; and I conclude by saying, what man has done, man can do.

SELECTION OF SERVANTS.

In the selection of your servants, seek those who are neat in their apparel and cleanly in their habits. Tell them you require it, and unless they conform strictly to your rules, you cannot employ them. It is a good plan to demand written recommendations from their previous employers. Avoid all that are known to be given to open bad habits, tattling from house to kitchen, using bad language, indulging in intoxicating drinks, and the awful practice of snuff rubbing, too much indulged in by our *Southern cooks*. Tell them of its bad effects, the stimulating effect, and injury to the brain; the coating of the stomach that prevents digestion, and engenders disease that often baffles the physician's skill; the sin of the deception that is practiced with the abominable habit, and *tax* on their wages, and give them, withal, the opinion of a celebrated divine, who, when asked if he thought snuff rubbing injured the brain, replied, he could not tell, as his opinion was, no woman that *had* brains would use it.

SOUPS.

TURTLE SOUP.

Kill and clean a turtle very early in the morning and lay it in cold water. Wash and scrape the shell nicely. If a loggerhead, the largest size will only make one gallon of good soup. If sea-turtle, use eight pounds. Put it in your soup-kettle at eight o'clock, if wanted at three, with two gallons of water. Put in a hock of ham and the shell with it, and boil briskly. As soon as the shell is hot, take it out and scrape all the meat out of the inside, and return the meat to the kettle. Tie up in a thin bag some thyme and sweet marjoram, and at eleven o'clock put it in with a tablespoonful of salt, pepper grains, and allspice. At one o'clock put in the juice of one lemon. Take out the hock when you put the spice in. Rub some brown flour smoothed with some of the soup, and thicken just before you wish it served, giving it one good boil, stirring all the time. Take out the bag with thyme and pour it in a tureen and add one pint of sherry or Madeira wine to the gallon. Cut a lemon in slices and put it in with the yelks of four hard-boiled eggs. Chop some of the turtle from the bottom of the kettle, season it with pepper and salt. Mix in a few bread crumbs and make it in little cakes with beaten yelks of two eggs. Fry it in butter and put them on the top of the soup. You can strain this through a colander if you choose, but it will be better if poured off carefully from the kettle.

BEEF SOUP.

Put on very early in the morning a piece of beef, and boil it in two gallons of water; put in a nice hock of bacon. At ten o'clock, put in one gallon of peeled tomatoes, one pint of butter beans, two Irish potatoes, two carrots, one pint of chopped cabbage, a teaspoonful of sugar, and twelve okras cut in slices, with two onions chopped fine. One hour after you put them in, add a pint of green corn cut off the cob and a spoonful of salt, with a pod of red pepper.

This is a nice soup, but you can make it richer by beating eight eggs light, and stirring in them enough of the hot soup to cook them, and then adding it to the soup pot as you take it off. If you wish it extra, after you put it in the tureen, stir in a half pint of wine and half a lemon sliced up. Chop some of the meat with a little cold ham. Make it up into balls with bread crumbs, and a yelk of egg; season them highly with pepper and fry them, then place on the top of the soup. Have toasted bread to eat with it.

Soup Made with Beef Shank.

Break the bone in a beef shank after it has been carefully washed in cold water, put it in a dinner-pot by eight o'clock in the morning, and nearly fill the pot with cold water. Let it boil briskly; at ten, put in one tablespoonful of salt, and two of onion chopped fine; cut up small some white cabbage and add next; then peeled tomatoes with green corn cut off the ear, some okra cut fine and one pod of red pepper, and boil steadily until it is wanted for dinner, at one or two o'clock. Some persons like one tablespoonful of sugar in this soup and a few butter beans. In winter use cabbage, and dried tomatoes or tomato sauce; when that is used, do not put the salt in the soup. If you require it very thick, rub one spoonful of browned flour smoothed with cold water, and stir it in the soup just before you serve it, or have some nicely boiled rice and put one spoonful in each plate of soup as you serve it at table.

Oyster Soup.

Take two quarts of water, or the liquor of boiled fowls; put in it three pints of oysters, salt and pepper to your taste, one tablespoonful of butter rubbed in the same of flour. Beat the yelks of four eggs and mix them with one pint of sweet milk and the liquor from the oysters (after it has been strained), and add them to soup. Let it cook a few minutes; then pour it in a soup tureen with a few slices of dry toasted bread in the bottom, and serve it hot. Very fine.

CHICKEN SOUP.

Put one or two nice large hens in your soup pot, with a piece of the hock from a ham, one teacup of nicely washed rice and a spoonful of salt, fill the pot nearly full of cold water, and after it boils (if you like them) add one quart of peeled tomatoes, and one pint of green corn cut from the ear, with a little thyme, chopped fine. Just before you dish it, rub one spoonful of flour and one of butter together and stir the soup well; give it a boil up and serve hot.

CALF'S HEAD SOUP.

Clean the head nicely, divide the chop from the skull, take out the brains and tongue, and boil the other part until it is tender put in a knuckle of veal or four pounds of lean beef. Chop three onions and put in, with a bunch of thyme and parsley tied in a muslin rag; beat twelve cloves fine, two blades of mace and a dozen grains of allspice; put that in a bag too (the flavor is all that is wanted and the soup is nicer without the grains), boil it in one gallon of water and boil down to three pints, then add half a pint of wine, some Worcester sauce or tomato catchup, with a few slices of lemon, and thicken it with brown flour rubbed smooth in butter. This is frequently called mock turtle soup, and is a good imitation.

CALF'S HEAD STEW.

Take the pieces of meat from the soup pot and chop them fine, put them in a saucepan with some of the gravy and stew it. Pick the brains and mix them with grated bread, pepper, and salt, and work them in small cakes with the yelk of an egg; fry them and put them in the soup after it is placed in the tureen. Put paste around the stew that is baked separately; put that in a dish, and add catchup and a few hard boiled eggs.

GRANVILLE HOUSE SOUP.

Put a large piece of beef on to boil early in the morning. At nine o'clock put in a stew-pan twelve onions, two turnips cut up, one head of celery, quarter of a pound of butter, and one quart of the water from the beef; let them stew an hour, then season high with black pepper and salt, and stir it in the soup. Before taking it up, stir in a pint of boiled cream, and have a dozen small onions, boiled in milk and water, to put in after it is dished. Serve it with Odenheimer sauce. The beef can be hashed up and stewed, put in a dish and garnished with sliced pickled cucumber and a hard boiled egg.

DRIED PEA SOUP.

Put one pound of peas and two slices of bacon to boil. (If bacon is not convenient, one large teaspoonful of butter or lard will answer.) Let it boil until the peas are tender enough to mash. Boil separately some mutton in slices, or pieces of beef, with salt and pepper, six carrots cut up, and six turnips, with one gallon of water. After they have boiled well for two hours, strain the peas in through a sieve, and let it boil nearly one hour more. This soup is very popular in Louisiana with whole or split peas.

FISH SOUP.

Any kind of fresh fish can be used for soup. Always stew them with vegetables and sweet herbs, and strain the liquor from them into a soup pot and add any seasoning you like. Celery and cayenne pepper adds much to the taste.

LOBSTER SOUP.

Put one dozen onions, one slice of beef and ham, and a small piece of butter in a stew-pan. When the onions are soft, mix them with some rich stock you have for soup; boil, skim, and strain it through a sieve. Beat the meat of a haddock that has been boiled, the spawn and body of a large lobster, or two small ones, in a marble mortar; add it gradually to the soup and stir it until smooth. Let it boil again and skim it, add some cayenne pepper, a glass of wine, and the tail and claws of the lobster, cut in fine pieces, and serve it hot.

Tomato Soup.

Cut up a chicken and four slices of bacon in one gallon and a half of water. After they have well boiled put in one gallon of tomatoes, with a tablespoonful of sugar, two small onions, salt and pepper, and boil until all are well done. Just before taking it up rub a large spoonful of flour in butter, thin it with some of the soup and stir it slowly in; let it have one boil and serve it hot. This is *excellent*.

Oyster Soup. No. 2.

Put two quarts of oysters with three quarts of water, three onions chopped up, two or three slices of lean ham, pepper and salt; boil it down to three pints and strain it from the oysters through a sieve. Put the liquor and one quart of fresh oysters in the pot; stir two gills of cream, four spoonfuls of flour, and the yelks of eight eggs together, and mix it in the liquor, boiling it a few minutes, then turn in all in a soup tureen and serve hot.

Soup Made with Tough Fowls.

Cut off the legs and wings and the breast from the ribs,—do not use the back,—wash the pieces and put them in a soup pot with a slice of bacon, one onion cut up, some pepper and salt. Tie up some thyme and parsley in a thin rag and drop it in, boil it gently three hours, (add two spoonfuls of rice if you like it,) thicken it with two spoonfuls of flour rubbed in butter, and if you wish it add to the thickening the yelks of two eggs and half a pint of milk. I prefer it without the milk.

Green Pea Soup.

Put two quarts of green peas in three quarts of water and boil them two hours; then strain them from the liquor, return that to the pot and put in a slice of nice pork or bacon, with one onion chopped fine, a little thyme, salt and pepper. When the meat looks done, thicken the soup with butter rubbed in one spoonful of flour and mixed smooth with some of the liquor before it is put in the pot. Toasted bread, buttered, must be sent in with it.

ASPARAGUS SOUP.

Take three large handfuls of asparagus, cut off one inch of the tops and lay them in water, chop the stalks and put them in a soup pot, with one onion cut up, pepper and salt, and three quarts of water; boil briskly. When the stalks are done, strain them from the liquor, put that back with the tops, a hock of ham and a fat chicken. Boil it until the chicken is done, and thicken it with flour and butter rubbed together, and wet with some of the soup or milk.

MACARONI SOUP.

Boil one quart of milk and one pound of macaroni cut in small pieces and scalded in hot water before it is put in the milk. When it looks tender take out part of it, add another quart of milk and boil it up, then add the other macaroni and a quarter of a pound of cheese; let it simmer awhile but not boil. Add a piece of butter rolled in flour, some salt and pepper, and have toasted bread to eat with it. Cold soup, kept from the meat soup the day before, and strained, can be used instead of milk.

VERMICELLI SOUP.

Break the bones of a knuckle of veal or a neck of mutton in small pieces, and put them in a soup pot; put in a hock from a ham, two onions, a bunch of sweet herbs, and a head of celery, with a quarter of a pound of butter. Let it cook for one hour over a slow fire. Skim it and put one gallon of water to it boiling hot; keep it boiling until the meat has left the bone, strain it, set it on the fire and add a quarter of a pound of vermicelli that has been scalded in hot water; season it with salt and cayenne pepper and let it boil fifteen minutes. Lay slices of bread in the bottom of the pan and pour the soup over it. This soup is elegant, made with two chickens, with their bones all broken up before putting them on to stew.

MILK SOUP.

Blanch one quarter of a pound of almonds and put them in half a gallon of milk with a stick of cinnamon; stir in two tablespoonfuls of sugar; when it boils up strain it. Beat the yelks of six eggs, set it on the fire and stir the eggs in by degrees until it thickens. Take it off instantly for fear it may curdle.

CREAM SOUP.

Break a knuckle of veal and put it on early in the day with two gallons of water let it boil until only two quarts. Then strain it and season it with white pepper, a little salt, mace, and lemon juice. Mix a tablespoonful of flour with one teacup of sweet cream and stir it in the soup; give one boil up and serve in a tureen with cover. Always boil cream and strain it before adding to the soup. I think the friend that gave me this and the following recipe learnt it from Mrs. Hale's Cookery.

CURRY SOUP.

Season two quarts of veal broth with two onions, a bunch of parsley, salt, and pepper; strain it and return it to the pot with one chicken cut up and skinned, and one tablespoonful of curry powder. Boil until the chicken is tender, and just as you dish it pour in one cup of cream with the juice of a lemon. Have rice boiled to serve with it.

NEW ORLEANS GUMBO.

Put one *large* spoonful of lard in your soup pot, and stir in it, until it browns, two large spoons of flour; cut up in small pieces one large, fat chicken, and put it in the pot with the lard and flour, and cover it over to stew. Cut up one pound of lean beef, very fine, and one slice of ham, two large onions chopped, teaspoonful of thyme, parsley and marjoram, one pod of red pepper, and one spoonful of salt; add them to the other ingredients, with four quarts of boiling water, and boil it briskly for two hours. When ready to dish it, take the pot off and stir in one large teaspoon of feela. Have some rice boiled nicely and sent to the table in a covered dish, and put one spoonful in the plate and then pour the gumbo in as you serve it. Have nice light bread or toast to eat with it.

Oysters may be used in place of chicken.

OKRA GUMBO.

One tablespoonful of lard and two of flour carefully browned in a pot; cut in fine bits one large chicken and put it in to stew half an hour, then add, chopped very fine, one onion, some thyme, parsley, and marjoram. Add three quarts of boiling water and two tablespoons of rice, and one hour before you serve it stir in half a pint of okra chopped small.

HAM-BONE SOUP.

Put in your soup pot one gallon of water, one fourth of a cabbage cut fine, four Irish or two sweet potatoes, half a gallon of tomatoes, six ears of corn cut off the cob, half a pint of butter beans, six okras and one pod of pepper. Let these boil well, and one hour before it is to be served, put in the ham-bone you had cooked a day or two, when nearly all the meat is off. Put pepper and salt to your taste, if you do not like red pepper.

* * *

If for pecuniary aid or pleasure you have to preside over a boarding—house, try to make the home of those under your roof as agreeable as circumstances will admit. Always make a contract, even in small matters. If they name their peculiarities, and you agree to bear with them, do not speak of them when cares perplex you. You have agreed to supply their daily wants and they to punctually pay for them. It is the business you have chosen, and therefore your duty is to try and please. Have your table supplied with what your means can afford, and everything needed in table service at hand, in a clean, orderly manner, never having to complain of your orders being disobeyed at the table. That you should have attended to before the meals were announced.

Preside at the head and see that your waiters are attentive to every want. If a delicacy is requested from your closet, give it cheerfully, by showing the pleasure it gives to have it at hand, without complaining of the trouble of housekeeping, and such little interruptions. You can add honor and dignity to any calling in life. There is nothing degrading in providing for the wants of your fellow-beings, presiding at the head of a hotel table or private boarding-house; and a lady can make a reputation, characterized by dignity and honor, that will last years after she has been numbered with the dead, and show the respectability of her family, by her modest deportment. If you are blessed with daughters, educate them in such a manner that their pleasure will consist in lightening their mother's toil. They can so conduct themselves in their private parlor or at the head of the table, as to enlist the praises of the passing stranger or the daily boarder, though they rise while it is yet night to give meat to the household.

FISH.

BOILED ROCK-FISH.

Clean the fish nicely and put it in a pot with cold water enough to cover it. You can pin a nice towel or not around it to keep it compact. If a large fish put half a teacup of salt in the water. If small, lessen the quantity to suit. Boil it slowly one hour; when the meat looks tender and easily leaves the bone it is sufficiently done. Serve it on a hot dish, and garnish it with hard boiled eggs cut in slices and put over the fish, with a nice butter sauce poured over to make it look nicely, and sprigs of parsley around the dish. If you have a fish-slice on your stove-boiler, put the fish in that, by all means, and steam it done; the flavor is preserved, and it is much nicer when cooked by steam. Always have drawn butter and sauces for fish.

BUTTER SAUCE.

Boil six eggs until the yelk is hard enough to rub smooth, and add butter when they are hot. Put one pint of the fish water in a saucepan, thicken it with a little flour rubbed smooth in cold water and then stir in four ounces of butter, with the egg, and give it one boil up. Serve in a sauce tureen.

BAKED SHAD.

Take some bread crumbs, chopped parsley, butter, pepper and salt, and mix them up with beaten yelks of eggs; fill the shad with this dressing, tie a string around it, put in a pan with bits of butter over the fish and a little water, and bake it in an oven. Rock and sheep's-head may be baked in the same way; takes longer time to cook rock than the others. Onion or garlic can always be added according to taste.

BARBECUE SHAD.

Take a fine large shad, put it in a pan, and season it with cayenne pepper and a small teaspoonful of sugar; put one large spoonful of butter and lard, mixed, on it, and a little salt. Mix vinegar and water, equal parts, and pour on enough to cover it. Bake slowly one hour.

FRIED SHAD.

Split the shad open and cut in cross pieces three or four inches wide; salt it, sprinkle a little meal through the sieve on it, and put it in hot lard to fry; when brown turn it nicely, so both sides will be well cooked.

SHAD AND ROCK ROE.

This may be fried in hot lard, or beat up with eggs and fried in small cakes. If boiled, wrap them in a cloth and throw in boiling water, and dress with butter sauce.

FRESH HERRINGS.

Clean them nicely and gash them half an inch apart on both sides, sprinkle a little meal or flour over them, and fry in hot lard.

SALT HERRINGS.

Soak them twelve hours before they are wanted; let them drain, and fry or broil as you prefer.

EELS.

When eels are good they have a glossy, bright appearance on the back, and a brilliant white underneath. Clean them nicely, take out the entrails, skin and cut off their heads and tails, cut them up in pieces as long as your finger. If boiled, flour them and boil until tender in salt and water with parsley in it, and serve with butter sauce and chopped parsley. If baked, dip them in egg and bread crumbs, and season with butter and sweet herbs; or to fry, leave out the butter and herbs.

ANCHOVY.

A small fish caught in the Mediterranean and exported for sauces and sandwiches. Wash them, remove the bones, and lay them between slices of bread and butter, or pound them with fresh butter and eat on toast.

SHEEP'S-HEAD.

This delicious fish is finer in the Norfolk, Virginia, market than any part of our country, and will not bear transportation without being packed in ice. After the fish is nicely cleaned and rinsed in two waters, put it on a fish-slice over a boiler of water, cover it and let it steam till perfectly done. When ready to serve, put in a dish with butter sauce poured over it. Garnish it with hard boiled eggs, cut in round slices, and curled, parsley, and have butter sauce in the tureen to serve with it. Odenheimer, Worcester, or tomato sauce as an accompaniment.

BAKED SHEEP'S-HEAD.

Prepare a force-meat of bread crumbs, pepper, salt, butter, a bit of fat bacon chopped fine, a little onion or shallot, with the yelks of two eggs. Rub the fish with butter and sprinkle pepper and salt upon it; place it in the stove pan or a long tin pan, and bake it till it is thoroughly done.

SPOTS OR HOG-FISH, WITH ONIONS.

Fry the fish at breakfast, cut slices of onions very thin and put them on every fish in layers; cover them with vinegar. Nice side dish for dinner or good for tea.

TO BOIL STURGEON.

Leave the skin on the piece you boil, and scrape it nicely; take out the gristle and dredge it well with flour, then put it in cold salt and water with a few cloves of garlic; boil and skim it nicely. When done, pour over it melted butter with parsley, and have sauces to eat with it, and drawn butter in a sauce tureen.

STURGEON STEAKS.

Cut them half an inch thick, lay them in salt and water a short time, then dredge with flour and fry quickly; pour melted butter and fried parsley over them.

STURGEON, PICKLED.

Clean and scrape it nicely, taking out all the gristle, cut it up in small pieces and salt it well; let it remain two days, then boil it, not quite done enough to eat. Boil some vinegar, with cloves, allspice, mace, black pepper, and a little cayenne. When the sturgeon is perfectly cold, pack it in a jar and pour the vinegar hot over it.

TO BAKE STURGEON.

Take a nice piece of sturgeon with the skin on, scrape it well, cut out the gristle, and boil it twenty minutes to extract the oil; take it up and pull off the large scales. Make some force-meat of bread crumbs, butter, salt, and a little chopped parsley and shallot; when the sturgeon is cold, stuff it with the forcemeat. Put it in an oven or stove pan with a pint and a half of water and a gill of wine, one of catchup, some salt and cayenne. Stew the sturgeon in this until done and thicken the gravy with butter rubbed in brown parsley; garnish it with sprigs of parsley.

STURGEON CUTLETS.

Take the tail piece of the sturgeon, skin it, and cut off the gristle; cut it in slices half an inch thick, sprinkle them with pepper and salt, dredge them with flour, and fry in hot lard; make a gravy of one pint of water, large spoonful of butter rubbed in brown flour, a little catchup and wine, and stew the outlets in it a few minutes.

TO PICKLE SHAD.

Clean and cut open nice large shad and salt them, let them stand three or four days, then cut them in pieces four inches wide (as to fry), put them in a pot with cold water and boil them till done through, but not soft enough to leave the bone. Put them in a jar when cold and pour boiling hot vinegar with allspice, a few cloves, and black pepper boiled in it, enough to cover the fish nicely. You can pickle them from the barrel when first put up, by soaking them all night before cooking.

CORNED SHAD.

Clean and split open a fresh shad, mix one teaspoonful of cayenne pepper and one of brown sugar, lay the shad open on a flat dish and rub it gently on the inside with the pepper and sugar. Next morning broil it nicely and put bits of butter on it, and you will find it superior to salt corned.

SALT CORNED SHAD.

Clean and split it open (always cut off the head), sprinkle salt over the inside and let it remain twelve hours; wash it off and broil it. Put bits of butter on it when hot.

QUAKER POTTED HERRING.

Wash nicely as many herrings as you wish; after having them scaled, cut off the heads and tails, and sprinkle a little salt over them, to stand a few hours;

drain them and wipe dry. Line a stone jar through with dough made of rye flour and water, rolled thin; put the herrings nicely in the jar, then boil cider vinegar enough to cover them, with a few cloves, some allspice, black pepper, and mace, and pour it boiling hot over the herrings. Cover the jar instantly with dough. The next day place them in a clean jar and tie up. They keep well, and cut in slices as souse-cheese. The vinegar eats all the bones up. You can add onion if you like it.

CAROLINA POTTED HERRINGS.

Put them in a stone jar with spices and salt sprinkled between and a layer of onions sliced; set the jar in an oven of cold water; fill it to the brim with vinegar and cover it with dough. Put fire under it and let it slowly cook nine hours.

CLAM FRITTERS.

Put into a pot of boiling water enough clams to make a pint when chopped up; when the mouths are open, take the clams out of the shell and put them in a saucepan; strain the liquor and put one half over the clams, with a little black pepper, and stew them half an hour, then take the clams out and chop them very fine, leaving out the hardest part. Beat six eggs and mix in gradually one pint of flour and one of milk; beat it smooth, free from lumps, then mix the clams in the batter; stir it well. Have some lard hot in a frying-pan, drop the batter in with a spoon and fry the fritter a light brown.

OYSTER OMELET.

Take the heart from twenty-five large oysters; chop them fine. Beat six eggs, leaving out the whites of two; mix with the oysters and season with cayenne pepper and salt. Heat three ounces of butter in a frying-pan, pour in the mixture, and fry quickly. Raise the edges up with a knife occasionally.

OYSTER FRITTERS.

Beat six eggs and stir in them six large spoonfuls of flour, with one pint of sweet milk and a teaspoonful of salt. Take the oysters (half a gallon) out of the liquor and wash them in cold water; strain the liquor through a coarse towel, add the oysters to the eggs and flour, then make it a thin batter with the oyster liquor. If large oysters, take up one at a time in a large kitchen spoon and drop in hot lard, prepared for them in your frying-pan; if not very large, take up two or three with the batter in the spoon.

STEWED OYSTERS.

Wash the oysters in cold water and strain the liquor through a coarse cloth. Put them in a sauce pan with a large spoonful of butter to half a gallon of oysters, teaspoonful of salt and a little black pepper. Boil them until they are plump, about ten minutes. Serve them hot in a covered dish for breakfast, dinner or tea. Always palatable.

OYSTER SAUCE.

Put in a saucepan two dozen large oysters and strain their liquor to them. Let them simmer, but not boil; then take them out, and put in pepper and salt, with one teaspoonful of flour rubbed smooth in butter, one teacup of milk, and let it all boil. When you take it from the fire, put the oysters in and serve it hot.

PICKLED OYSTERS. 1.

Rinse your oysters in their liquor, strain it on them, and give one boil up, then take them out of the liquor to cool. Prepare vinegar by boiling it with black pepper, little salt, mace, cloves, and nutmeg, and when perfectly cold, pour it over the oysters and keep them in a stone jar.

PICKLED OYSTERS. 2.

Wash your oysters in cold water, put them in a porcelain kettle, with salt to your taste, put in some grains of black pepper and blades of mace, give them a good boil up, and when perfectly cold put half vinegar and half of the liquor they were boiled in and pour over them. These keep well and are much liked.

OYSTER ROAST.

Have a hot fire and place the oysters on it and before it. When they begin to pop and open their months, place them with tongs upon waiters or flat wooden trays made for that purpose; send them to be eaten hot. If you have invited guests, have an oyster or large case-knife, a coarse towel, a large plate and saucer by each guest, and for every two have a bucket or pan to receive the empty shells. Have on the table plain and pepper vinegar, black pepper, salt, butter, and thin biscuits or crackers. If you eat butter with them, put it on before taking from the shell. Sauces may be added to the vinegar and pepper.

OYSTERS FRIED.

Have in your frying-pan some boiling lard or butter. Select fine large oysters, and wash them in cold water, putting in a few at a time and taking them out quickly; place them on a dish and sift a little corn meal over them; drop in the hot lard one or two at a time and fry them a light brown. Serve hot.

TERRAPINS.

Salt-water terrapins are the only kind I ever prepared. Put the terrapin in a pot of boiling water as you do a crab. When it is perfectly dead, take them out and remove the outer skin and toe-nails; boil them again in warm water, with salt in it, till they are tender, then take off the shells and clean them very carefully; remove the sand-bag and gall as nicely as you can, and put the shells in cold water; scrape them clean and scald them. Then put all the meat and entrails, cut fine in a saucepan with butter, pepper, cayenne, salt, and a few bread crumbs with a little Madeira Wine, and the yelk of eggs boiled hard to mash like flour; give it one boil up, fill the shells and set them in an oven to brown. This was a favorite dish of a friend of mine who was a great epicure and declared he ate black snakes prepared like terrapin. If you prefer the stew, cook it longer and serve on brown toast. Always allow one egg to a terrapin.

SHRIMPS.

Boil the shrimps with a little mace in the water, then bake them with butter and vinegar, or drop them in hot vinegar to pickle.

Having spent my early days in the finest fish country in the Southern States, and basing my recipes on the experience of skillful cooks, I can recommend them all as good.

TROUT.

Scale them nicely, sift a little meal over them, and fry in hot butter. If you use lard in preference, sprinkle salt over the fish. If you bake it put it in a pan with slices of meat and parsley, or bread crumbs sprinkled over, seasoned with butter, pepper, and salt. They are not so good boiled as fried.

PERCH, SPOTS, AND HOG-FISH.

Clean these nicely, sprinkle a little salt on them, then a dust of meal, and fry them in enough hot lard to cover them. Too nice to write about in an inland town.

ROACH, SMELTS, GUDGEONS, MINNOWS.

Sprinkle a little flour or meal over these and fry in boiling lard.

TO BROIL MACKEREL.

Clean them nicely (if salted, soak them all night in clear water), grease the gridiron, put the fish on skin side down, broil till done and butter it.

Lobster Salad.

Boil the coral of a lobster half an hour; pound, and rub it smooth. Make a dressing of two hard boiled eggs rubbed smooth in two tablespoonfuls of vinegar; add one tablespoonful of English mustard, three of salad oil, one of white powdered sugar, tea spoonful of salt, same of black pepper, one pinch of cayenne, and the yelks of two raw eggs. Mix this well with the lobster and pour the sauce over the whole. Put nice white heads of lettuce in the centre of dish with the salad, and hard boiled eggs, cut, around it.

To Preserve Fish for Transportation.

Take the fish fresh from the water and fill the mouth with bread crumbs saturated with brandy; pour a little in the stomach. Pack it in straw in a short time after and it will keep fresh ten days. When wanted for use put the fish in fresh water, and in a few hours they are ready.

A Nice Salad Dressing.

Yelks of four hard boiled eggs, three spoonfuls of mustard, two of sugar, one of salt, two tablespoonfuls of cream and five of vinegar; rub the yelks of eggs hot in the vinegar and add the other ingredients.

Salad Dressing, With Oil.

Mix one spoonful of black pepper, half the quantity of salt, in two tablespoonfuls of oil. When well mixed stir in four tablespoonfuls more of oil and five of vinegar. Prepare any salad you wish and pour it over just as you use it; add a little cayenne and sugar or mustard if you like.

Scolloped Lobsters.

Boil the lobster, take the meat and chop it fine, season it with pepper, and salt, Worcester sauce, or catchup; add a tablespoonful of vinegar, small piece of butter, and enough cream or milk to moisten it; put this in a saucepan and let it boil. Then put it in a buttered dish, sprinkle bread crumbs or powdered cracker over it and bake it brown.

DEVILED CRABS.

Boil the crabs and pick out all the nice meat, wash and scrape the shell, put the meat in a dish, season it high with salt and pepper, and slight sprinkle of cayenne. Grate some bread crumbs, and mix a few with the crabs and stir it all up with yelk of egg. Fill the shells with the mixture and put a piece of butter on each; put them in an oven or stove and bake them.

CRABS SERVED PLAIN.

Boil them in hot water, pick out all the white meat and put it in a covered dish with pieces of ice on the top. Send it to the table to be seasoned according to taste.

LOBSTER PATTIES.

Bake some puff paste in patty-pans. Take the meat of one or two boiled lobsters, mince it fine, and mix it with the coral smoothly mashed and hard boiled eggs grated; season it with a little salt, cayenne, mace or nutmeg, and a little lemon rind grated. Moisten the mixture well with cream, fresh butter, or salad oil put it in a stew-pan with a very little water, let it come to a boil, take it off and fill the crust baked in the patty-pans.

CRAB PATTIES.

Boil hard crabs, clean them nicely and pick out the white meat; season them with butter, pepper, and salt, and hard boiled yelk of egg grated; put in a few bread crumbs, give the mixture one boil, and fill crusts baked in patty-pans.

HARD CRABS, BOILED.

Throw them in boiling water and cook a few minutes. Eat them with vinegar and pepper.

FRESH COD-FISH.

I learnt to prepare this in Boston. To boil it, lay it in a kettle of cold water, with salt and a bit of saltpetre, and cook it thoroughly done; serve with melted butter and any sauce you prefer. When fried, flour the pieces and sprinkle cayenne on them and fry brown. To stew, season it high with pepper and salt, and add a little wine and lemon, or some nice sauce with butter rolled in flour.

COD SOUNDS.

Boil them in milk and water, and serve with egg sauce after they have been soaked half an hour in warm water, scraped and cleaned. Always parboil them before broiling.

BAKED COD OR HADDOCK.

Carefully take the skin from the middle part of the fish, make a dressing of bread crumbs, a little of the roe parboiled, pepper, salt, and butter, with egg (and lemon peel if you like it), stuff the fish, sew it up and put it in a pan, put a little lard and bits of butter over it, and serve with any sauce you like.

TO CRIMP COD.

Lay small pieces in half vinegar and salt for four hours, then cook it any way you prefer,—boiled, fried, or broiled.

SALMON.

This fish we never have fresh at the South. I have eaten it at Saratoga and Niagara, boiled and dressed with butter, and baked just as other fish. It requires longer boiling than any other fish, to get it sufficiently done. Serve with sauces. The canned fish is fresh, of course, but not equal to its flavor when just from the water.

CAT-FISH.

There is a strong prejudice against cat-fish, but they make a delicious stew seasoned with salt, pepper, butter, and a little parsley (shallot if you like it). They are very fine when taken on the Sounds in large fisheries.

CAT-FISH PIE.

Cut the fish up and stew it with salt, pepper, and butter for a few minutes, then put it in a pan lined with paste, cover it with the gravy, and bake with a top crust.

COD-FISH BALLS.

Boil three pounds of salt cod-fish slowly, after soaking it in cold water the night before. Boil some Irish potatoes and mash them fine, whilst warm; add a large spoonful of butter, in the proportion of one third cod-fish and two thirds mashed potato; make it up with four eggs and a cup of milk, then make cakes of it in your hand as you would a biscuit, about an inch thick, and fry it brown in hot lard or pieces of salt pork. Boil some eggs hard, cut them in halves, and put a piece in centre of the ball and send it to the table on a flat dish.

CHOWDER.

Fry in a large pot some pieces of fat pork, well seasoned with pepper. When done, remove the pork and put in some slices of peeled onions. Then some fresh fish, cod, rock, or black fish, with a layer of cut Irish potatoes; add one pint of water and let it stew half an hour, then add one pint of milk thickened with a little flour; let it boil up, and serve hot.

BOSTON CHOWDER.

Fry four tablespoonsful of chopped onion with some slices of fat pork, and break up two pilot biscuit in it; then put one tablespoonful each of sweet marjoram and sweet basil, half a bottle of port wine, one fourth of a bottle of catchup, a half grated nutmeg, a few cloves and grains of pepper, six pounds of fresh cod and sea bass, cut in slices. Boil it steadily for an hour, stirring it carefully. Serve in a large covered dish.

Sturgeon may be cooked in the same way.

STEWED HALIBUT.

Cut your fish in pieces four inches square having cut out the bone, season with a little salt and let it stand half an hour. Take it out of the salt and add some grated nutmeg, cayenne pepper, a little ginger, pint of vinegar, and a spoonful of butter rolled in bread crumbs; put it in a baking dish, set it in oven and let it cook slowly till well done, basting it frequently with the liquid. When nearly done add a tablespoonful of capers.

SAUCE FOR FISH.

Stew an onion in some of the water the fish is boiled in, and add one teaspoonful of grated horseradish, with two of essence of anchovies. When the onion is soft take it out, and put in a piece of butter just before you pour it in the tureen or over the fish.

ANOTHER FISH SAUCE.

Rub one quarter of a pound of butter with two tablespoonfuls of flour, into half a pint of water from the fish that is boiling. Add half a teacup of cream beaten with the yelks of six eggs, and three tablespoonfuls of Odenheimer or tomato sauce; warm it enough to cook the flour, and put thin slices of lemon over the top.

BROWN SAUCE FOR BAKED FISH.

Take one spoonful of butter, one of flour, and one onion if you like it, fry it a pretty brown, then slowly stir in two spoonsful of catchup, walnut, or Odenheimer, and add a glass of port wine as you take it up.

So many sauces are in use at the present day it is useless to add any more, as drawn butter and yelk of egg rubbed together with sauces are sufficient.

APPLE SAUCE.

Peel nice apples which are a little sour, put them in a tin or porcelain saucepan (cover them close) without any water, set the pan in boiling water in another vessel and keep a brisk fire under it. When soft, mash them with butter and sweeten to the taste. Some persons prefer it without sugar, with goose or other meats. This is a nice way to preserve the flavor of the apples for pies or custard.

SAGE, ONION AND THYME SAUCE.

Chop an onion, some sage leaves, and a few leaves of thyme in half a tumbler of water, let them stew together ten minutes with pepper and salt and a few bread crumbs. When ready to serve stir in one large spoonful of butter.

FROGS.

This ugly, noisy animal is considered equal to young chicken by some epicures, and I give a receipt from early recollection when my father enjoyed them *alone*. Take the hind legs of the large bull-frog, skin them and throw them in boiling water and let them remain ten minutes, then put them in cold water to cool, wipe them dry, sprinkle a little salt and corn meal over and drop them in hot lard to fry until a light brown.

To Stew Frogs.

Skin the hind legs as above and parboil them for a few minutes, then fry them a light brown in butter. Chop a little parsley, thyme, and onion (or garlic), put in a little salt and pepper, mix it in a little wine and water, and pour it on the frog legs; let it stew until they are tender. Beat the yelk of one egg to a frog, stir it in and serve them hot.

Muscles.

These are better in the fall and winter than any other season. You can fry them like oysters. After they have been well soaked in water and washed, put them on the fire in a saucepan and remove the shell as soon as they open. Save the liquor, season it with butter and pepper and stir in a little flour; let it boil up. Then add the muscles, with a little parsley and yelks of eggs beaten, give them one boil up and serve with slices of lemon.

Fish Pie.

Boil a large rock-fish and pick it up. Add to it three eggs, two tablespoonfuls of butter, one of flour, and make it in a batter with milk. Add salt and pepper, and bake it in a paste.

Rock Chowder.

Cut rock-fish in pieces about four inches wide. Put in a dinner pot a layer of fat meat, then one of biscuit or bread, then one of onions, with salt, red and black pepper, then a layer of fish. Repeat until all is in, cover with water, and boil it five hours.

Clam Chowder.

Cover the bottom of an iron pot with pieces of fat pork that has been in salt, and fry all the grease out. Then put in a layer of clams and a layer of sliced Irish potatoes until you have the amount required; season it with pepper, and put water enough to moisten it. Cover it close and cook over a hot fire thirty minutes. Cover a dish with crackers and pour the chowder hot over it.

FISH COOKED WITH OIL.

Cut fish in pieces an inch thick and season it with pepper and salt; let it lie one hour, dry it with a towel, flour it and fry it brown in oil. Put in your saucepan equal parts of vinegar and oil, with a little garlic, mace, pepper, and salt, and let it boil and then cool. When the fish and liquor are cold, slice some onions, lay them in the bottom of the fish kettle, and then a layer of fish with another of onions until you have all in. Pour the liquor over it and slowly cook it all until the onion is quite soft.

FISH STEWED WITH WINE.

Cut fish in pieces and put it in a kettle with one tumbler of wine and water mixed, three onions sliced, a slice of bread toasted brown, salt, pepper, and a lump of butter; cover it with sufficient water to cook it and stew it gently. Just before you serve it, pour the gravy in a saucepan, roll some butter in flour to thicken it, add some catchup and walnut pickle, stir it smooth and pour it over the fish to heat. Serve it hot, add an anchovy to this, if you like, when you first put it on to stew.

WHITE FISH SAUCE.

Put one glass of white wine, and two of water in a saucepan, with a little nutmeg, grated lemon peel, and two anchovies. When it has boiled five minutes, strain it and add a spoonful of vinegar. Roll nearly one pound of butter in flour, stir it in, boil it up and pour over a nice boiled rock, sheep's-head, or any other fish you prefer.

* * *

As many persons wish to board to avoid the cares of housekeeping, a few words of advice may not be out of place. Boarders generally feel they have a right to demand any and everything they wish, whether it is convenient or not for their demand to be supplied; and if their wishes are not complied with, go at once to the landlord with a complaint. If they have never known the cares they seek to avoid, there may be some excuse. There are times, particularly in small towns and villages, when necessary articles cannot be procured. The housekeeper and landlord of a hotel have to depend on the same market; and company with one, is as the boarder with the other. How often housekeepers, when company drops in, are dependent on their neighbors for a kindness, which a landlord would not feel justifiable in asking. We should never exact more than we are willing to dispense. Few persons display the noble gift of gratitude they owe to their landlord, thinking the money he receives is his only due. Not so. When that trait of character, with a kind manner is displayed, no boarder will have to complain of inattention. The constant exercise of their minds for the good of others, makes the duty to please hard to perform.

Husbands are often subjected to inconvenience by some trivial circumstance when their means would not justify any other mode of living; and a shell of a house, with bread and water, are considered preferable to the various comforts enjoyed, if every wish is not instantly complied with. The cold dinner on the Sabbath day is complained of, when a moment's reflection should teach them to "go and do likewise." The command given for *no* work to be done, does not exempt any. The laborer must have rest to prepare for the bread of life, and such examples should be imitated. The desired change is made, the novelty wears off, and housekeeping has perplexing cares. The wife relents and finds, when too late, she did not exercise that good gift, "The very bond of peace," as she ought to have done, and the complaint against her sex receives additional force from her hasty action. May the young women of the rising generation remove that *odium*, showing women can dwell peaceably together in one house by hearing with each other's infirmities.

MEATS.

GATE'S RECIPE FOR CURING HAMS.

After the ham is perfectly cold, mix some salt, saltpetre and red pepper pods in a tray, and moisten it with warm water and a little molasses. Rub the hams well in this and pack them in a barrel, with a handful thrown in on each layer, and occasionally a handful of coarse salt. Let them remain closely packed for four weeks. Take them out of the brine, dip them in *fresh* tan ooze (that is made from red oak bark), lay them down with bone side up, and cover around the bone thickly, with cayenne pepper. Hang them up to smoke with hock down, and smoke with hickory chips. I tested this recipe ten years, and never lost a ham or had one with a bug in it. Wash it in two or three waters before putting it on to boil. Always have the door open, or some way for the smoke to escape when curing meat. The best plan is to have an inside slat door with a lock, so the strong door can be left open part of the day, that secures your smoke-house.

PICKLE FOR CURING BACON.

Take five gallons of water, seven pounds of salt, one pound of sugar, one pint of molasses, two teaspoonfuls of saltpetre, and stir it well; rub the thick part of the ham, shoulder or middling with a little salt, and pack it in a clean barrel,—hams first, then shoulders and middlings. Pour the brine over, and if not enough to cover it well, make more the same way. Let it remain from four to seven weeks in the brine, according to size; then drain them, sprinkle pepper around the bone, and smoke with hickory wood, or dry in the air as you prefer. Makes sweet meat and keeps well.

ADMIRAL POCOCK'S RECIPE FOR CORNED BEEF.

Cut up quarters of beef in pieces to suit the size of your family. Lay it one hour in cold water, then spread it to drain; have a *clean* barrel and (after the water has drained from the beef) place it in the barrel with a layer of coarse salt between each layer of beef (if fine salt has to be used put a slight sprinkle). Have in a large iron pot six gallons of water, four quarts of salt in winter and six in summer, two ounces of pulverized saltpetre, half a pound of brown sugar and one pint of molasses. Boil and skim off the thick scum, set it aside to cool, and when *perfectly cold* pour it over the beef in the barrel, and put clean rocks on the beef to keep it under the pickle. This quantity of pickle will answer for one quarter of beef weighing eighty pounds. Steaks can be used out of the barrel for eight days without being too salt, if nicely washed off in cold water. I have tested this twenty years.

SAUSAGE MEAT.

Chop the pieces of fresh meat you do not cure as bacon. To twenty-five pounds, put half a pound of sugar; pepper and salt to your taste. Mix it well and keep it dry. Sugar keeps it from getting strong.

MCMORINE'S CORNED BEEF.

Cut up your beef in pieces the size you wish after it has hung up to tender. Put some fine salt in a wooden tray, with one teaspoonful of saltpetre finely powdered, to one quart of salt; wet it with molasses, and rub each piece of beef well with it. Have a clean cask or barrel, and pack it in with a layer of coarse salt (or slight sprinkle of fine) between each layer of beef. It will soon make pickle enough to cover it. Keeps well and is nice when boiled for dinner, or to broil for a few days before the salt strikes in. Use four quarts of salt to sixty pounds of beef.

DRIED BEEF.

After curing the ham of beef by Pocock's or McMorine's recipe, letting it remain in the pickle *ten days*, take it out, dip it in a pot of *boiling* water, and hang it up in your kitchen, where it will get air on all sides. It keeps well and is convenient to broil for breakfast or tea. Two weeks will be long enough to hang it to dry.

HAM BOILED WITH HERBS.

Put your ham on in a pot of cold water; when it boils, put in one bay leaf, with a bunch of thyme and parsley; boil slowly for two hours, then take it and remove the skin, spread grated bread crumbs over it and set it in an oven for half an hour to brown.

NEW HAM, BOILED.

Put a new ham on two hours earlier than you would one that has been cured. After it has boiled hard for one hour, dip off the liquor and pour cold water in the pot and boil again briskly. Boil cabbage and turnips with it and dish them separately.

HAM BOILED IN WINE.

Boil a ham in clear water one hour or more according to size; take it out of the water and rub it off with a clean cloth and remove the skin; put it in a kettle, pour wine over it and keep it closely covered, steadily boiling one hour. It is very nice browned in an oven for half an hour with brown sugar, sprinkled over it.

FANNIE'S STUFFED HAM.

Boil the ham until done, remove the skin and save the juice. Take some bread crumbs, parsley chopped fine, black pepper, butter (and onion if you like it), and mix it up with the juice of the ham; then take the ham on a dish and make incisions with a carving knife, top or underneath, and with your finger stuff the force-meat in. Cover the ham with it or grated bread crumbs, dust pepper all over it, place it in an oven or stove, and bake twenty-five minutes. Nice for a spring dinner when hot; and elegant, cold, for a meat supper.

BONED HAM.

Soak a nicely cured ham the night before you wish to cook it, in tepid water. Next day, place it in a large dinner pot of water the same temperature, and boil it briskly eight or ten hours. Take it up in a wooden tray, let it cool, and carefully take out the bone; cut it clear at the hock and loosen it around the bone on the thick part, with a thin, sharp knife, and slowly pull it out. Then press the ham in shape and return it to the boiling liquor. Take the pot off the fire and let the ham remain in it, until cold. It is like beef tongue when cut across in slices.

FRIED HAM WITH EGGS.

Cut some nice slices of ham, take off the skin and throw them in cold water; wash and rinse them; have your frying-pan hot; put the ham in and fry until well done; with a fork take the slices out and lay them on the dish they are to be served in; then break some eggs, one by one, and drop them whole in the juice from the ham. As soon as the white looks done, take them up and put them nicely on the ham.

ROAST HAM.

Soak a ham in tepid water the night before you wish to roast it. Four hours before you wish to serve it, set it before a moderate fire in a tin kitchen, turn the spit frequently, and let it roast two hours. Then take it up on a dish or pan and take the skin nicely off, scrape all the fat out of the roaster, return the ham and let it roast two hours more, basting it often with the drippings in the bottom of the roaster. When it is done take the ham up on a dish, put the 4 drippings in a saucepan, stir one tablespoonful of flour in a teacup of water, pour it in the sauce and boil up. Serve this in a sauce tureen.

BOILED HAM.

Wash a ham nicely in warm water; rub it well with a wet cloth. Have a large dinner pot on the fire, fill with cold water and put your ham in; let it boil slowly until the water is very hot, and then boil briskly. Turn it in the pot occasionally, and allow four hours to cook it thoroughly, if over ten pounds; three will do if under that weight.

ROAST BEEF.

Cover the beef you intend to roast, the night before, with black pepper. Pepper sweetens the meat and salt extracts the juice. Next day wash it off and season it with a little salt. Put it in a tin kitchen before a hot fire, with the bone side to the fire. When nearly done turn the spit and let the fleshy part go next to the fire, and baste it with the drippings in the bottom of the kitchen; stick a fork in it and if the juice looks red, let it cook a little longer. Stir one tablespoonful of browned flour with water until smooth, and thicken the gravy in the pan with it. Place the meat in a hot dish and pour a little of the gravy over the top, balance in a sauce-boat. Eat Odenheimer or tomato sauce with it.

MUTTON AND LAMB.

Roast mutton and lamb in the same way, well rubbed over with lard and seasoned with pepper and salt, and cooked well done.

VEAL.

Always stuff veal to roast or bake with a forcemeat made of bread crumbs, sweet herbs, bits of fat bacon, pepper, and salt, and garnish with crisped parsley.

MELISSA'S STUFFED BEEF.

Take a nice piece of roasting beef and put it on to boil. When nearly done, take it off the fire, make incisions in the beef and stuff them with a force-meat made as follows: Bake a piece of plain corn bread (meal and cold water mixed), take the crumbs and mix it up with two eggs, two onions chopped fine, pepper, and salt, with a little chopped sage and parsley, wet it with the grease that you skim off the water the beef was boiled in, put it in the incisions and if any is left over the top of the beef, place it in an oven with the grease from the top of the water and brown it. This is a delicious way of preparing fat beef.

Randolph's Beef Alamode.

Take the bone from a round of beef, fill the space with a force-meat made of crumbs of loaf bread, four ounces of marrow, one head of garlic or two onions, a little thyme and parsley chopped fine, a little nutmeg, cloves, pepper, and salt; mix it to a paste with four eggs, stuff the lean part of the round with it, in incisions made with a carving knife, and if any is left make balls of it. Sew it up in a linen towel, put it in a tin just large enough to hold it, pour one pint of red wine over it and cover with a sheet of tin, put it in a warm oven and bake it three hours (a brick oven is best but out of date). When done, skim the fat from the gravy, thicken it with browned flour, add some catchup and put the balls over it. Good hot or cold.

Bouilli Beef.

Put six pounds of a brisket of beef in a pot of cold water enough to cover the beef well; let it boil until the scum rises and skim it nicely. Add two carrots, two turnips, and one onion cut in dice form; stick one onion full of cloves; let this simmer three hours; then add one tumblerful of red wine, two teaspoonfuls of mixed mustard, one tablespoonful of tomato soy or catchup, and let it simmer one hour. Take the beef out and stir a tablespoonful of flour in the gravy, give it one boil up and turn it over the beef, then put pickled cucumber cut up fine all over the top.

If you choose, in summer, you can add tomatoes, okras and one or two potatoes. It is extra nice.

Fried Beefsteak.

Have some lard boiling hot, in your frying-pan, sprinkle a little salt and pepper on the beef and then dredge it with flour, put it in the hot lard and fry it quick. Some persons think it is better to fry with a lid on the pan or spider. Always beat your steak well with a beef mallet when it is to be fried and see that it is cut across the grain.

POTATO BEEF.

Boil some Irish potatoes, and mash them nice and smooth with milk and two beaten eggs; put a layer of this on the bottom of a pie pan, with a layer of beef and then potatoes until the pan is full; put bits of butter on the last layer of beef and then potatoes over the top. Cut your beef very thin and only use the lean; bake it slowly.

BEEF PATTIES.

Cut up bits of cold beef and season it with salt, pepper, a bit of mace, and any sweet herb you like; add cold gravy if you have it, if not, bits of butter and lard, and a little water with a teaspoonful of flour stirred in it. Make a nice plain paste, not very rich, roll it out the size of your pie plate and line your plate with it. Put the beef with some of the gravy in the centre of the plate, and fold the paste from each side to meet in the middle, pinch it together, prick the top with a fork, and bake it a light brown. Cheap and very nice.

BEEFSTEAKS.

Cut your steaks half an inch thick and beat them well with a beef mallet (or hammer), have your gridiron nicely cleaned and greased on the kitchen dresser, put the beef on it, then put it over bright, hot coals to broil; turn it over often; have a hot dish before the fire with a little butter, pepper, and salt in it; turn the beef over and over in this, then put bits of butter on the top and touch them with boiling water from the kettle, just enough to make it dissolve easily. If you have a hot water pan to fit under the dish, put it over it filled with boiling water, and cover the steak over. You will find this extra nice.

MUTTON CHOPS.

Cut them from the rack of mutton, with one bone in each, broil them on a gridiron, then season with pepper and salt, make a gravy with one gill of hot water, large spoonful of butter, and one spoonful of catchup; boil it up and pour it over. Twist curled paper on the end of the bone when sent to the breakfast table.

VEAL CUTLETS.

Cut off the flank and take the bone out, then take slices the size of the fillet and half an inch thick; grate some bread crumbs, and mix them with two yelks of eggs that have been beaten; put it on the veal and press it with a knife or cake turner, and let them stand to dry, then fry them in hot lard a light brown. Take them from the lard and stew them in gravy seasoned with wine, lemon, and curry powder; let it cook fifteen minutes, then thicken with butter and browned flour. Leave out curry powder if you choose.

VEAL CHOPS.

Cut your chops from the best end of a rack of veal, one bone in each. Prepare crumbs of bread; dip the chops in beaten yelks of eggs and then bread; grease pieces of writing paper with butter, wrap it around the chops and carefully broil; do not let the paper burn. Broil on a hot spider instead of gridiron when you use paper. Have a nice white sauce to put over them, highly seasoned.

BAKED BEEF TONGUE.

Make a stiff paste of coarse flour and water; roll it out thin and inclose the beef tongue in it after it has soaked one day and night and been nicely cleaned; put it in an oven and bake it slowly for five hours. When done, remove the paste and serve it hot with Irish potatoes mashed fine and put in a nice roll around it. This is the best way to cook it when to be eaten cold.

BOILED BEEF TONGUE.

Wash the tongue well and scrape the root; put it in soak the day before you wish it, and change the water once or twice. Put it in a dinner pot with cold water and boil it six hours; take it up, and trim it nicely, and serve hot with Irish potatoes mashed around it, and sprigs of parsley over the thick part by the root. When you want to press it, boil from four to six hours and cut all the root off.

CALF'S TONGUE.

Salt the tongue in a brine of salt and water with a little sugar and a pinch of saltpetre in it (three days or longer if you wish), boil it tender, peel it and cut it in slices around chickens or ducks, or use it as you do beef tongue; it is more delicate.

HOG TONGUE.

The tongue of the hog is usually left with the jowl and salted with it. Where you have a good many hogs killed, you can spare some to corn, and they will be nicer. Scrape the tongue nice and clean and rub a bit of saltpetre on each one and a teaspoonful of molasses; let it stand on them two hours, then rub salt on and pack them with salt between in a keg. They keep well and answer to boil in a family in place of pieces of bacon, and are a very nice relish for breakfast or tea.

HOGS' BRAINS.

Pour boiling water over the brains and let them remain in it a short time; then skin them and beat them with egg broken in and seasoned with salt and pepper. Have hot lard ready in your pan, put them in and stir them all the time until done.

FRIED TRIPE.

After tripe has been boiled tender, cut in slices four inches square. Make a batter of four eggs, four tablespoonfuls of flour, and one pint of milk; dip the tripe twice in the batter and fry it in hot lard. It is very nice fried without the batter, with a little vinegar poured over it just before it browns.

CATTLE FEET.

Clean them nicely and soak them three or four days, changing the water every day. Have them scraped nicely and boiled in salt and water. Pour that off after it has boiled three hours, and put clean hot water to them and boil until very tender.

HOGS' FEET.

When boiled and put up in vinegar for souse, split them open and dip them in a thin batter made of flour, egg, and water, and fry them in hot lard; or split them, grease the frying-pan, and warm them with vinegar poured over them in a pan. Eat them cold if you prefer it.

LAMB ROASTED OR BAKED.

Take the fore quarter of lamb and season it with salt and pepper; put it in a tin kitchen before the fire and roast it, basting frequently with lard, and make a gravy with the drippings, or rub it with lard and put it in a Dutch oven or stove pan to bake, with a little water; cook it slowly until well done. Never parboil it for baking; it extracts the taste of the meat and makes it stringy. Mint chopped very fine, put in vinegar with a little sugar, makes an agreeable sauce.

BOILED LAMB.

Wrap the hind quarter of lamb in a coarse towel, put it in a pot of warm water and boil it slowly until tender; have a little salt in the water. Take it up and dress it with a nice butter sauce, cut hard boiled eggs in rings and put over it with bits of parsley scalded in hot water; add capers to your sauce or mint sauce to eat with it, as with the roast and baked.

ROAST PIG.

Have your pig killed and cleaned the evening before you wish it or very early in the morning; have it well scraped and wash it in cold water changed two or three times; cut the feet off close to the first joint, take the heart and liver, and put them with the feet in a saucepan to stew. Fill the body of the pig with Irish potatoes mashed fine, seasoned highly with pepper, salt, tablespoonful of butter and one of lard; fasten the legs together, sew the body up and rub it all over with salt and pepper. Put it in a tin kitchen before a hot fire, turn the spit often, and occasionally rub a piece of lard over it, tied in muslin, to make the skin crisp. You can suspend it in front of the fire with a string on a strong nail, and spider under it to catch the drip pings, or place it in a stove pan or Dutch oven to suit your convenience. The feet should be cut up, liver and heart chopped fine and boiled in clear water with a few sage leaves, then take them out and season highly; rub some bits of butter in flour, stir it in, and stew until tender; then take the drippings from the pig in the pan or oven, and thicken it with flour, give it a boil up, and serve in tureen for gravy.

Another dressing may be prepared with crumbs of bread scalded and seasoned with salt, pepper, and butter, a little sage sifted in, and a small onion, chopped fine, and stuff in the same way.

Another, prepared with corn meal baked in plain cakes, scalded and mixed with yelks of eggs and highly seasoned with butter, pepper, salt, and lard, sage and sweet marjoram sifted in to taste, is very much liked. Always cook it a pretty brown and send the pig to the table with a lemon, apple, or small orange in his mouth.

TO BAKE QUARTERS OF PIG.

Cut the skin cross ways, wash it nicely, and rub it with pepper and salt, (little dry sage if you like,) put it in the oven with a little water and lard, and bake it brown.

PORK AND BEANS.

Take a nice piece of corned pork, wash it clean, and put it in a pot with one quart of hominy or navy beans and let them boil one hour. Take the pork out and boil the beans an hour longer, then put them in a pan and put the pork in the middle and bake three hours.

PORK CUTLETS.

Cut them from the leg, take off the skin and beat them with a pestle; have some bread crumbs, sage, and onion chopped fine, and some yelk of egg beaten; dip them in the egg and then in the bread crumbs with seasoning. Fry them with a small piece of lard until a light brown, turning them often. After you take them up, sprinkle a little flour in the gravy, give it one boil up, and pour over them in the dish.

BROILED PORK STEAKS.

Take some nice pieces of loin, season it well with pepper, salt, and powdered sage, put it on your broiling irons or spider, and turn it often until it is thoroughly done. Cut a piece to try it, and if it looks red, it is not done enough. Make gravy as for cutlets.

TO ROAST A LOIN OF PORK.

Cut the skin in narrow strips, and rub it all over with salt, pepper, and dry sage finely powdered. Make incisions between the ribs, and stuff it with a dressing made of bread crumbs, chopped onion, pepper, and salt mixed up with beaten yelk of egg. Put it before the fire on a spit and baste it with lard. It may be baked in an oven or stove after it is dressed, but roast is the sweetest.

PORK STEW.

Backbones, spareribs, or piece of the leg of fresh pork makes a nice stew. Stew it in clear water one hour, then add salt, black pepper, and sage, and stew it gently for one hour. Cut up a little red pepper if you like and add sweet or Irish potatoes, out small, or a few turnips.

CORNED PORK.

After it has been salted one week, boil a piece of corned pork two hours and then out in a cabbage, and boil one hour more. It is nice with the skin removed and browned before the fire.

PIG'S HEAD STEW.

Cut the head open and take out all the brains; boil the feet with it until all is tender, then take out all the bones, mince the tongue fine, and chop the brains. Take some water from the pot you boiled the head in, and put it with the meat; season it with a little dry sage, cayenne, or red pepper pod chopped fine, salt, and black pepper, and a little tomato catchup; stew it twenty minutes, broil the liver nicely, put the stew in a dish, and the liver around it. This is a good receipt for shoat or full grown hog's head stew.

BLOOD PUDDING.

Catch the blood as it runs from the hog, and stir it constantly until perfectly cold; then thicken it with rice or oatmeal, add some beef fat chopped small, season it highly with salt, pepper, a little sage, and chopped red pepper pod. Fill large skins, stick them with a fork, to prevent bursting; boil and smoke them.

LIVER PUDDINGS.

When putting up your pork (as we term it in hog killing time), boil the livers very tender, chop them fine and season with pepper, salt, sage, and cayenne, as we do sausage meat. Take some of the large skins, stuff them about nine inches long, tie the end securely and stick them with a fork to prevent bursting; put them in a pot and boil slowly for an hour. When cool, pack them in stone jars and they will keep well and require no further cooking.

SAUSAGE MEAT.

Take all the spare meat and tenderloins from your pork and grind it in a sausage grinder or chop it. Season it highly with black pepper, salt, and powdered sage. Boil one or two pods of red pepper, and pour the tea over it; work it all up; cook a small piece to try, and if not seasoned high enough, add what it needs. Pack it in a jar, or stuff skins with it after they have been soaked and cleaned nicely; hang them up to dry. Smoking makes them hard.

SAUSAGE MEAT.

If you want it extra nice, take two nice fresh hams and one shoulder; take off the skin and have it chopped nicely, season it with salt, pepper, sage, and a very little sugar. If you like spiced meats, use with that a few cloves, some mace, and nutmeg. Keep it in a dry, cool place, and fry it in balls, or stuff the skins, when you first make it, for dried sausages.

BEEF SAUSAGE MEAT.

Chop or grind four pounds of beef and two pounds of suet together, after the suet has been picked; season it highly with salt, pepper, and cayenne, make it in balls, and fry it. If you wish to stuff beef chitterlings with it, add cloves and a little garlic, and stuff the skins; put them in strong-salt and water brine for two weeks, turn them often, then wipe them dry, and smoke them.

TO FRY LIVER.

Cut your liver in nice pieces, put it in cold water and let it boil until it looks nearly done, take it out and drop it in hot lard, and season it with pepper and salt after you take it out.

* * *

The beauty of a well ordered home is beyond calculation. Woman is the priestess ministering before its altars and the incense arising from her heart is full of bliss or anguish to all around her. Here the parents can draw close in counsel, and consider measures for their government and prosperity. Here, in unmolested gladness and security, children gather and revel in the very exuberance of infantile life. Here, the husband finds rest for his wearied frame after toiling through the day. The wife, with her little world of cares, perhaps struggling with a sigh, is strengthened by the thoughts of the happy home provided for her, to inspire love and gratitude, and draw forth the sympathy of the pleasant circle, formed in that sacred retreat, which shelters her from the world and protects her from the strife of many minds. Then be thankful; be grateful to God for blessing you with a home. Be it ever so humble, there is no place like a happy, cheerful home.

POULTRY.

CLEANING POULTRY.

Turkeys, geese, chickens, and ducks, are better killed the day before we wish them, and during the winter they may remain several days unhurt. The best way to kill them is to hang them up by the legs tied together, and cut the throat with the head hanging down. They bleed better and die much quicker than when the head is chopped on a block and thrown down to struggle until life is extinct. Geese and ducks have the finest feathers; they are picked carefully and never scalded, as chickens are, to make them clean easily. Make a paper bag of an old newspaper and put it by you to save the feathers for beds and pillows, and when they are cured they can be packed in bags for use; sun them often or dry them in a moderate oven. Turkeys must have all the large feathers picked out, the wings cut off to the first joint, and then they can be scalded to get the smaller feathers off. It is more tedious, but I think it much nicer to pick a fowl without scalding in hot water, particularly before the entrails are removed. After it is picked, and singed over a blaze or a piece of lighted paper, make an incision at the lower part of the breast-bone, and remove the entrails; be careful in taking the gall-bag from the liver, as the least particle of that would spoil the taste of the bird. Cut the gizzard open and take out the inner skin, clean the heart and liver and throw them all in cold water, with a little salt in it. Have a nice rag and wash the bird in two or three waters, using a little salt in the last, as it cleanses it better. The French prefer poultry rubbed clean to having it washed, but I give the manner of cleaning it as we are accustomed to in our country. Cut the feet off to the first joint, and fasten the legs in the incision made to draw the entrails out. Tie a string around the neck and suspend them in a cool place until they are needed for the spit. Chickens are often cooked as soon as dressed; and when necessity requires it, wash them in water until it ceases to look bloody, and lay them in salt and water until you have to cook them. Pay strict attention to the back and side-bone of all birds, removing all but the black meat *in* the side-bone.

To Fatten Turkeys and Ducks.

Give turkeys plenty of fresh air, and charcoal in their food, and keep them in clean coops. Beef suet, chopped fine, hastens the fattening. Pork scraps ought not to be given the last ten days, as it makes the fat oily and soft. Ducks fed on meal, with chopped celery leaves, have a fine flavor; and to fatten them quickly, feed every two hours. Never confine a duck to fatten it. Always have clean water near them, and feed early in the morning and late in the evening.

Roast Turkey.

Wash the turkey well inside and out, and see that all the pin-feathers are well drawn. Twist a piece of paper, light it and pass the blaze over it quickly (if you have no blaze in your fire to singe off the fine feathers), then wash it off again. Break some pieces of cold, light bread in a bowl, put one teaspoonful of salt, half a teaspoonful of black pepper and tablespoonful of butter with a small piece of lard, in the bread; pour over it enough warm water to make it up like a dough. Put your turkey in a pot and give it one scald up, then take it on the tray and fill it with the dressing made of the bread, and rub salt and pepper on it. Fill the craw first, and with your kitchen needle, take a stitch through it to keep the dressing in. After it is stuffed, grease the turkey well with lard, and place it in your tin kitchen before the fire. Cook slowly, basting it with the juice that drips from it. Turn the spit often, and when it begins to look a little brown, cook a little faster and turn the spit. After it is well cooked, set the kitchen one side, and pour the drippings in a saucepan. Stir in a half pint of water two tablespoonfuls of browned flour, and mix it in the drippings from the turkey; add a little salt and pepper, and send it hot in a sauce tureen to the table, with the turkey on a large dish, or a chafing-pan dish over the pan for hot water, that usually is sent with the chafing dishes for beefsteak; fill the pan with boiling water and it will keep it hot until all are served. Oysters are often added to the dressing to improve it, and when they are, add a little more butter. Celery chopped fine and mixed in is very much liked, or a few nice pieces laid on it, imparts a nice flavor. Never forget to remove the string that you used to sew the stuffing in.

Serve it with cranberry sauce.

ROAST GOOSE.

Wash it thoroughly with salt and water. Prepare some Irish potatoes by boiling them nicely and mashing smooth with a tablespoonful of butter or lard. Chop two onions that have been parboiled and add them to the potato; then season highly with pepper and salt, and a little powdered sage. Roast it slowly at first and baste it with butter or lard; dredge it with flour just before you take it up to make it brown nicely. It will answer to bake dressed in the same way, but will require a pint of water in the oven or stove pan. When done, thicken the gravy with one spoonful of flour rubbed smooth with water and seasoned with pepper and salt. Apple jelly is nice to serve with it.

WILD GOOSE AND DUCK.

Parboil wild geese and ducks with one or two carrots placed in them to remove the fishy taste; throw the carrots out, and rub them with salt; let them remain fifteen minutes, then rinse them in warm water. Rub them over with lard or butter, season with pepper and salt, and roast or bake. They are seldom stuffed as tame fowls. Ducks are improved by covering them with onions before baking, and a goose with a little sage.

GREEN GOOSE PIE.

After cleaning it nicely from pin-feathers, cut it up, and put it in salt and water for an hour or more, as you choose. Have a nice soup pot, and line it with a nice plain paste. Put a layer of goose, salt, and pepper, and then small square pieces of paste. Do this until all the goose is in, then put a layer of paste over the top. Cover it well with water and let it cook three hours slowly.

TO BAKE A GOOSE.

Always let a goose hang until tender; try it by putting your thumb under the wing to see if the skin breaks easily. Prepare a dressing with one cup of bread crumbs, one of mashed potato, two onions chopped fine, pepper, salt, and sage, with the yelks of two eggs. Stuff the goose with this, and if not very fat, put a piece of butter or lard in the dressing. Rub it all over with lard, sprinkle a little flour over it, pepper and salt and bake it slowly at first, then quick, until a dark brown. Baste it often with the gravy from its fat.

BROILED TEAL.

This is a fowl nearly allied to the common wild duck, but smaller and more delicate. Split it open in the back (and if at all fishy have some carrots, tie them in, and give it one boil up), salt and pepper it, and broil on your irons or spider well greased, bone side down. Cover it with butter and send it hot to the table, and you have a delicious relish.

CANVAS BACK DUCKS.

These are a large kind of wild duck, and are considered *the dish* for an epicure. They should hang until tender (always use the carrot inside to remove the fishy taste if they smell at all like it). Prepare some chopped onion, one to a duck, a little scraped bacon, a little sage and parsley, with a sprig of marjoram and thyme, salt, and pepper; put it inside of the duck, cover the duck with thin slices of bacon, wrap it in white paper and tie it around. Roast, if possible, before a brisk fire. If you have to bake them, put a pint of water and a small piece of butter in the pan, and when nearly done, thicken the gravy slightly with browned flour. Wine added to the gravy is very nice when poured hot over the duck, with a few slices of lemon laid on the breast after it is dished. Worcester or Odenheimer sauce is an agreeable accompaniment. Crab-apple or guava jelly gives zest to the whole.

BAKED DUCKS.

English Hud, or Muscovy ducks can be cooked the day they are killed (though better to have them cleaned the day before). Mash Irish potatoes soft that have been nicely boiled; while hot put a large spoonful of butter or a small one of lard in the potato. Chop an onion fine that has been parboiled, and add it, with salt and pepper to the taste, and a little fine powdered sage. Fill the body of the duck with this dressing, put a cake of it on the breast, and bake them with a large spoonful of lard and a little water in the oven.

BOILED TURKEY.

Prepare the turkey as you do to bake. Make a dressing of bread crumbs, pepper, and salt, with hot water and milk poured over to make it soft. Chop a little parsley and put in, or fill it with oysters; fill the crop with this dressing. Put it in a pot of warm water with a little salt in it and boil it until well done, but not so tender as to fall to pieces. A good plan is to keep towels to put boiled fowls in, with long strings sewed on, so it can be tied around conveniently. Take some of the water it is boiled in, put a quarter of a pound of butter in it, rub the yelks of six hard boiled eggs smooth and mix them in the butter, with one tablespoonful of flour. Give it one boil up, and pour it over the turkey, with eggs cut in pieces over it. Celery is a great addition to the dressing, or a few seeds in the sauce. Always boil the turkey hen.

FAVORITE DISH WITH CHAPEL HILL STUDENTS IN OLDEN TIMES.
OPOSSUM.

After having the possum nicely cleaned, put it in salt and water for six hours. Rinse it well and put it in an oven with weak red pepper water and give it one boil up. Prepare a dressing of bread crumbs, salt, butter, pepper, and a little sage, if you wish to stuff it like a pig; if not, put it in an oven or stove pan with one pint of water and three nice slices of bacon on the possum and bake it. When it is nearly done, place small sweet potatoes around it and add more water (from the kettle) if it is needed, and bake it until well done and the potatoes soft. Put butter, pepper, dry sage, and salt on it, place it in the centre of a flat dish and put the potatoes around it. Serve it with Worcester or Odenheimer sauce when it is cold. It is a rich dish, and seldom eaten hot.

BARBECUE OPOSSUM.

After the possum is nicely cleaned, rinse it well with salt and water and put it in a pot to parboil, with a pod of red pepper in the water. Then put it before the fire in a tin kitchen, or lay it on crossed sticks in an oven, with a piece of fat bacon over the top. Mix some vinegar with a little mustard, butter, pepper, sage, and salt. Make a nice clean mop with linen, on a stick, and baste the possum with vinegar often; dip the mop in and rub it all over both sides, and bake it a little crisp.

BAKED CHICKEN PIE.

Clean and cut up your chickens and put them in a pot to stew, covering them with water. Put butter (large spoonful to two chickens) in it, with salt and pepper. While it is stewing, make a rich puff paste with lard and flour, roll out a piece and line a baking pan, stir a tablespoonful of flour with water and stir it in the chicken, then pour it all in the pan with the paste in it. Roll out a piece of dough for the top and butter it, sprinkle flour over it, and roll again; do this twice, then put it on the pan and put pieces of dough twisted across the top and in rings between; stick it well in the centre with a fork, press the edges with the fork, and bake it slowly. You have, then, a North Carolina pie.

STEWED POT-PIE.

Line the pot with paste and then put in pieces of chicken with thin pieces of paste between; lay in a few slices of fat meat, season with salt and pepper, cover with water, and stew two hours.

CHICKEN WITH RICE.

Take a large fat hen; put it in a bag with one teacup of nicely washed rice; put it in a pot of cold water and let it boil two hours; slip it nicely out of the bag on a dish, and cover it with a nice sauce, made of butter and hard boiled egg rubbed together, some of the water the chicken was boiled in, and a spoonful of flour well seasoned with salt; serve it hot. If cool, keep the water the hen was boiled in and make soup with it the next day. Very nice for oyster soup.

ROAST OR BAKED CHICKEN.

Prepare a nice dressing of bread crumbs, butter, pepper, and salt; pour enough hot water over it to work it up. Fill the chickens with this (and after baking put some on the breast-bone and legs), rub them over with lard, and hang up before the fire to roast, or put in your oven to bake, with a piece of lard and a little water. When done, take them up, pour some water in the drippings, dredge it with flour, give one boil up and pour a little on the chickens; balance in sauce tureen.

CHICKEN SALAD.

Boil two nice large chickens until very tender (the day before you wish to use them), take out all the bones, and remove the tough skin, and leave out the back; chop the meat fine with a cleaver. Boil eight eggs hard, peel them while hot and put in a half pint of cider vinegar the hot yelks, rub them smooth in the vinegar, then add half pint more, one tablespoonful of English mustard rubbed smooth, teaspoonful of sugar, same of salt and black pepper, tablespoonful of fresh butter melted or two of olive oil. Have one pint of chopped celery, or more if you like, and work the chicken and celery up with it; chop the white of the eggs fine and add them or not as you choose; add more mustard and sugar if you like.

BOILED TURKEY SALAD.

Prepare the dressing as above, and chop the white meat of the turkey, and mix with celery as for chicken. It is richer and preferred by many.

SALAD WITH CELERY SEED.

When celery cannot be had, chop your chicken or turkey, and put half the quantity of fine chopped cabbage that has been lying in celery vinegar one hour, put a few fresh seeds in the dressing prepared as chicken salad, and mix in the same way. It has been preferred by some at a feast; a little more mustard and small dust of cayenne can be added to this. White heads of lettuce prepared as the cabbage, answers, if that cannot be had.

IRISH POTATO SALAD.

Take cold Irish potatoes that were peeled when hot, cut them in thin, round slices, boil some eggs hard, mash the hot yelks in vinegar and season it with mustard and salt, with a pinch of sugar; put them in a salad dish, pour the sauce over them, and garnish with the white of egg cut in rings. It is excellent for a Sunday dinner—particularly with cold roast beef.

FRICASSEED CHICKENS.

Cut the chickens in pieces, put them in a pot with one or two slices of bacon or pork, sprinkle pepper and salt on each layer, cover them and let them simmer till tender; then take them out and put in a dessert spoonful of butter and same of flour, return them and stew a few minutes longer. Spread some toast, bread or crackers on a dish, put the chickens on it, and pour the gravy over them. If you prefer it brown, pour off the gravy and let it brown in the pot.

BROILED CHICKEN.

When you have cleaned your chickens nicely, lay them in skimmed milk for two hours, then dust them with flour and lay them in cold water. Take them out, sprinkle pepper and salt on the inside, and lay them open on the broiling iron after it has been nicely greased. Cook them nearly done, then turn them to brown nicely, put them in a dish, and pour drawn butter over them.

BOILED CHICKEN.

Clean it whole and lay it in milk two hours; wash it off in clear water and dust it with flour. Put them in cold water and boil half an hour (if young and tender), then let them stand closely covered half an hour in the water, and dress them with butter sauce.

CHICKEN FRIED IN BATTER.

Clean and cut up young chickens, and lay them for an hour in salt and water. Make a batter with flour, egg, and water with a little milk, put the chickens in, and take the pieces up with a large spoon and fry in hot lard.

PLAIN FRIED CHICKEN.

Clean and cut up young chickens and lay them in salt and water as above. Dredge flour over them, put them in boiling lard, cover the spider over, and fry them brown. Take them out when done, put some flour in the gravy and stir in as much water as you wish, boil it up and pour over the chicken.

CHICKEN FRIED WITH TOMATO.

Fry chicken as above, and just before done, cover it with tomatoes that have been stewed and seasoned. Cover them over and let them simmer fifteen minutes; then pour all in a dish together.

BEEFSTEAK WITH TOMATOES.

Fry nice pieces of steak cut up the size you want to serve it; before it is done, pour tomatoes over, stewed as for chicken. Let them cook and serve in a dish together.

BRUNSWICK STEW.

Put in your soup pot a nice fat chicken or hen (or two half grown), cover it with water salted to taste, and let it stew until it begins to look tender (the hen will have to be put on earlier than the young chickens); cut up one gallon of ripe tomatoes and season them with butter, a little onion, small cup of sugar, slice of fat bacon, pepper, and salt, as you would to stew; put them in the pot with the chicken, and one hour before you serve it, cut the grain off of twelve ears of green corn and add to it. The chicken should be cooked so it falls to pieces, and when dishing it, pick out the bones. Squirrels make a nice substitute for young chickens, and young duck will answer, or young turkey.

LOUISIANA SQUIRREL PIE.

Parboil the squirrels in salt and water; line a baking dish with nice pastry, put the squirrels in pieces through the pan with a slice of bacon and two hard boiled eggs, fill the pan with cream, and season with black pepper; cover it with a crust and bake it.

FRIED SQUIRRELS.

After they have been cleaned, hang them up a day or night, cut them in quarters, sprinkle salt and pepper over them, with a little meal or flour, and fry them in hot lard. Take them out and make a little thickening with flour and cream or milk, and stir it a few moments in the drippings they were fried in, with sprigs of parsley scalded in it. Pour the gravy over them and then the parsley.

SQUIRREL BARBECUE.

Parboil the squirrel, and lay it in a spider with a piece of butter, and turn it over often. Have some vinegar and mustard well rubbed together with a little salt and pepper and a pinch of sugar. When the squirrel begins to look cooked, pour this over it and turn it frequently until as brown as you wish. One gill of vinegar, teaspoonful of mustard and fourth of a teaspoon of sugar, pinch of salt and pepper to one squirrel.

BROILED SQUIRREL.

Parboil the squirrel whole for a few minutes, grease the broiling iron, put it on and turn it often over a hot fire. Season drawn butter with pepper and salt, and moisten the squirrels with it. No gravy.

MACARONI WITH BEEF.

Stew four ounces of macaroni with a large onion in milk, line a baking dish with it and cover it with grated cheese; slightly broil pieces of beef and season them high; fill the dish with layers of macaroni, beef and cheese. Cross the macaroni over the top and put bits of butter over it. Bake it slowly until a light brown. This is very nice.

VERMICELLI AND SEMOLINO.

These are much used to thicken soups and are preferable to macaroni for that purpose.

WELSH RABBIT.

Cut some nice cheese up fine in a saucepan well greased with butter, stir it until it melts; beat up five eggs and stir it in; then put a teaspoonful of made mustard and a gill of wine in it, and stir it a few minutes longer. Toast some bread and spread it over it.

CHEESE STEW.

Cut up some nice cheese and put a little ale with it and a small piece of butter, and stew it until all is melted. Serve on toast.

ROAST CHEESE.

Mix grated cheese, yelk of egg, and bread crumbs together, season to taste, spread it on bread with bits of butter, and brown it in an oven.

MACARONI.

Boil your macaroni in half milk and water until very tender; take it out and put it in a baking pan with a layer of that and one of grated cheese until it is full, put bits of butter over the top and bake it a pretty brown. Season it with salt and a little pepper.

TO STEW MACARONI.

Put as much macaroni as you want for dinner in cold water ten minutes; wash it out and put it in tepid water in a saucepan. When it is soft, drain it out and nearly cover it with milk. Add salt and cayenne pepper to your taste, with a dessert spoonful of butter and teacup of grated cheese; stir it over the fire a few minutes, then put it in a baking dish, put bread crumbs over the top, and let it brown in an oven. Take it out as soon as it browns, and keep it hot over the kettle.

MACARONI PIE.

Stew the macaroni tender, put a layer in the bottom of a baking dish, then some grated ham, with bits of butter, then macaroni and some pieces of wild duck, birds, or squirrels that have been stewed and the bone taken out; put the gravy with it and bits of butter, put another layer of macaroni crossed over the top, season a cup of cream with pepper and salt and pour it over the pie; put a puff paste on and bake it.

* * *

Seek employment; it strengthens mind and body, and matures a character that will shine bright and beautiful in moral excellence and active virtue. The Author of every good and perfect gift gave us six days for labor and the seventh for rest. He would not have so ordained, if He had not known it was for our good and would enable us to resist the temptations of *Satan* "who finds mischief for idle hands to do." "He created mind and matter, the soul and the body, gave them vitality and beauty and laws for their government, and stamped on them His own image, the sense of duty, and the instinctive dread of responsibility." Listless minds and idle hands invade and violate the rules and precepts of political economy no less than the order and laws of morality and religion.

> "Work for some good,
> Be it ever so slowly,
> Cherish some flower, be it ever so slowly,
> Labor! All labor is noble and holy!"

CURED MEATS, ETC.

To Cure Scotch Hams.

Procure mutton, pork, or beef hams, and take the bones carefully out. (If beef, get the joint called the buttock and have it out pretty far down, taking out the bones and sinews with as little cutting as possible.) Mix equal quantities of sugar and molasses, and smear the meat over with it to stand thirty hours. Then make a pickle of salt and water strong enough to bear an egg, with two ounces of saltpetre dissolved in it. Put the meat in this pickle for nine days, and then add two ounces of saltpetre to the pickle. Keep it in five days longer, and then hang it up for twenty-four hours. After this, roll the meat in a mixture of ground white pepper and half an ounce of cinnamon; tie it up tightly in a round form. Cut slices from this as you want it to boil or broil. Keeps well and is a delightful relish. Venison hams can be cured the same way.

Save fresh meat bones, pound them on a large stone, and mix with grain to feed hens.

To Try Lard.

Take the leaf fat from your fresh pork, when cutting up to cure for bacon, cut it in squares an inch thick, and put it in a large iron pot over the fire, and cook it until the pieces are a *light* brown. Be careful never to have a blaze under the pot. Strain it through a colander, in tin lard stands, with a *coarse* cloth over the top of the stand. Drain it in another vessel, and then press the pieces of meat for common purposes. The pieces are generally saved to make crackling bread.

To Make Common Lard.

Take the flabby pieces of meat that are not fit to be salted. Put them on the fire with a half pint of water and slowly cook it until the meat looks done. Strain it out and set it in a cool place. If allowed to freeze, it will lose the strong taste.

CHITTERLINGS.

This dish is a great favorite on plantations, and should be carefully prepared. After they are emptied and nicely cleaned, turn and scrape them and put them in warm water. After soaking all day in that, put them in salt and water to soak for two days. Then wash them out nicely in warm water again. Select out what you want for sausages and then plait the balance and boil them until perfectly tender. Sprinkle a little salt over them when hot, and put them in a jar for use, and cover them with melted lard or vinegar as you prefer.

HOG'S-HEAD CHEESE.

Put hog's heads in salt and water for two days, then wash and scrape them clean, and boil until all the bones come out. Take it up, pick all the bones out and chop it fine; season it with sage, pepper, salt, and a little cayenne, with a small spoonful of spice. Put it in a cloth or a tin pan, cover it, and put heavy weights on to press it. When cold, take it out of the mould and cover it with vinegar. Cut it in shoes for the table as cold souse, or beat it up and fry it, with or without batter.

BEEF'S-HEAD CHEESE.

Split the head in half, take out the eyes, and soak it all night; then boil it tender and make it as hog's-head, or put it in the liquor after the bones are taken out. Season high and stew it until all the water is out, then pack it tight in a jar and press it, and keep it to slice for supper.

CRIPPLE.

Take two hog's faces, boil them until the meat leaves the bone, put it in a colander, pick the meat from the bone, then strain the liquor and put it back in the kettle with the meat, and if not enough to cover it, add boiling water. Add pepper and salt to your taste, one tablespoonful of ground allspice, same of cloves, marjoram, and thyme; boil it fifteen minutes after it commences to boil, then thicken it with buckwheat or seconds sifted fine. Pack it in a jar, and when cold, cut it in slices to fry. This was given me by a lady from Baltimore as one of her favorite dishes.

BETTIE'S SAUSAGES.

Put six pounds of lean and two of fat pork together and grind it in a sausage grinder, or chop it fine with a cleaver. Put it in a tray with four tablespoonfuls of salt, same of black pepper, six of powdered sage, and two of red pepper. Mix thoroughly and keep it in a cool place.

BOLOGNA SAUSAGES.

Chop veal, pork, and ham fine, season with pepper, salt, and sweet herbs. Prepare beef chitterlings by soaking them three days after they have been nicely cleaned, changing the water every day; then put them in tepid salt and water twenty-four hours, scrape them the second time, and wash them out in cold water. After they are stuffed with the meat, boil them tender and dry them.

GAME.

Birds may be preserved several days by washing them clean after being picked and dropped in boiling water long enough for the water to pass through, and then salt them. If any game is tainted, wash it in vinegar and cook it, and it will not be discovered. Broil, fry, and bake birds as you fancy. Always parboil ducks, geese, or any game that smells fishy, with carrots inside; remove the carrots and when cooked the smell will not be perceptible.

TO CLEAN BEEF TRIPE.

Rinse it clean in cold water, put it in a tub, sprinkle lime over it and cover it with tepid water, to stand four hours. Then scrape it and if it does not clean easily, sprinkle a little more lime on it and let it remain an hour longer. Scrape it nice and clean and wash it in several waters; put it in salt and water for three days, changing it the second day. If you want it very white, after you take it from the salt and water and rinse the salt off, lay it in buttermilk to whiten for four hours, then wash it clean, and cook as you like it.

LOUISIANA DOUBE.

Take a round of beef and make incisions in it with a knife or sharp stick; stuff them with thyme, onion, parsley, and red pepper. Put two tablespoonfuls of lard in a kettle just large enough to hold the beef, put it in and let it fry slowly for three hours over a slow fire, frequently turning it. When it has been cooking three hours, put one spoonful of lard in a separate vessel and thicken it with browned flour. After it has browned, pour one quart of boiling water to it and pour that over the beef; let it cool slowly all day until the jelly congeals. When cold, keep it one day in vinegar and stick it with cloves, and you will have a delicious relish for tea or lunch.

A FRICANDEAU OF BEEF.

Take a nice piece of lean beef, lard it with bacon, season with pepper, cloves, mace, allspice, and a clove of garlic. Put it in a stew-pan with a pint of broth, a glass of white wine, a bunch of parsley, sweet herbs, a shallot, four cloves, pepper, and salt; stew it until perfectly tender, and cover it close. Skim the sauce and strain it and let it boil until reduced to a glaze; glaze the larded side with this and serve the meat with sauce.

BEEF ROBART.

Take thin slices of a sirloin of beef, fry it in butter a few minutes, then put it in a stew-pan with some gravy, a shallot, anchovy essence, mushrooms, and oysters; thicken the gravy and serve with fried sippets of bread.

ENGLISH STEW.

Cut up cold beef or any fresh meat in slices; pepper, salt, and flour them and lay them in a pan; sprinkle pickled cucumber or cabbage cut fine over the meat.

Stir one teacup of water, a little vinegar, the pickle, and half a teacup of catchup together; pour it over the meat, and cook in the stove or oven half an hour.

BROWN STEW.

Cut up some pieces of beef or cold meat of any kind and season them highly with cayenne, black pepper, salt, and butter; dredge a little flour over it. Put in a saucepan a spoonful of lard, and when it is warm stir in a spoonful of flour; stir it over the fire until it browns. Put the meat in with a little chopped onion, marjoram, and thyme; set it in one corner, and let it stew slowly half an hour; then put a little boiling water on it and let it cook five hours. This is a Louisiana stew.

TO STEW AN OX TONGUE.

Salt a tongue with saltpetre and common salt for a week, turning it every day; then boil it until tender enough to peel. Always take the root off before it is salted. Stew it in gravy and season with tomato, sage, cayenne pepper, a few cloves, and mushroom catchup if you like, and stew it until perfectly done.

SPICED ROUND OF BEEF.

Take a nice round of beef and rub it well with three tablespoonfuls of saltpetre, same of sugar, two teacupsful of salt, and one of ground allspice and cloves mixed. Put it in a vessel as near the size as you can. As soon as the pickle forms, turn it over every day. Let it remain three weeks before using it. When you cook it, put cross sticks in the bottom of the pan or oven to prevent its touching.

COLD PICKLE FOR BEEF.

In hot weather it is good to have a nice pickle always ready to drop beef in, particularly if you have not an ice-house convenient. Mix in two gallons of water half a gallon of coarse salt, one tablespoonful of pulverized saltpetre, and one quarter of a pound of brown sugar. If a scum arises after standing a week, give it a scald up, carefully removing the scum. Strain it in the vessel you keep it in, and when cold add a little more saltpetre and sugar. Before putting fresh meat in cold pickle, give it *one* scald in boiling salt and water, and drop it in hot. I know this to be good from experience.

MEAT JELLY.

Three ounces of gelatine, four eggs, tablespoonful of salt, half a glass of brandy or wine, one quart of cold gravy or soup, and a little pepper. Mix well, boil ten minutes, strain and set it on ice.

MRS. W.'S FRENCH STEW.

Put four ounces of salt pork out small in a stewpan, with some parsley, thyme, onion or a clove of garlic, sweet basil, a *few* cloves, and two or three carrots cut in rings. Let it simmer a few minutes; then, after having covered the beef with a little gravy mixed in half wine and brandy, place it in a moderate oven with rings of onion over the top and paste around the sides and top. Cook it from six to eight hours, pour the gravy over it, and you have a rich, nice stew that improves common beef.

MRS. W.'S BAKED BEEF.

Season a nice piece of beef with butter, pepper, salt, and slices of onion rubbed over it. Put it in a pan or oven with one quart of water; grease a piece of paper and cover the beef well with it to prevent its baking hard. Baste it often over the paper, and remove that and replace a fresh piece if it scorches. Serve with Odenheimer sauce.

MRS. W'S HAM WITH JELLY.

Soak a ham twenty-four hours. Cover it with onions, carrot, parsley, thyme, celery, and one or two cloves; pour half a pint of wine over it, and put it in a towel fastened around tightly. Cook it five or six hours in a kettle of water, cold when first put on. When done, remove the towel, put it in a dish, and put meat jelly all around it, with carrots and turnips cut fancifully after being boiled, and placed over the ham.

To Collar Breast of Veal to Eat Hot.

Bone the veal; take some thyme, marjoram, salt, pepper, nutmeg, a little mace, shred suet, crumbs of bread, and a score of oysters. Beat all these in a mortar to mix them together, strew the mixture thickly over the veal, then roll it up into a collar, sew it tightly in a cloth, and boil it three hours. Serve it with white sauce and force-meat balls.

Venison.

Wash it well with milk and water and dry it in a cloth, till there is not the least damp remaining; then cover every part with ground pepper and you can keep it several days to roast or fry. Cook it as you do lamb, and eat jelly with it. If you wish to stew it when cold, put some of the gravy in a stew pan with a little wine, currant jelly, and lemon juice, with a little flour. When it is hot drop the venison slices in and heat it through. The steaks are nice broiled or fried with butter and eaten with jelly.

Mutton to Eat Like Venison.

Take a fat loin of mutton, hang it for three days, and then bone it; rub it with sugar, a glass of port wine and some vinegar and let it remain four days. Then wash and wipe it dry, season it with pepper and salt, and put half a pound of butter on it. Put it in a dish with crust around the edge, cover it with a thick crust and bake it in a slow oven.

Turkey Salad.

Prepare a dressing of four eggs beat very light, boil two cups of vinegar with a piece of butter size of a goose egg; when the butter melts stir in the eggs. Continue to stir until it boils, then add one tablespoonful of mustard, one of sugar, teaspoonful of salt and pepper. When it is cold pour it over a turkey that has been chopped up fine.

CROQUETS.

Chop very fine cold fowl or any fresh meat. Beat light several eggs (in the proportion of three or four to a chicken), mix together and season highly with pepper, butter, and salt (a little pickle cut up is an improvement), make into lady fingers, dip in beaten yelk of an egg, rub in grated bread crumbs, and fry a light brown.

MUTTON CUTLETS.

Season with pepper and salt and lay them into melted butter; turn them often, then dip them in bread crumbs and broil over a clear fire, or fry them in hot lard.

TO BONE A TURKEY.

Take a sharp thin knife and carefully remove the flesh from the bone of the wing, scraping it downward as you proceed without cutting it to pieces. Do not tear or break the skin. If any breakages, sew them up before cooking. Loosen the flesh from the breast-bone next, then the back and thighs. Draw the skeleton by the neck from the flesh, as the hand from a glove, and then restore the mass to its original form by hard stuffing with force-meat, or any stuffing you prefer. Bake it two hours and tastefully cover it with guava or currant jelly. Stew the giblets until done in half pint of water, cut them fine, beat the yelks of three eggs, stir it in *the water* with a gill of wine, pour it over the giblets in a sauce tureen and send it as an accompaniment. Sprigs of curled parsley, dipped in hot water, may be put between pieces of jelly around the dish. This was a favorite dish at Elizabeth City parties.

SAUCE MAYONNAISE.

Put into a quart bowl the yelks of two fresh eggs, with a little salt and cayenne. After they are stirred well together, add one teaspoonful of best salad oil, and stir it until it looks like cream, with a half pint of oil slowly added. After it is well mixed and no oil visible, stir in two tablespoonfuls of sharp vinegar and one of cold water. This was a favorite dressing for boned turkey and salads of a particular friend ten years ago in Elizabeth City.

ANOTHER PICKLE FOR CORNED BEEF.

Put six gallons of water on the fire with three ounces of saltpetre and when it is dissolved and the water boiling, dip your beef, piece by piece, into the boiling saltpetre water, holding it for a few seconds only in the hot bath. After it has all been immersed and becomes cool, pack it in a clean cask. Put nine pounds of salt, three pounds of brown sugar, one quart of molasses, and one ounce of pearlash in the water with saltpetre in it, and boil it, carefully removing the scum the molasses and sugar causes to rise. Dipping it in hot saltpetre water contracts the surface by closing the pores, and prevents the juices from the meat going out into the pickle. Beef cured in this manner preserves its color, and cuts almost as juicy as a roast.

TO FRY CHIPPED BEEF.

Chip one pound of dry beef that has been cured by the above recipe and hung to dry; parboil it five minutes (in cold water when you first put it on), drain the water from the beef; place it on the fire with a large lump of butter, dredge it with flour until covered; pour on a pint of rich milk, stirring with a spoon until it thickens, and send it hot to the table.

TO COOK CALF'S LIVER.

Cut the liver in slices and fry it in butter when done, take it out and put it in a saucepan, dredge flour over it, pour on a glass of claret wine with four small onions chopped, little parsley, pepper, and salt; let it boil briskly until the sauce is done, and serve it hot.

To Cook Beef's Heart.

Clean the heart nicely and cut the inside out, and chop it fine; mix it in a force-meat with bread crumbs, onion chopped fine, and a little chopped bacon. Fry it in butter partly done, then season it with pepper and salt, add one pint of rich gravy, with one carrot cut fine, and stew it nearly dry. Take it out, put it in a pan, stir the yelks of three eggs with it, sprinkle bread crumbs over the top and bits of butter, and put it in an oven to brown. Boil two eggs hard, slice them, and cover the top with them when sent to the table. If you like spice with meats, you can use a small quantity of cloves and nutmeg with it.

Scotland Neck Sausage Meat.

Twenty pounds of meat, fat and lean mixed, seven tablespoonfuls of salt, four of black pepper, two of sage, one of red pepper, and one teaspoonful of saltpetre.

Giblet Stew.

Take the pinions of turkeys or geese, cut them in two parts, the neck in four pieces, slice the gizzard and liver, and put it in two quarts of water, with some pepper, salt, marjoram, an onion, some catch up, and an anchovy. When they are tender, stir in one spoonful of cream and thicken it with flour and butter.

Onion Sauce.

Boil the onions, chop them on a board, add butter and cream, give it one boil, and pour it hot over ducks or anything you like.

To Cook Pigeons or Partridges.

Fry the birds in butter or lard until slightly browned. Take them out and fry some onions cut in four pieces a short time in the gravy. Put them in a stew-pan with the gravy and enough hot water to cover them. Pepper and salt and cook them one hour. This way is much liked by persons that love onions. Add two tablespoonfuls of flour to the gravy half an hour before you wish to serve it.

TO SMOTHER BIRDS.

After they are nicely washed, and split open, put them in boiling water for ten minutes. Then season them highly with salt, pepper, and a little mustard mixed thin with vinegar. Put a little water and one dessert spoonful of butter to one bird, in an oven or stove pan, and sprinkle a little flour in it and stir it until it is mixed. Then put the birds in, cover them, and let them simmer slowly nearly two hours, turning them often until nearly done; sprinkle a few bread crumbs over, and brown the top, and when dished, pour the gravy over them.

BIRD PIE.

Take young pigeons, robins, or any small birds, and stew them with butter, pepper, and salt until tender. Line a baking dish with nice paste and partly cook it, then place the birds in, pour the gravy over, add the yelks of hard boiled eggs, cover it with a crust nicely trimmed on the top, and bake.

VEGETABLES.

CAROLINA SWEET POTATOES.

Pare off the specks, wash them nicely and put them in an oven or stove pan with a little water (one teacupful). Cover them and bake in a slow oven at first and then quickly. They are delicious baked slowly in a large brick oven. Some persons bake nearly a barrel in this way and warm them as they are wanted, or eat them cold with a glass of milk.

SQUASH.

Peel the squashes, if old, and cut them in quarters, put them in the pot with a piece of meat and boil to mash up, or put them in a saucepan with bits of meat, and as they cook mash them and stir often. If boiled, stir some cream in them and put black pepper over the top.

WINTER SQUASH.

Cut them up and stew them with pieces of meat, or parboil them, mash, season with cream, pepper, and salt, and bake them. Some persons like a little onion mixed with squash before it is stewed or baked.

CAULIFLOWER AND BROCCOLI.

These vegetables are not much used; generally cooked in salt and water, and dressed in cream or butter with pepper.

STUFFED CABBAGE.

Parboil a nice cabbage whole, tie it in a towel, and fasten it tightly. Then drop it in with a nice ham boiling for twenty minutes. Take it out and plunge the cloth with it in cold water, and let it stand to cool. Untie the cloth carefully, lay it open, and take the heart out with a piece of the stalk; do not disturb the upper leaves. Save the piece you cut out. Make a dressing of it mixed with bread crumbs, cayenne pepper, one or two whole spices and black pepper, a few celery seeds, yelks of two hard boiled eggs and butter. If you have a steamer, put it in for half an hour over boiling water on the fire, carefully fitting the piece of stalk in where you cut the heart out. If no steamer, wrap it in the towel and boil it fifteen minutes. The flavor of the ham improves it, and some use it instead of butter, when it had to be parboiled in clear water.

RADISHES.

This root must be placed in cold water until wanted, and then put on the table in glasses to eat with salt. They are very good cut in round slices and put in good vinegar for an hour or two.

WATER CRESS OR PEPPER GRASS.

Wash clean and put it in salt and water and send it to the table with other salads.

TURNIPS.

Boil turnips peeled and cut in quarters when you want to mash them. They are very good boiled with corned beef and sent in around the dish nicely mashed and formed in a roll, with black pepper on the top.

SUCCATASH.

Take one quart of Lima or butter beans and put two quarts of green corn with it. Cover them with water and let them stew an hour or more; then season highly with butter, pepper, and salt, and serve hot in a covered dish.

CABBAGES.

Pick all the outer leaves off and quarter the head; put it in a bag made for the purpose, and two hours before you wish it, put it in with a ham that has been boiling and let it boil one hour. Take it out, dip the bag in cold water, and return it to the pot after it is cold, and boil again until wanted. I always used thin cotton bags for vegetables and found them very useful. If cabbage is to be boiled without meat, put red pepper in the water, and salt, and serve with butter, or a nice gravy made from cold ham essence.

BEETS.

These should always be boiled in a separate vessel from other vegetables.

SPINACH.

Boil this in clear water half an hour. If you wish it to look very green, put a small lump of pearlash or saleratus in the water. Drain it well and dress it with poached eggs and butter.

PARSNIPS.

Boil the parsnips whole in clear water, and then split them and put butter over, or mash fine and fry in batter like egg-plant.

POKE-ROOT SPROUTS.

When this first springs like asparagus, boil and dress the sprouts with butter, pepper, and salt.

SALSIFY.

Scrape or grate this root, and mix it with batter to fry in hot lard as egg-plant, or cut in thin round pieces, stew it done, and cover it with cream, pepper, and salt. If you have to use milk, boil it with a piece of butter and pour it on hot. You can slice it lengthways, fry or broil, and dress with butter.

ONIONS.

Remove the outer skin, and put them in an *onion kettle*. When nearly done, pour off the water and add fresh boiling water with milk in it if you have it. Pour drawn butter over them.

FRIED ONIONS.

Cut them in thin slices and season them; have a piece of fat bacon frying to get the juice, take it out, and put the onions in and stir until a pretty brown.

BROILED TOMATO.

Peel, and take the seed out, cut them through the middle, season with pepper and salt, sprinkle meal over them, and broil on a warm griddle.

BAKED WHOLE TOMATO.

Take large Linden tomatoes, peel them nicely with a knife, cut them through the middle, take out the seeds and fill the cells with a dressing made of fine crumbs, sugar, butter, pepper, salt, and a drop or two of vinegar. Fit the halves together and tie them with a string. Fill a baking pan with these, mix a little sugar and water and pour in, and when done, take a large spoon and arrange them on white plates or small dishes, and they not only look pretty on the table, but are as nice as tomato can be made.

CORN PUDDING WITH TOMATO.

Cut the corn down the ear, and scrape it down with a knife, having only a few whole grains. Beat three eggs with a quart of milk and season it with butter, pepper, salt, and stir the corn in. Then stir in one pint of tomato that has been stewed with sugar in it, stir it well, and bake it. You can leave the tomato out if you choose.

CORN FRITTERS.

Take twelve ears of half-grown corn, cut the grains through with a knife, then cut them from the ear. Beat four eggs, mix them with four tablespoonfuls of flour, and thin with one quart of milk. Season it with salt and pepper, stir the corn in and drop one large spoonful at a time in hot lard, and fry them a light brown. Try it and see if it is not like oysters.

TURNIP SALAD.

Cut this in the last of September when young, and boil it well done with fresh corned pork. Put it on a dish with the pork in the middle and the tiny little turnip roots put all around. This is the way it is preferred in the eastern part of this State, and in the middle and west, the salad that springs from the root that has been covered all winter is used as a great dish before spring vegetables are ripe.

ASPARAGUS.

Cut this when two inches high, run the knife under the ground three or four inches. Put it in cold water as you scrape it off. Put it in a bag for the purpose and boil it hard twenty minutes or longer if required. Put drawn butter over in a covered dish, and you have the nicest of all spring vegetables. If you want it to grow large, press a large mouth bottle over the first shoot, and press dirt around it. It will grow to a larger size and be tender.

BAKED TOMATOES.

Peel and cut up one gallon of tomatoes, put a layer on the bottom of a baking dish, then a few crumbs of loaf bread with sugar, pepper, salt, and bits of butter; do this until the pan is full. Set it in a stove or oven and cook slowly two hours. Green corn, cut off the ear after the grain has been split with a sharp knife, and sprinkled over each layer, adds very much to the dish. Do not use as much crumb of bread when you put corn in and a little more butter.

STEWED TOMATOES.

Peel and season them with salt, butter, pepper, and sugar; add a few bread crumbs, and stew them slowly one hour.

SNAP BEANS.

Take a sharp knife and shave the string off on both sides, put them in a bag and boil them two hours with a piece of meat, or in plain salt and water. When boiled without meat, pour cream over them, and black pepper.

LIMA OR BUTTER BEANS.

Gather them and put them in salt and water half an hour, then put them on in cold water and boil them tender; serve them hot, covered with butter.

FRIED IRISH POTATO.

Slice the potato very thin and sprinkle a little salt over it. Have lard boiling hot and fry them crisp. Some persons sprinkle a little flour or meal through a sieve over them before putting in the lard to fry.
Nice with beefsteak.

FRIED CUCUMBERS.

Peel large cucumbers and slice them half an inch thick; season them with salt and pepper; sprinkle meal over them and fry them with hot lard or a slice of fat bacon.

STEWED IRISH POTATOES.

Cut up one dozen Irish potatoes in round pieces half an inch thick, nearly cover them with water in a saucepan, cover it and let them stew until tender. Drain off the water and let them steam a few minutes, then cover them with milk. Rub a little flour in butter, put it in with salt and pepper, and when the milk comes to a full boil, pour them out in a covered dish. This is a great breakfast dish in Louisiana. Cold gravies left from the day before are often used instead of milk.

FRIED CORN.

Cut enough corn from the cob to make one quart, season it with a piece of butter size of a hen's egg, pepper and salt, put it in a saucepan with a very little water and cook it half an hour, shaking it occasionally to prevent burning.

FRIED APPLES.

Wash apples, not very sour, take out the stem, core, and calyx (do not peel them), cut them in thin slices, and put them in a frying pan with some butter or gravy of baked pork and a little water. Cover them with a lid, set them on the stove or fire, and stir them occasionally. Sour apples will not fry well, they tear to pieces.

FRIED SWEET POTATOES.

Peel the potato and cut it in slices quarter of an inch thick; sprinkle a *little* salt on the slices and try them in hot lard, or pieces of fresh meat. Put butter over them or not as you choose. It takes very little grease to fry them brown.

TO BAKE NAVY BEANS.

Boil one quart of beans in three quarts of water until they begin to crack, drain the water off through a colander, put a piece of pork in the middle of a pan and beans all around and under it, cover it with water and two tablespoonfuls of molasses, and bake it slowly until the pork is done. It is not so rich if the pork is parboiled.

FRIED POTATO CAKES.

Boil Irish potatoes and mash them fine, season with butter, pepper, and salt; flour your hands, make up small rolls of potato, and mash them until quarter of an inch thick. Fry them in lard or bake them brown on a greased griddle.

IRISH POTATO PUDDING.

Boil and mash potatoes, season with butter, pepper, and salt, thin with sweet milk, and bake in a pan to eat with meats.

BEET PUDDING.

Boil beets nearly done, grate them and stir in milk, eggs, and a little butter, with one spoonful of flour to a quart of milk. Bake in pans. Some prefer the beet boiled tender and mashed up.

TURNIP FRITTERS.

Boil and mash them fine, mix them in a batter of flour, milk, and egg, with a mite of sugar, and fry in lard.

CYMBLING FRITTERS.

Peel the cymbling and cut it in half inch slices, slightly parboil it in salt and water; beat up a batter with two eggs, a little flour and milk, dip it in the batter, and fry a light brown. This is a very good substitute for egg-plant.

EGG-PLANT IN BATTER.

Peel the egg-plant early in the day, slice it and salt each slice; let it stand until ready to fry for dinner. Then make a batter of flour, egg, and milk, pour it over the plant, and fry it in hot lard, taking up one piece at a time. Slightly parboil it before putting it in the batter.

EGG-PLANT FRIED.

Peel, cut, and salt it as above and parboil it; then sprinkle meal over it slightly, and fry in hot lard.

EGG-PLANT STUFFED.

Boil them whole in salt and water, scrape the inside out and mix with it some bread crumbs, little chopped onion, pepper, and salt, with yelk of egg and small bit of butter. Stuff the shell with this mixture and bake it.

TOMATOES SLICED.

Peel the tomato and cut it through the centre, in three slices; sprinkle white sugar over it, then cover with claret wine. Vinegar is often substituted for the wine, but does not impart the rich flavor the wine does, resembling strawberry.

OKRA.

Take young okras three inches long and boil them in water with a little salt, until done; the seeds always look dark when the okra is cooked sufficiently. Put them in a covered dish with butter and black pepper over them, and send them hot to the table.

OKRAS FRIED.

Cut them in thin cross slices, sprinkle meal over them, and fry crisp in hot lard.

OKRA FRITTERS.

Cut the okra in very thin slices, almost as thin as a wafer, make a batter of flour, egg, and water, or a little milk; put the okra in with a little salt, and fry them in hot lard.

COLD SLAW.

Shave nicely one head of cabbage two hours before dinner. Put in a porcelain saucepan one pint of good vinegar, teaspoonful of English mustard, tablespoonful of sugar, teaspoonful of salt, and a lump of butter size of a walnut. While this is boiling, beat two eggs and stir them in. When it boils up, take it off, and stir in a teaspoonful of celery seed. Pour it hot over the cabbage and work it all up together. Put it in a cool place or on ice.

COLD SLAW.

Cut cabbage very fine. Boil some eggs hard and rub the yelks smooth while hot in vinegar. Add mustard, salt, and cayenne pepper to taste, with olive oil if you like, and a few celery seed, with a teaspoonful of sugar, and stir the cabbage in the mixture. Add vinegar if needed to make it moist.

LETTUCE DRESSED.

Cut the lettuce fine and prepare a dressing as for cold cabbage. Use a little more sugar.

LETTUCE WITH OIL.

Rub the yelks of three eggs with one tablespoonful of olive oil for ten minutes, then stir in a tablespoonful of sugar, one of mustard, and small bit of salt. Have heads of lettuce nicely washed, open, and pour the mixture in, or cut it up fine and pour over it.

CUCUMBERS SLICED.

Put your cucumbers in cold water until you are ready to prepare them; peel off the green skin, cut them in thin slices with a slicer made for the purpose, or very sharp knife; put them in a deep plate with salt sprinkled between, let them stand ten minutes; then turn another plate over the top, shake them hard and drain off all the water. Cover them with good cider vinegar and sprinkle black pepper over the top. Prepared in this way they are easily digested. Onions sliced and mixed with them are much liked by some. The best plan is to have onions sliced and put in a separate plate for each one to add as they like.

SOUR-KROUT.

Take a cask with a hole in the bottom, size of a bottle cork. Lay cross sticks on the bottom of the cask and cover them with grape-vine leaves. Cut up fine, sound cabbages in thin slices, cut round, pack it in the barrel with a layer of salt on each layer of cabbage, nearly to the top. Put a piece of coarse cloth that has been soaked in strong salt and water and dried, on the top, then cross sticks with weights upon them to keep the cabbage packed; tie a cloth over the top and put gimlet holes around the cask to let the air pass through the top. Take the cork out of the bottom every week for a month, and let the brine run off. Rinse the cloth off and add a quart of salt over the top every time the brine is taken off. This will keep a long time, and was highly relished in West Virginia during the war, when vegetables could not be had.

TO COOK SOUR-KROUT.

Take it out of the cask with a wooden spoon and soak it three hours in cold water, rinse it in another water, and put it on with a nice slice of bacon and cook it until the bacon is done.

TO BOIL IRISH POTATOES.

Take off a piece of the peel from each end, and put them in boiling water with salt in it; let them boil fast for half an hour. Pour the water off and cover them closely for five minutes, then send them to the table in a covered dish. If peeled, pour butter over them.

NEW POTATOES.

Always scrape them nicely and lay them in cold water for an hour. Put them in boiling water with a little salt in it and boil fifteen minutes, pour the water off, let them dry, and when served put butter over them.

MASHED POTATOES.

After boiling old potatoes, put them in a wooden bowl and mash them soft with a potato pestle; put in butter while they are hot; pepper, and salt, then stir in a little cream or rich milk, and set the dish they are served in over hot water until wanted.

EDIBLE MUSHROOMS.

They appear very small at first, are round in form, on a little stalk. They grow fast, and the upper part and stalk are white. As the size increases, the under part gradually opens, and shows a fringed fur of a very fine salmon color, which continues more or less till the mushroom has gained some size, and then turns to a dark brown. These marks should be attended to, and likewise whether the skin can be easily parted from the edges and middle. Those that have a white or yellow fur should be carefully avoided, though many of them have the same smell, but not so strong as the right sort. This, with the following recipes for mushrooms, a friend gave me, having learned them from Mrs. Hale's valuable cookery.

TO STEW MUSHROOMS.

The large buttons are best for this purpose and the small flaps while the fur is still red. Rub the button with salt and a bit of flannel; cut out the fur, and take off the skin from the others; put them in a stew-pan with a little lemon-juice, pepper, salt, and a small piece of fresh butter; let it simmer slowly till done then put a small bit of butter and flour, two spoonfuls of cream, give them one boil, and serve with sippets of bread.

To Stew Mushrooms—An Easy Way.

Cut off that part of the stem that grows under ground, wash them carefully, and take the skin from the top. Put them into a stew-pan with some salt, but no water. Stew them till tender, and thicken with a tablespoonful of butter, mixed with one of brown flour.

To Broil Mushrooms.

The largest are the best. Have a clear cinder fire; make the gridiron hot, and rub the bars with suet to prevent the mushrooms from sticking; place them on the gridiron with their stalks upwards; sprinkle them slightly with salt and pepper and serve them on a hot dish, with a little cold butter, under and over them. When they begin to steam, they are sufficiently done.

Louisiana Green Pea Recipe.

Wash the peas and put them in a clean spider, cover them up and set them over the fire; let them steam in this way half an hour. Then put in a spoonful of butter and two of cream, and serve them hot. The flavor of the pea is far better than when boiled in water. If they are not soft, let them cook a little longer, but not add the butter until just before you take them up.

Tomato Fritters.

Stew them done and season (as for the stews), beat up a batter with egg, milk, and flour, stir the tomatoes in and fry them in hot lard.

DRINKS.

During the late war, many new drinks were substituted for the favorite beverages from coffee and tea, that could not be procured, and many persons confessed they did not consider them as necessary to a meal as they had been trained to think. Then why should we train children to use them? The effect is stimulating to the nervous system without nourishing it. Heat is said to be a stimulant to the nerves of the mouth, teeth, throat and stomach, inducing constant reacting debility, which, according to the law of the nervous system, is in exact proportion to the degree of stimulation. Weak and delicate persons, and children, suffer from habits that form a love for stimulating drinks, when they have to bear the infirmities of the strong. Water is the most natural drink, when pure and good. Rain water is considered the purest when obtained from a cistern dug in the vicinity of a large dwelling, with conducting spouts, lined with water lime. It can be purified by alum being used in proportion of two grains to one quart, or through a simple filterer, made in a cask of sand and charcoal, with a piece of blanket over the top, that is to be removed and washed every time the cask is refilled. When such simple preventives from disease are at hand, there is but little excuse for not using them. Good, sweet milk, when cows are properly fed, with healthy food, and have fresh air and exercise, is decidedly healthy for both adults and children. Delicate infants should be fed from the milk of one cow that is fed on sweet food. The decayed vegetables and offal from the kitchen, that has not been preserved by keeping it in salt and water, is not only bad for the cow, but affects the health of the child, from its bad effect on the milk. Every housekeeper should give this particular attention. The love of coffee is universal. It forms a pleasant beverage, and those who indulge in it cannot be convinced of its injurious effects. The immoderate use of it is said to produce various diseases, tremor, anxiety, palpitation of the heart, and feverishness, and often the vision is affected by it. Green and black tea are used by many in preference. Persons thin in flesh should never indulge in green, from its creating vertigo, and being opposed to active nutrition, giving rise to sleeplessness and tremor, if strong. It sometimes relieves headache from its sedative influence, but is not recommended by physicians as highly as the black. Chocolate contains oil, and is difficult to digest, but devoid of the disagreeable qualities of tea and coffee. Cocoa has less oil than chocolate, and its shells, not being so rich, are better adapted to weak digestive organs.

To Make Good Coffee.

Procure the best and wash it clean, roast it until it is of a golden brown color, mix the whites of three eggs with each pound of coffee while warm, and tie it up tightly in a jar. Grind the quantity you wish to make fresh every time. Put it in a thin muslin bag made for this purpose, drop it in the coffee-pot and pour boiling water on it. Cover it immediately and boil five minutes.

Coffee Number Two.

Parch nice clean coffee, with half a teaspoonful of lard to the pound, let it toast until you can break the grain, stirring it all the time; grind it as you wish. Take a teacup of coffee and the white of one egg, and stir it to a paste with cold water. Put it in a tin boiler and pour three pints of boiling water to it, put it on the fire and boil it five minutes, pour a cupful off and back in the top of the pot, and let it set a few minutes before pouring it off.

Coffee Number Three.

Parch your coffee as directed above, grind it and put it in a tight tin coffee box: Buy a block tin coffee-pot with a strainer. Put your coffee in the strainer and pour boiling hot water on it. It is clear, needs no egg, and has the pure, rich aroma of the coffee. When it has ceased to drip, pour off a cupful and pour it through the top again, to get all the strength from the coffee. Wash the pot nicely every time it is used. These pots are used in place of a costly urn.

Coffee Number Four.

Pick and wash your coffee, and carefully toast it a golden brown (a coffee roaster is said to preserve the aroma better than the spider usually used), and grind it as you need it. Put water on to boil, and when hot, put the coffee in by the spoonful, stirring it all the time until all is in and it boils up to the top; put white of egg in or egg-shells crushed to clear it, boil it ten minutes, then pour a little cold water in it and set it aside to settle. Pour it off in the pot or urn you use at the table. Use a large cup of coffee to a quart of water.

* * *

"She stretcheth out her hands to the poor, yea, she reacheth forth her hands to the needy."

How few mothers in our land of plenty train their daughters to practice self-denial, by giving up what they consider *actually necessary* to their comfort and happiness, even for one day out of seven, to enable them to administer to the wants of the poor around them. It was my happy lot to be trained by a saint upon earth, my mother. My gentle, loving, Christian mother, left an undying monument, not of gift or stone wrought by human agency, but one gilded with Christian virtues so pure and bright, that her name, at the head of an *incorporated Dorcas society*, will be handed down to generations yet unborn, and "her children ever call *blessed*, when her praises are spoken." She never forgot the poor. From my earliest recollection a well filled plate was sent to them daily, from the luxuries in which her family indulged. Often have I seen her leave delicacies untasted on her plate, and carefully set aside for her evening walk to the poor, who were perhaps craving such things on a bed of sickness.

If any prayer has ever been offered up with true sincerity, it is this, that with the mantle of her virtues thrown around me, I might have the power to impress upon the women of my day the claims of the poor—which are urgent upon them, not only for the well-being of moral and social government, but for the spiritual and temporal welfare of beings who possess immortal souls as well as we, created by "the common Father of us all." Hence, "He that giveth to the poor lendeth to the Lord!" Their duty to the poor should be one of our first instructions to the young, and the penny or bread never denied to charity at the door. Charitable acts will make a happy, cheerful home; encourage them by daily goodness. Be your means ever so small, some good may be done. It does not require the wealth that perisheth like a flower in the noonday sun, to accomplish such acts. It requires instilling in the hearts of the young, the love

91

of good deeds and the love of that pure happiness enjoyed by those only who seek to make all happy around them in discharging daily their duty to their God, their neighbor, and all mankind.

92

BREAD.

OARSE BREAD.

Take one quart of seconds, three large spoonfuls of coarse corn meal and a gill of molasses, mix with warm water and a gill of hop yeast until it is a thick batter, and put it to rise; when light, bake in a quick oven.

CAROLINA BISCUIT.

Take two quarts of flour, sift half a teaspoonful of salt in it, then work in a large tablespoonful of lard, make it into a pliant dough with cold water, work it hard, then place it on a break table and beat the dough for half an hour; flour your hands, pinch off small pieces of dough, and make them up in the palm of your hand into round balls, pinching one side together, then put them on your biscuit board and flatten them until half an inch thick with the rolling pin; have your spider or oven and lid hot enough to brown flour; place them in, add small embers and bake quickly. If done on a stove, be sure to have the pans heated and flour sprinkled lightly on the bottom. These biscuit are not good with soda, and must be worked well to make them bake nice and smooth. In Carolina few tables for breakfast or supper are set, without these hot biscuit.

MIXED BREAD.

Put a teaspoonful of salt and a large spoonful of yeast into a quart of flour; make it up into a soft dough with corn meal gruel; when well risen, bake it in pans or a mould.

BATTER BREAD.

Take six tablespoonfuls of flour, three of corn meal, and a little salt sifted together, make it into a thin batter with four eggs and milk. Bake it in tin shapes in a quick oven, and send to table hot, to eat with butter.

LOAF BREAD WITHOUT LARD.

Put a little salt and a coffee cup full of yeast into two quarts of flour, and make up with milk-warm water. Put the dough to rise, and an hour before baking work it over and make it into two loaves. Let it rise in a warm oven for an hour and then bake quickly.

TABB'S MUFFINS.

Beat five eggs, sift in one quart of flour, alternating with one quart of milk; add one large spoonful of lard and butter melted, beat hard, and bake immediately in tin shapes.

POCKET-BOOK ROLLS.

Rub in one quart of flour a dessert spoonful of lard, and one of butter, with a teaspoonful of salt. Add one cup of yeast (or cake of leaven dissolved) with a teaspoonful of sugar, and make it into a dough, with one cup of milk and three eggs. Do this at eleven o'clock; at four o'clock flour your biscuit board and roll the dough out in a sheet half of an inch thick; spread butter all over it with a knife, then cut it in strips three inches wide and six inches long. Roll each end to meet in the middle as a pocket-book of olden times, put them in your stove pan or oven as you roll them out, and let them rise until you are ready to prepare your tea; then bake them and send them to the table hot. If properly done you can unroll them and put the butter inside. They are nice for breakfast or tea, and look pretty on the table.

CRACKERS.

Take one egg, one pint of sweet milk, one teacupful of lard, small teaspoonful of salt, and flour enough to make a stiff dough. Rub the flour and lard together, then add the egg and milk, add flour and knead well; then add to this half the quantity of light dough reserved from your loaf bread, and set it to rise. When light, roll it out an eighth of an inch thick, cut it in squares, prick it with a fork, and bake to a crisp.

CARAWAY COOKIES.

Rub two cups of sugar, and half a cup of butter together, add half a cup of milk and one egg, with one tablespoonful of caraway seed. Mix in one spoonful of lard in a quart of flour, work it all together, roll it in thin cakes, and bake quick.

MUFFINS.

One quart of flour, three eggs, one cup of yeast, one spoonful of lard or butter, and a little salt. Make it at night and bake in tins for breakfast.

SWEET POTATO ROLLS.

Boil and peel two nice size sweet potatoes, beat two eggs and mix in the potato, with a dessert spoonful of sugar, small piece of lard and butter, put in when the potato is hot. Stir in one teacup of good yeast or one cake of leaven dissolved in cold water, then work in flour with tepid water made salt to the taste,—three quarts of flour and one pint of water make a soft dough,—put it to rise, and make it in rolls for breakfast. Eat hot with butter.

NICE ROLLS.

Rub four ounces of butter in two pounds of flour; rub smooth one boiled Irish potato and beat the whites only of six eggs; mix them with the potato and a gill of good yeast or half cake of leaven, work all up in the flour, and wet it with milk; make it a stiff dough and let it rise one hour, then make it in rolls and bake in a quick oven. These can be made for breakfast by rising early, and before baking; break them as you do biscuit.

ASH CAKE.

Stir up meal and water to a stiff dough, make a round cake one inch thick, rake out a hot place on the hearth and bake it on hot ashes.

FLOUR ASH CAKE.

Rub two spoonfuls of butter in a quart of flour and make it in one round lump of dough, with cold water; rake open a place on a hot hearth and bake it in hot ashes.

VIRGINIA ASH CAKE.

Stir up some corn meal with cold water and a little salt to a stiff dough, take up one large handful, and pat a cake about one inch thick, brush the ashes from the hottest part of the fire-place, put a colewort (or collard) leaf on the hearth, lay the cake on it and put another leaf over it; then cover it all over with hot ashes, and bake one hour and a half. Always let ash cake without leaves dry, after it is put on the hearth, before the ashes are sprinkled on. This bread is a great favorite with a glass of nice buttermilk, and was given me by a bachelor in a stage-coach in Bedford County.

PLAIN CORN BREAD.

Sift one quart of corn meal in your tray; put in a teaspoonful of salt, make a hole in the middle, and work it to a soft dough with one pint of cold water. Take it in the hand and make it in a ball, and then put it on a hot griddle with a little meal or flour sprinkled over it, pat it with the hand to fit the griddle, and have it half an inch thick. When the under part has browned, slip your knife under, and turn it quickly; as soon as the other side is brown it is done. Put it in a plate, and set the plate on the tea-kettle to keep hot, until you cook as many as required for the family; send them hot to the table. The same dough will make a Carolina johnny-cake. Take the centre board of a flour-barrel head, flatten the dough across it and set it before the fire, with a stone or flat-iron to support it, cook it brown, and cut it in pieces two inches wide, to send to the table.

CORN MEAL MUFFINS.

Sift a quart of meal, put in one teaspoonful of salt, stir it up with one pint of hot milk and a large spoonful of butter or lard; when a little cool stir in four well beaten eggs; bake in well-greased muffin rings or small tin shapes.

FANNIE'S SALLY LUNN.

Beat separately the whites and yelks of five eggs, put one teaspoonful of sugar, one cup of milk, one cup of butter, one teaspoonful of soda in the milk, and one teaspoonful of salt, with the eggs; then one gill of yeast and one and a half cups of flour. Put it in a greased pan to rise and bake it in the pan for tea.

BETTIE'S WAFFLES.

Boil one pint of rice, mix with it two pints of flour, teaspoonful of salt, one tablespoonful of melted butter, three beaten eggs, and as much milk as will make a thick batter. Bake in muffin rings, waffle irons, or small pans.

MILK YEAST BREAD.

Put three quarts of flour in a tray, make a hole in the middle and put in one tablespoonful of lard, one teaspoonful of sugar and one of salt, with half pint of milk yeast; work it up well with lukewarm water to make a pliant dough; set it to rise. Four hours after you put it to rise, knead it over with a little flour, make it in loaves, and let it stand two hours, then bake in a moderate oven.

BATTER YEAST BREAD.

Take half a gallon of flour, and work in a dessert spoonful of butter, or lard, then make it up with the yeast for batter bread. Make it in one large pone and put it in an oven in a warm place; put warm ashes underneath and let it rise nearly to the top before you put it to bake.

CORN MEAL BREAD.

Make as above recipe and bake it in small pones. It is sweet and healthy.

NICE LOAF BREAD.

Make up a sponge at night, with a pint of sweet milk, a pint of warm water, one teaspoonful of salt, one teaspoonful of sugar, small piece of butter, and flour enough to make a stiff batter. Let it rise until morning, then dissolve a piece of saleratus size of a grain of corn in boiling water, and flour enough to make it mould hard. Fill your pans half full, let it rise until they are nearly full, and then bake in a quick oven.

SALLY LUNN.

Three pounds of flour, warm one quarter of a pound of butter in one quart of milk, put one teaspoonful of salt, six eggs well beaten and one teacup of yeast in it, and work the flour up with it; Set it to rise and bake it in tin pans well greased, or, for variety, part in a pan and balance in muffin rings.

UNBOLTED FLOUR MUFFINS.

Take one pint of milk, two eggs, and one tablespoonful of yeast, add two tablespoonfuls of molasses, and flour enough to make a thick batter. Bake in muffin rings or shapes.

FRENCH ROLLS.

Put one teaspoonful of salt into one quart of flour, sift it, beat three eggs and put one tablespoonful of sugar in them; work a tablespoonful of lard in the flour, then pour in the eggs and a small teacup of potato yeast, made by the recipe in its respective place. Make them at eight or nine o'clock in the evening, put them to rise, and next morning make out rolls and bake for breakfast.

SARATOGA ROLLS.

Beat six eggs together, put half a cup of sugar in it, one cup of lard and one of butter, then add three teacups of baker's yeast from recipe for that. If the yeast is at all sour add a little soda. Beat it well and stir in gradually one gallon of sifted flour. Work it well, making it a soft dough, and put it to rise. Two hours before baking, make the rolls out, place them in your pans or oven to rise and bake in time for breakfast or tea.

BEAUREGARD BISCUITS.

Rub a dessert spoonful of lard and one of butter into one quart of flour, beat four eggs and put in it with one teaspoonful of sugar, a little salt, and half a cup of hop yeast. Let it rise six hours, then make the dough into biscuits and bake them. If the eggs are not sufficient to make a soft dough, use water to make it pliant.

BEAUREGARD BREAD.

At tea-time, stir a pint of flour and half pint of good hop yeast together, and set it to rise in a warm place. Next morning at nine o'clock, beat six eggs together with a coffee cup of sugar; work a tablespoonful of lard and same of butter into a half gallon of flour, put a teaspoonful of salt in it, then pour the sponge made of the flour and yeast and the eggs in the middle of the flour, and make it up into a pliant dough. If stiff, add another egg, no water. At three o'clock work it over, make it in loaves, and set it to rise until ready to bake for tea. Good, hot or cold.

MRS. LANDIS'S RUSK. N. C.

Boil and mash fine, two Irish potatoes with a dessert spoonful of lard; put them in half a gallon of flour with half a pint of yeast, and set it to rise. An hour before you wish to bake it for tea, break six eggs on the dough and put a coffee cup of sugar with them; work all well in the dough, make it in loaves, and bake it half an hour in a quick oven.

PLAIN LOAF BREAD.

Take one pint of flour and half a pint of good hop yeast and stir it together about five o'clock in the afternoon; at nine put one half gallon of flour in a tray, put the sponge in the middle of the flour with a piece of lard as large as a walnut. Knead it all up with tepid water made salt with two teaspoonfuls or more to taste; work it well, and put it in a jar to rise. At four next morning knead it over with a little flour, make it in two loaves, and set it in a warm place or oven until ready to cook breakfast; then put it to bake, and when done, wrap it in a nice coarse towel. If you have no sugar in the yeast you use, stir a large teaspoonful in before putting it in the flour. My cook never lost one pound of flour out of the barrel, with bad bread; and this was her recipe, made with the yeast by her name,—Aunt Matilda's,—as Southern cooks were always called. I give it to her memory.

MRS. COUTERIER'S RUSK. S. C.

One yeast cake dissolved in a glass of water, five eggs well beaten, one tablespoon of butter, one teacup of warm milk, two cups of sugar, a little ground cinnamon, flour enough to make it very stiff. Let it rise, and then make into rolls with a little flour, kneading as little as possible; set it to rise again, and afterwards bake quickly.

CLARA'S SALLY LUNN. S. C.

About eleven o'clock in the morning dissolve the quarter of a yeast cake with a dessert spoonful of sugar, in a little water. Take a pint and a half of flour, a heaping tablespoonful of butter, two eggs well beaten, and mix with enough rich, sweet milk to make a moderately stiff batter; beat well and set to rise till about five in the evening, or an hour before cooking; then beat up well and pour into a greased pan; let it rise again till ready to bake. Bake quickly.

* * *

FOR HOUSEKEEPERS.

A good plan for housekeepers is, to give orders immediately after each meal for the next.

At tea-time tell your cook what you wish for breakfast, and give her all she may need to deposit in the kitchen safe. If she has none, nor any good place to keep it in the kitchen, let it be put where she can get it in the morning without disturbing the duties of your toilet or necessary care of young children. Have a measure for your flour, meal, coffee, tea, lard, etc., and require her to bring them to you regularly. At breakfast, give orders for your dinner, and let her then have what she may require to prepare it. Having done this, you will not be disturbed by Kittie's wanting meal for bread, or lard to fry with, and thus having to excuse yourself from a visitor to wait upon your cook, or to hurry through a visit because you have not given out dinner. After dinner see if you have bread enough for tea, and if not, let her have whatever you wish prepared, and you will then, from acting wisely, enjoy the evening without interruption.

MUFFIN BREAD. NO. 2.

One pint and a half of flour, four eggs well beaten, tablespoonful of lard, coffee cup of yeast; grease your pan, put it in to rise, and when very light bake it in the pan. Rub the flour and lard together before mixing it.

MUFFIN BREAD. NO. 3.

Three pints of flour, one pint of milk, four eggs well beaten, tablespoonful of butter, a gill of yeast, and a little salt. Make it at night for breakfast, or at ten o'clock for tea.

MUFFINS.

Three pints of flour, teaspoon half full of salt, mix it with lukewarm water so stiff a spoon will stand in it. Put half pint of yeast in the flour. Make it at night, and bake in small pans for breakfast. These muffins are a little tough, but sweet and healthy.

MUFFINS. NO. 4.

One quart of flour, one pint of milk, a lump of butter the size of a walnut, a spoonful of lard, and two cups of meal. Bake in patty-pans.

COTTON BREAD.

One quart of meal, one pint of flour, three eggs, and a tablespoonful of lard. Grease a pan, pour in the mixture, and bake it.

MUSH CAKES.

One quart of meal made into mush, one pint of flour, and a spoonful of lard; drop in the oven or pan with a spoon.

MUFFINS. NO. 5.

One quart of seconds, three eggs, tablespoonful of lard, teaspoonful of saleratus, and milk enough for a stiff batter. Bake in rings.

MUFFIN BREAD FOR TEA.

At twelve o'clock beat four eggs very light (separately) stir in a quart of flour, one gill of yeast, and a little milk. At four o'clock stir in a tablespoonful of melted lard, pour it in a pan, and bake in time for tea.

ANOTHER RECIPE FOR MUFFINS.

Eight spoonfuls of flour, four of meal, one spoonful of lard mixed up with four eggs, and sufficient milk to make a thick batter. Bake it in a small pan or muffin rings.

MUFFIN BREAD.

Beat separately four eggs, stir in them three pints of flour, and a teaspoonful of lard, with a teacup of yeast, and milk sufficient for a thick batter. Make it at night for breakfast, and at ten o'clock in the day for tea. Before baking, beat it hard; then with a spoon, drop it in your oven, or tin pans for a stove, as you do corn muffins.

DROP CAKES.

Dissolve one teaspoonful of saleratus in a cup of cream; stir in one quart of milk, and flour enough to make a stiff batter. Beat it very smooth, then dip your spoon in milk, and place your batter at short distances in a buttered pan, and bake them.

CREAM OF TARTAR BISCUITS.

One quart of flour, with a teaspoonful and a half of cream of tartar sifted in it, dissolve a teaspoonful of saleratus in water and add to it, then work it up with a large tablespoonful of butter or lard.

TO MAKE BUCKWHEAT OR JOHNNY CAKE.

Put a teaspoonful of soda in one quart of buttermilk, add flour enough to make a thin batter, with one egg. If you have not the buckwheat flour, use Indian meal, and bake it in a quick oven.

FRENCH ROLLS. NO. 2.

One pound of flour and one of butter worked together with one egg, a gill of yeast, and as much lukewarm milk as will make a soft dough. Cover it with flour and put it to rise until light; flour your hands and make it in small rolls and bake in a quick oven. These are very nice and rich for tea, with invited company.

VELVET CAKES.

Take one quart of flour, add a gill of yeast and pint of warm milk, mix well, set it to rise for two hours, then work in one large tablespoonful of butter, flour your hands, and make it in small cakes, and bake in a quick oven.

MUFFINS.

Beat three eggs, add one pint of warm milk and a gill of yeast, stir well into it two pounds of flour. If your batter is very thin, add a little more flour. Butter your rings and bake them quickly.

YELLOW SULPHUR SPRINGS BREAD.

The Yeast.

Boil one handful of hops in a quart of water until strong. Mix it while hot with a pint of flour and put in half a teacup of old yeast. This quantity will last two weeks.

The Ferment.

Boil one dozen Irish potatoes well done. Mash them without peeling them. Pour the potato water over it and stir to a paste; add as much cold batter cake, then a half teacupful of the hop yeast. In cool weather it will keep several days; in warm weather make it fresh every morning. Then—

To make the Bread.

Take one quart of sifted flour. Pour half a pint of ferment through a colander and stir to a batter. Let it stand two hours. Add a teacup of warm water and work in all the flour except enough to work it over in the morning. Put it in a warm place to rise. In the morning, add a little lard. In the summer half an hour will rise it after it is made in loaves, and an hour in winter. Bake one hour.

SALLY LUNN.

Take five eggs, one half pint ferment, same of milk, and as much flour as will make a thick batter to stir with a spoon. Let it stand all night. Add half an ounce of butter and a little salt. Beat it hard and pour it in a pan. Bake it for breakfast in a quick oven one hour.

CLARA'S CHEESE TOAST.

Put into a hot pan, several large slices of good cheese pared and a small lump of butter. Beat up two eggs with salt and pepper, and add to the cheese, stirring quickly; put in a little milk. Have ready some thin slices of well toasted bread and spread the cheese upon it while hot, and you will have an excellent lunch.

GERMAN TOAST.

Cut nice slices of loaf bread. Beat up four eggs for twelve slices. Dip the bread in the egg on both sides, and fry it in hot butter. Never put the butter on until you have all prepared. The salt in the butter makes it burn quick, and gives the toast an unpleasant taste. This is very nice for breakfast.

MILK TOAST.

Toast nice slices of cold bread and put them in a covered dish. For six slices, boil half pint of new milk with one tablespoonful of butter and pour it boiling hot over the toast. Place the cover on immediately. It is not good cold.

RISEN SHORT-CAKE.

Stir one quart of flour, a little salt, one cup of yeast, one teaspoonful of soda and two eggs in enough milk to make a pliant dough, at night for breakfast, and morning for tea. Next morning knead in one tablespoonful of lard and bake it like short-cake, on a griddle or in an oven. Cut in square pieces.

Although some of my recipes are given with an alkali and acid, which combined evolve carbonic acid by a more sudden process than yeast fermentation, yet I would urge upon all housekeepers a return to primitive days, when medicated flour was unknown, and the labor of making light bread and cakes was preferable to the injurious effect upon the health from the use of them. Sal volatile will certainly lighten by the disengagement of carbonic acid gas, which the gluten of the flour will retain. When using soda, pearlash, or saleratus with sour milk, always wet the flour with some of the milk, and then dissolve the alkali and pour it in. The effervescence takes place in the mixture, and much of the carbonic acid generated is saved for the flour before it is lost in the sour liquid. Soda, pearlash, and saleratus may be dissolved in warm water, but sal volatile makes light when the gas is disengaged by heat, and should never be put in hot water; the heat of the oven volatilizes it, and the lightness is induced by the gas expelling. It may not be necessary for me to say in this age, yet I must, that the most wholesome and nutritious articles of food are composed of but few elements, simple, unstimulating, and easily prepared.

South Carolina Biscuit (Mrs. Stewart).

One quart of flour, one large tablespoonful of lard, a small lump of soda, a little salt, four tablespoonfuls of buttermilk. Make into a stiff dough with either sweet milk or water, beat well until blistered, make into small biscuits with the hand, and bake quickly.

Mrs. Stewart's Waffles.

One pint of flour, two large tablespoonfuls of hominy, rice, or mush, a half tablespoonful of lard or butter. Make into a thick batter with sweet milk. If sour milk or clabber is used, add a little soda and make the batter stiffer. Bake quickly in waffle irons, and send to the table hot, in a covered dish, with butter over them.

Clara's Buttermilk Cakes.

One pint of corn meal or wheat flour stirred into enough buttermilk to make a thick batter, one egg well beaten, half a teaspoonful of soda and a little salt. Fry immediately on a hot griddle, well greased, butter them, and send hot to the table.

VELVET CAKES.

To one quart of flour add a pint of warm milk and a gill of yeast; stir it well, and put it to rise for two hours. Then work in two large tablespoonfuls of melted butter, flour your hands well, and make the mixture into small cakes; rub a pan with butter, and put them to bake in a quick oven. Send hot to the table.

RISEN BISCUIT.

Make up a quart of flour at night with a gill of good yeast and lukewarm salt and water into a pliant dough. Next morning work in a large spoonful of butter; knead it well and make into biscuits. Place them in your stove pans or oven, and bake quickly.

RISEN SHORT-CAKE.

Put a little salt in one quart of flour and sift it; add one cup of yeast, and a teaspoonful of saleratus or soda, and two eggs. Make it up with milk, and put to rise. Next morning knead in a large spoonful of lard, and bake it like short-cakes.

STRAWBERRY SHORT-CAKE.

Rub a large spoonful of lard and one of butter in one quart of sifted flour; put in a little salt, and make a dough with cold water. Roll it out in thin cakes about the size of a breakfast plate; put in a layer of strawberries with a light sprinkle of sugar, then another cake of dough, another layer of strawberries and sugar, with a top layer of dough. Bake it slowly in an oven or stove, and eat for lunch or for dessert, with sugar and butter sauce.

NICE ROLLS.

Take one quart of flour, large spoonful of good yeast, two eggs, a little salt, and half pint of sweet milk. Knead it well, and set to rise. Next morning, work in an ounce of butter, make the dough in small rolls, and bake them.

DROP BISCUIT.

Beat eight eggs very light, add to them one pound of flour and one of sugar. When perfectly light, drop them on a tin sheet, or spider, and bake them quickly. Nice for tea.

CAROLINA EGG-CAKES.

Sift one quart of corn meal, put a teaspoonful of salt in it and scald it with half a pint of hot water; stir it until it cools, then break in three eggs and continue stirring, and sprinkle in slowly one tablespoonful of flour; thin it with one pint of sweet milk to a thin batter that will run easily; have your griddle very hot, grease it well with lard, and fry quickly in small cakes. Serve hot to be buttered at the table.

RICE BATTER-CAKES.

Boil a teacup of rice very soft; when cool, stir it in one quart of flour; beat five eggs and stir in with half a pint of milk. If the batter is not thin enough to run as you drop it on the griddle, put a little more milk or rice water, add a teaspoonful of salt, give it a hard beat, bake on a hot griddle well greased, and butter them. Serve hot.

RICE CORN BREAD.

Scald your meal, break in some eggs, put in cold rice and piece of lard, thin with water and a little milk, bake in pans or shapes.

NICE BREAKFAST CAKES.

Beat ten eggs, add three pints of milk, a tablespoonful of butter, two teaspoonfuls of salt, and half a teaspoonful of saleratus. Sift some Indian meal and make a thick batter, pour it in tin shapes or cups, and bake for half an hour in a quick oven. You can make these with buttermilk or milk that has been skimmed for butter. Send them hot to the table.

RISEN WAFERS.

Beat three eggs, add one pint of sweet milk, one large spoonful of yeast, same of butter, stir in enough sifted flour to make it as stiff as you can stir with a spoon. Have your wafer irons well greased. After it is well risen, put in a small lump of the dough, shut the irons together and bake it on hot coals; turn it in a few minutes to bake both sides alike. If your irons are well heated and greased, it takes but a minute or two to bake them.

CREAM GRIDDLE-CAKES.

Mix one pint of cream and one of sweet milk with three eggs and a teaspoonful of salt, make it into a thin batter with flour, and bake it on a griddle in cakes like buckwheat; butter them hot. If the cream or milk is at all sour, use a pinch of soda to correct it.

AMES SALLY LUNN.

Measure seven cups of sifted flour, and warm a pint of milk with half cup of butter in it. Make a hole in the flour and stir a cup of yeast, the milk and butter, and a salt spoonful of salt, with three well beaten eggs in it. After it is nicely mixed pour it in pans to rise, and bake it for tea. Be careful it does not sour.

THORPE'S SALLY LUNN.

Four teacups of warm water, one cake of leaven, four eggs well beaten, one large spoonful of lard, half a teacup of sugar, a teaspoonful of salt. Mix three pints of flour in it and set it to rise at night. Next morning stir in one pint of flour and bake it like loaf bread.

CREAM RENVERSEE.

Mix three tablespoonfuls of flour with a gill of cold milk, and then add a gill of scalded milk. Put it in a saucepan over the fire and stir until it begins to thicken, then take it off and add four ounces of white sugar and the yelks of four eggs, with a teaspoon of lemon extract or any flavor you like. Then beat the whites of the eggs to a stiff froth and stir it in the mixture; place it in a buttered pan or mould and set it in a kettle of boiling water to rise. After it has risen bake it in a mild oven, and when cool, turn it out on a dish upside down.

CREAM CAKES.

Ten cups of flour with half teaspoonful of soda sifted in it, six eggs beat with six cups of sugar, two cups of sour cream, and two of butter worked up in a mass. Roll out in thin cakes, cut with a tumbler or shape, and bake in stove pans or a moderate oven.

SPONGE CAKE.

One pound of flour, one and a half of sugar to sixteen well beaten eggs; flavor with lemon.

BUCKWHEAT CAKES.

Put a teacup of wheat flour into one quart of buckwheat; sift them together, add half pint of good yeast and one small spoonful of salt; make it into a batter with lukewarm water at bed-time, and let it rise in a warm place. Next morning, if it should taste at all sour, beat a pinch of soda in it; if not sour, do not add soda. Have a large griddle very hot; grease it well with lard tied in muslin; bake the cakes fast, butter them, and send to the table hot.

BUCKWHEAT CAKES. NO. 2.

Mix one cup of corn meal with one quart of buckwheat; break in two eggs and beat well, adding gill of good yeast, teaspoonful of salt, and sufficient cold water to make it a proper consistency. Put it to rise and bake as above directed. Mix milk and butter hot and pour over them.

BUCKWHEAT IN HASTE.

Put a teacup of flour to one quart of buckwheat, and a large spoonful of yeast powder; sift them together and make a batter with water or half milk; add a little salt. Bake and serve as above directed.

FLANNEL CAKES.

Beat six eggs very light, stir in them two pounds of flour, one gill of yeast, small spoonful of salt, and sufficient milk to make a thick batter. Make them at night for breakfast, and at ten in the morning for tea. Have your griddle hot, grease it well, and bake as buckwheat. Butter and send them hot to the table, commencing after the family are seated.

CORN-MEAL BATTER-CAKES.

One quart of meal, half tablespoonful of lard, pour a pint of boiling water on it, and stir until a little cool. Then break three eggs in it, a pinch of salt, and thin with milk. Bake them on a hot griddle and eat hot.

NICE PUFFS.

Put one ounce of fresh butter in a quart stew-pan; when hot put in four spoonfuls of flour; stir it over the fire for five minutes; stir in by degrees one gill of milk boiling hot. When well boiled take it off and stir in six eggs, a pinch of salt, a little nutmeg, a handful of currants, little lemon peel chopped, and a little sugar flavored with orange-flower water. Take pieces of the dough the size of a walnut, make in balls and fry them in hot lard until they burst, sift powdered sugar over them, and eat with wine sauce.

HETTIE'S PUFFS.

Take three ounces of almonds that have been blanched and pounded fine, with quarter of an ounce of butter and two ounces of loaf sugar; wet with rose-water until a thick paste, spread the paste on buttered tins, and bake them in a slow oven. When cold, put a spoonful of jam in each and cover with whipped cream.

NENA'S PUFFS.

Roll out puff paste very thin, cut it into round pieces, lay jam on each fold of the paste, rub the edges with egg and close them, put them on a baking sheet or carefully in the oven, ice them, and bake quarter of an hour.

JEANETTE'S PUFFS.

Boil one pint of milk with half a pound of butter; after it is boiled add three quarters of a pound of flour, stirring the milk and butter in the flour, return it to the pot and stir it until it does not stick to it. Let it cool, then add the yelks of nine eggs, beat the whites to a stiff froth and add them last; grease tins, snow-ball shapes, or cups, fill half full, and bake quick.

NANNIE'S PUFFS.

Put in a saucepan half a pint of water, with one quarter of a pound of butter, stir it till it boils, then mix in four tablespoonfuls of flour. Stir it well together and add the beaten yolks of four eggs, then the whites; let it cool, and with a spoon drop it in boiling lard and fry a light brown. Sugar them while hot or eat with a little sauce for a plain dessert.

LARGE HOMINY.

Pick some ears of white flint corn that is perfectly dry and have it well beaten in a large wooden mortar; put it in a flat tray and toss it about to get clear of the husk. Wash it well in one or two waters and put it in a dinner pot of cold water, filling the pot to the brim. Let it boil steadily for four hours, then wash clean some white hominy or navy beans, and put in with it, and boil three hours longer. Always have hot water ready to add to it, if it begins to boil down before the hominy is soft. If put on early in the morning, it will be ready for a nice side dish for dinner. Take it up and mash it with a wooden pestle, salt to taste and a spoonful of lard or butter stirred well in it. In cold weather it will keep good four or five days, and is always nice to fry for breakfast or dinner. Mash it well and fry it in hot lard, and turn it out with a brown crust.

SMALL HOMINY.

This is prepared at the corn mill. Select nice white corn, and have it sent to be ground coarse. To prepare it for breakfast, take the quantity you wish very early in the morning, wash it in two or three waters and skim the husk off that rises, or pour the water off carefully with the husk on it; then put in a small iron pot three quarts of water to one quart of hominy and boil it till perfectly soft; stirring it every few minutes to prevent its burning. Be careful not to scrape the bottom, as a cake generally forms that would spoil the hominy if mixed in; that answers for feeding poultry or pigs. If it looks dry before it is soft, add a little hot water. Send it in a covered dish to the table, and eat with butter or with milk after it is cold.

HOMINY CAKES.

Take one pint of small hominy that is cooked soft. Mix with it one pint of wheat flour, teaspoonful of salt, and a little milk with or without eggs. Fry them on a griddle and eat as buckwheats.

CORN BREAD (MRS. B.'S).

Mix three pints of corn meal in one quart of sour milk. Add three well beaten eggs, one teaspoonful of soda and one of salt. Beat it well, and bake in pans half an inch thick.

SWEET POTATO CORN BREAD.

Boil soft two large sweet potatoes. Mash them while hot with a small piece of lard or butter. Work it in finely sifted corn meal until tolerably stiff, and then work in enough water to make it a soft dough. Let it rise three hours or longer if you choose, and then bake it in a spider, or for a stove, in a tin pan.

TO DIVIDE LOAVES OF BREAD.

Make up dough after the receipt for French rolls. As soon as you have worked it well after the second rising, divide it as you wish. Cut off one pound and roll it round and twelve inches long, pointing both ends smoothly. When you have shaped it, take your rolling pin and press it lengthwise on the middle, and gently roll it until the dough each side is nearly two inches above it. Have a nice kitchen towel floured, and turn it over the bread as soon as you take the rolling pin out, and set it to rise, smooth side up; when well risen turn the bread over, letting the smooth part go in the pan, and bake it. It looks well for a change and gives more crust to those who prefer it. The recipe for French rolls came from White Sulphur Springs, Va., and cost ten dollars.

CRUMPETS.

Take one quart of dough from your risen bread very early in the morning. Beat three eggs separately and mix them with the dough. Then thin it with milk and water until the consistency of batter cakes; beat it well, let it rise until breakfast, bake them on a hot griddle, butter, and send to the table hot.

SWEET POTATO BUNS.

Boil sweet potatoes soft, peel them and mash while hot, in flour, like bread. Add spice and sugar with yeast. When well risen, work in butter and make the dough up in small rolls and bake. You can use any quantity, according to judgment. One quart of flour, coffee cup of potato, tablespoonful of sugar, and six grains of allspice with dessert spoonful of butter, is a good rule for a small family.

OXFORD CRACKERS.

Rub four ounces of butter in one quart of flour, make it in a paste with rich milk, knead it well, and roll as thin as paper; cut them out by a saucer and bake quickly, to look white when done.

SODA CRACKERS.

Rub six ounces of butter in three pints of flour that has two teaspoonfuls of cream of tartar sifted in it; dissolve one teaspoonful of soda in a cup of cream, beat two eggs, and work it in the flour; use milk to make it the proper consistency to roll, and add a little salt.

RICE BATTER CAKES.

Boil a teacupful of rice very soft, and let it cool; break four eggs in it, a teaspoonful of salt, and thicken it with wheat flour: add enough milk to make a thin batter; grease your griddle when hot, fry fast, butter, and send to the table during breakfast or tea.

RICE WAFFLES.

Nine eggs well beaten, nine large spoonsful of flour, one teaspoonful of salt. Have a teacup of rice boiled very soft, and when cool, beat it in the flour and eggs. Add one and a half pints of milk; grease your waffle-irons nicely with lard, fill them with the mixture, and bake in a hot fire. Butter and send to the table covered.

BUTTERMILK WAFFLES.

One quart of buttermilk, three eggs, and tablespoonful of lard, half teaspoonful of soda, flour enough to make a thick batter; fill your irons and bake as above directed.

CRACKLING BREAD.

Scald two quarts of corn meal, and stir in one pint of cracklings; make it a thick batter with cold water. Make it in round balls, flatten the tops, and bake in a quick oven.

PASS OVERS.

Two cups of flour, two cups of milk, and two eggs stirred together with a little salt and baked in patty-pans.

CORN FRITTERS.

Grate six ears of corn and mix it with two eggs, one spoonful of butter, and season with pepper and salt. Fry a light brown, and you have a mock oyster.

SCOTLAND NECK SALLY LUNN.

One quart of flour, half a pound of butter, one gill of yeast, one tablespoonful of white sugar, six eggs beaten separately; make it in a stiff batter, and set it to rise. Use a little milk if the eggs do not make it the proper consistency. After it rises beat it again, put it in a mould to rise the second time, and when light bake it.

BREAKFAST CAKE.

Beat five eggs separately, stir in three pints of milk and a quarter of a pound of butter, teaspoonful of salt, and a gill of yeast, with enough flour to make a thick batter. Make them late at night, and cook for breakfast like buckwheats.

MRS. LEE'S BREAD.

To one quart of best family flour put one egg and lard the size of an egg, two large tablespoonfuls of yeast (by her recipe), one teaspoonful of salt, and one of sugar. By this rule, bread can be made and the dough kept good for three days, and sufficient taken off to bake fresh each day. Mrs. L. says, if kept cold in winter or in an ice-house in summer it will lie dormant, and may freeze without injury. If frozen hard enough to be cut with an axe it will not be damaged, and will rise readily, as soon as placed near the fire. If made in this way to save labor, and a change of temperature causes it to rise, it must be worked down immediately. It is only in this risen state that it can be injured or become sour.

EGG PONE.

Take one pint of boiled rice, and when cool break six eggs in it. Sift one quart of meal and scald it, add one large spoonful of mixed lard and butter, and one teaspoonful of salt. Stir the rice and eggs in the meal with one quart of milk and bake it in tin pans. Send it to the breakfast table hot to eat with butter.

CORN MEAL DROP CAKES.

Scald one quart of meal and stir a dessert spoonful of lard in it. When cool break two eggs in, and stir in milk enough to make a thick batter. Grease a spider or stove pan and drop them in from the spoon to bake until brown. Clabber, with a mite of soda in it, will answer in place of milk or buttermilk.

* * *

"Let your light so shine that others may see your good works."

Every woman who is at the head of a household, is, in a measure, responsible to the Good Being for the salvation of those under her immediate care.

Start not, gentle reader; you have been intrusted with the care of souls, and to you they look for that training "in the way they should go" while working out their eternal salvation. Do you rise early to administer to the temporal wants of your family, and give not one thought to their spiritual food? Do you exercise that patience and forbearance with your children and hirelings which you are in constant need of? If not, remember that your account is to be rendered to Him who gave you the "light," and the power to make it "so shine" in your daily walk and conversation "that others may see your good works," and be constrained to "glorify your Father which is in Heaven."

EGGS AND BUTTER.

POACHED EGGS.

Strain some hot water from the tea-kettle in a spider or broad stew-pan; when it boils put a little salt in the water. Break your eggs, one by one, in the hot water and set it on the fire; when it boils up again, they will be done. Take an egg-slice or skimmer and run it carefully under each egg; put them in a covered dish, and pour butter over them.

FRICASSEED EGGS.

Boil one dozen eggs hard, peel them nicely, and cut them in slices, season some bread crumbs with salt and pepper and beat two raw eggs. Sprinkle a little flour over the sliced egg, dip it in the raw egg and then in the bread crumbs, on both sides, and fry in boiling lard. After the egg is all fried, put some parsley in the lard, and fry it to garnish the egg with. Very nice for a variety.

BOILED EGGS.

Have water in a saucepan boiling hard, put your eggs in and let them remain five minutes. If you wish them hard, boil them five minutes longer.

SCRAMBLED EGGS.

Put a piece of butter in a saucepan, and melt it over hot water, then break your eggs in, and set them on the fire, and stir them constantly, not allowing any to stick to the pan. It is a good plan to beat them a little before putting them in the pan to cook.

EGGS WITH CHEESE.

Put a small piece of butter in a saucepan, and then some bits of cheese; stir it well, and as soon as it melts, put in the eggs you wish, after beating them a short time; stir it well, and send to the table hot.

EGG OMELET.

Beat separately six eggs. If you have no omelet pan, put a frying-pan on the fire, and warm a spoonful of butter in it (be careful about butter being warmed over steam or a slow fire, as it burns easily and imparts an unpleasant taste), mix the eggs, pour them in the hot butter, and fry quickly. Never season an omelet until you take it on your plate.

EGG OMELET WITH HAM.

Beat six eggs together, chop some lean ham very fine, and mix it in the egg. Fry in hot lard instead of butter.

EGG OMELET AND OYSTERS.

Chop the soft part of the oyster fine and season it with salt and pepper; mix it with beaten egg, and fry as above in butter.

OMELET WITH HERBS.

Chop a little celery, two onions, some parsley and sweet marjoram; beat six eggs, mix it all together, and fry in boiling lard. Always turn an omelet over when you put it on the dish. Never turn it in the frying-pan.

FRENCH BUTTER.

Set pans of milk for the cream to rise; when it is a thick scum, take it off with a perforated skimmer, put the cream in a thick, clean bag, put that bag in another thick, coarse one, and bury it one foot and a half deep in the earth. Let it remain twenty-four hours; the cream will then be hard; break it with a wooden pestle, and wash the buttermilk out. This is said to make butter of a superior quality, and the butter separates more perfectly than the ordinary process.

GRANVILLE BUTTER.

Strain new milk in a large stone jar in the evening and set it in a warm place, carefully covered over. Next morning add the new milk, and as soon as it begins to curdle, churn it until the butter separates; then take it up, work it well, salt it, let it stand several hours, wash it in cold water, work it until all the milk and water is out, add a little salt, and then pack it in a stone jar.

PASQUOTANK BUTTER.

Strain the milk in pans; when the cream rises and is thick, skim it off and put it in a churn that has been well scalded. Churn slowly until the butter separates, then pour it out, work the buttermilk out of it, salt it, and let it stand a few hours. Then work it again, wash it in cold water, and salt to taste.

* * *

In the next generation, foreigners may be introduced into the South to discharge domestic duties. Their mode of living will be different from ours, and it will be hard to accustom ourselves to the change.

"If a stranger sojourn with you in your land, ye shall not vex him, but the stranger that dwelleth among you shall be unto you as one born among you, and thou shalt love him as thyself." Remember this, and be kind to them, and give them the light of your knowledge.

You must always preserve your proper authority and control over your household matters. Give your orders in a lady-like and determined manner, and you will be sure to command respect.

When anything occurs to vex you, through the neglect, incompetency, or impertinence of your new servants, act like a Christian, be watchful, careful, conscientious, and slow to speak. Do not give them any cause for suspecting that you doubt their honesty, but be vigilant, and "look well to the ways of your household." Tell them that it is your habit, and you shall continue to carry your keys, and give out what you wish prepared for each meal, in measures according to the size of your family—that your husband has intrusted these things to your care, and you intend to discharge your duty to him faithfully.

Be patient with them, making every allowance for their deficiency in training; give them good books to read, make them as comfortable as possible, and always pay them their wages promptly. In matters of religion, their faith may differ widely from ours, but we must remember that they were trained to believe as they do, and we should allow them the blessed privilege which we enjoy, that of worshipping God in a free country, according to the dictates of our own consciences.

I can testify to the fact that these rules, if strictly carried out in the management of servants, will result in attaching them to you, and the interests of your family, for of those who once called me mistress, there was one whose love was so great that she refused to leave when declared free, and clung to me until Death claimed her as his own.

YEAST.

AUNT MATILDA'S HOP YEAST.

Put a large handful of hops in a gallon of water, boil it until a light brown color, with two Irish potatoes sliced in it: when the potatoes are soft, strain it in a wooden bowl, stir one quart of flour into a paste with cold water, and when the hop tea is cool, stir it in. Then return it to the pot or kettle and put it over the fire to thicken, stirring it all the time; as soon as it is heated through, pour it again in the wooden bowl to cool, occasionally stirring it. When perfectly cold, put it in a stone jug with stopper put in very lightly; set it in a warm place to rise, placing the jug in a pan to catch the yeast that runs over. When it has done rising, you can pour that back, as the jug should only be two thirds full. Use one half pint to half gallon of flour; two spoonfuls of honey or a cup of sugar can be added before putting it in the jug, a teaspoonful of sugar to half pint when used. This yeast never fails.

YEAST FOR CAKES OF LEAVEN.

Put a large handful of hops in a pot with three quarts of water and three Irish potatoes: let it boil tolerably strong (down to half gallon), strain it boiling hot over a half gallon of sifted flour, stir it well, and when cool add half pint of yeast or one yeast cake, and put it in a bucket to rise. When very light and porous, before it begins to fall, make it up in small thin cakes with corn meal, and place them on a board to dry, turning them every day. After they are perfectly dry, put them in a thin bag and hang them in a cool place, where they will have air. In the summer time, use one of the cakes to one quart of flour for bread, rolls, or buckwheat cakes; dissolve it in a teacup of cold water, and add a small teaspoonful of sugar. For all purposes for which yeast is required to make risen bread or cakes, these can be used, and are less troublesome and more economical, as they keep well for several months.

BAKER'S YEAST.

Put one dozen large potatoes and a large handful of hops in a pot to boil; don't peel the potatoes. When they are soft, put one pint of flour in a jar, put the potatoes on the flour, and then the hops boiling hot; mash them all together and roll in a ball. Put it aside until cold, and the water the potatoes and hops were boiled in; when both are cold work them together, and let it rise to the top and then fall. After it falls, it is ready for use; stir it well and strain it. Does not increase by rising.

POTATO YEAST.

Take one pint of mashed Irish potatoes and work in it one pint of flour and one pint of water. Add one gill of good hop yeast and teaspoonful of salt; let it rise until the next day, and then use it for French rolls. Keep the yeast in a cool place, as it sours very easily. This quantity will last one week in a small family.

PEACH-LEAF YEAST.

Take three large leaves and three medium size Irish potatoes, boil them in two quarts of water. When the potatoes are done, take out the leaves and throw them away; peel the potatoes, and mash them up in one pint of flour, adding sufficient water to make it a paste, then pour on the hot peach-leaf tea and scald for five minutes; add half a cup of old yeast, and it will be ready for use in a few hours.

NAG'S HEAD YEAST.

Boil half an ounce of hops in four quarts of water ten minutes. Put one pound of flour and half pint of malt in a bucket, and pour one quart of the hop tea on it to make a thin paste, then strain the other three quarts over it from the hops. Let it stand until milk warm, pour a pint of old yeast in it, stir it well, and let it stand until it rises and falls. Use one half pint to a quart of flour for good plain rolls or loaf bread.

MILK YEAST.

This is made for immediate use. Stir in a pint of new milk a teaspoonful of salt and a large spoonful of flour, set it by the fire for one hour, and then make up your bread with it. It is convenient for loaf bread or biscuit when one wishes to make them up in haste.

MISS BETSEY'S YEAST.

At four o'clock in the morning, stir a cup of flour in one pint of water about as warm as new milk; put in a little salt. Set it by the fire to rise, and stir it often. When it is very light, it is ready for use, and will make two loaves of bread very light for tea.

HOP YEAST.

Boil a large handful of hops in two quarts of water until it is a strong tea. Strain it in a jar with a pint of flour and stir it till very smooth; when cool put in a gill of yeast and set it in a warm place till light, and then stop tightly. Always make fresh yeast, before all you have is used, so you can have some to set the new with.

YEAST CAKES.

Take some of the above when fresh, and thicken it with meal or flour, till very stiff. Roll them out and cut in thin, small cakes, and dry in the sun. Soak them in milk an hour before you want to make bread. Use one cake size of a half pint tumbler to a quart of flour. Be careful in winter not to let them freeze, and keep dry.

QUICK YEAST MADE WITH MILK.

Take one teacup of milk and two large spoonfuls of flour and stir them together. Set it near the fire and let it rise one hour. This quantity will make one gallon of flour in good bread.

READY YEAST.

Put in a pitcher one spoonful of sugar, two spoonfuls of flour, and three of water, stir them well, and add one gill of hop yeast or a piece of leaven dissolved in a gill of water; set it to rise in a warm place. Make up bread with it as other yeast. Before it gives out, stir the same quantity of sugar, flour, and water, and put it in with the little that sticks to the pitcher and set it to rise. It is always ready, and never sours.

ANOTHER SIMPLE YEAST.

Stir a pint of flour in one quart of lukewarm water, put in one teaspoonful of salt and one cup of brown sugar and one cup of yeast. Put it to rise, and when well risen, keep it in a cool place.

MILK YEAST FOR BATTER BREAD.

At sunrise stir one pint of warm water, one teacup of sweet milk and a teaspoonful of salt together, and make a thin batter with flour. Set it in a warm place in winter, and in the sun in summer. If near a fire, turn it often and keep it tightly covered, stir it every now and then, until it begins to rise well. At eleven or twelve o'clock make up bread with it.

MRS. SCOTT'S YEAST.

Monday morning boil two ounces of good hops in four quarts of water for half an hour. Strain it and let the liquor cool down to the warmth of new milk. Then put in a small handful of salt and half a pound of sugar. Stir one pound of family flour with a little of the hop tea until smooth, and then mix in the tea and let it stand until Wednesday. Boil three pounds of Irish potatoes, mash it fine and stir in. The next day strain it, and put it in jugs or bottles. Keep it in a cool place, and it will keep good for two months. The last generally the best. Always keep it in a warm place when it is being made, and stir it often.

MAGIC YEAST.

Twelve hours before you wish to use it, stir one tablespoonful of brown sugar, two of flour and three of water together, and add a small piece of leaven or one spoonful of hop yeast to make it rise. Use two tablespoonfuls of this to one quart of flour. Let the yeast remain in the jar, and before it is all used add the flour, sugar, and water as at first, and you will always have nice fresh yeast that makes beautiful bread. Keep two jars, and occasionally change them so you can have it sweet and fresh.

FLOUR YEAST.

Mix half a pint of flour with one pint of cold water. Put it in a saucepan and can it to a thick paste, stirring it all the time. Then pour it in a bowl and stir in one cup of hop yeast, dessert spoonful of sugar and one of salt, and set it to rise.

HOP YEAST.

Boil half a pint of hops in two quarts of water till the strength is extracted. Rub half a pint of flour smooth with cold water, strain the tea and mix it in; let it cook slowly like mush from five to ten minutes. Let it cool, and then add a gill of yeast and two nicely mashed boiled potatoes, and put it in a stone jug or bottles to rise. A tin coffee-pot should be kept to boil hops in, as the bitter taste is hard to remove from a kettle.

BUTTERMILK YEAST.

One quart of buttermilk, two teaspoonfuls of sugar, one quart of meal, two gills of hop yeast. Let it rise eight hours: then stir in one quart of meal, make it out in thin small cakes and dry them in the sun; use one for a quart of flour.

MRS. LEE'S YEAST.

Boil six Irish potatoes and a handful of hops in half gallon of water; when cooked, mash the potatoes. Strain the hop tea and mix with the potatoes.

Thicken with half pint of flour. Return all to the kettle and bring to the boiling point; add a heaping tablespoonful of salt, and set the preparation with half pint of yeast. This will keep good one week in a cool place.

* * *

Unforeseen circumstances may make a change in your life of which you little dreamed, when your heart and hand were pledged at God's altar, to one raised in the lap of luxury, with self-indulgence.

It is in the power of woman to make "her children rise up and call her blessed; her husband, also, he praiseth her."

The beautiful home of your bridal days, with all that wealth could accomplish, to beautify the grounds around your richly ornamented dwelling, surrounded by highly picturesque scenery, filled with sumptuous furniture, and with every convenience, may have to be placed under the sheriff's hammer, and exchanged for a simple cot furnished with unpolished wood. If such be your lot, make that home happy, by cultivating a cheerful, happy disposition.

When your husband's business hours are over, he always ready to meet him with a smile, your hair and dress neatly arranged, the fire burning brightly in winter with the "tidy little ones" around a nice, *clean* hearth, and as the opening bud expands its petals in gorgeous colors, with summer's sweet flowers, teach them to meet papa with a bouquet, gathered from the plants cultivated by your own hand around the cottage door, to elevate and refine the feelings, while creating a taste for the beautiful works of nature and making the air redolent with their sweet fragrance.

PUDDINGS AND PASTRY.

REMARKS ON BOILED PUDDINGS.

Procure a tin mould, melon or any shape you prefer, and see that the top fits very tight, a common tin bucket with a closely fitting top, or make a pudding bag, nine inches wide and eighteen inches long, of close coarse linen or twilled jeans; have them always in place and put up, nicely cleaned. When you wish a boiled pudding, before you begin to make it, have a clean pot or kettle of boiling water on the stove or over the fire-place. Make your pudding, scald the bag in the pot of water or some taken from it, turn it while hot and dip it in flour, then turn it again and pour the mixture in. If a simple batter, tie it close. If made of bread or Indian meal, let it be loose to allow for swelling. See that your water is boiling hot when you put it in and turn it frequently whilst boiling to prevent its sticking to the pot, and have water kept above the pudding: for this purpose have some boiling in your tea-kettle to add to it. When ready to send to the table, have a nice china dish with a cover, dip the pudding-bag in cold water and turn it out smoothly in the dish; untie the string, and roll the bag back, and it can be taken out without being broken. If you use your tin mould or a bucket, do not let the water be above the top of the mould, and see that the top of the bucket is tied across to the handle. I name the bucket, as moulds are not very common, and a bucket makes a very good substitute. Always plunge the mould or bucket in cold water as you do a bag, and turn the contents out quickly.

REMARKS ON BAKED PUDDINGS.

For a pudding of bread, custard, or corn meal, have your pan nicely cleaned and place it in a moderate oven, pour the mixture in the pan after placing it in, and bake slowly. If for a stove, warm your pan before pouring the mixture in, and moderate the heat by the stove dampers. If a batter or rice pudding, bake in a quick oven or well heated stove, so it will cook before the rice or eggs settle and cook hard.

PEABODY ENGLISH PUDDING.

One pound of flour, one pound of butter, one pound of sugar, two pounds of raisins, two pounds of currants, two gills of French brandy, eight cloves pounded fine and sifted through muslin, two nutmegs grated, one teaspoonful of cinnamon and allspice mixed, three lumps of sugar rubbed on a lemon and orange pounded fine, and twelve eggs. Beat the eggs light with the sugar, cream the flour and butter together and stir it well in the eggs and sugar; cut one pound of citron in small strips and flour it with the raisins and currants, put the spices and lemon sugar in the brandy, and add. Then stir in the fruit slowly, one at a time, first raisins, then currants, and then citron; handful of each till all are mixed. Put it in a pudding mould, and boil it six hours; keep hot water to add as it boils down. This cannot be surpassed for a Christmas or dinner party. Stick it with blanched almonds, pour half a pint of French brandy over it, and set it on fire, on the table.

WINE SAUCE FOR PEABODY PUDDING.

Pulverize one pound of the best loaf sugar, and stir it half an hour with nearly one pound of *fresh* butter; stir in one wine-glass best French brandy and two of best sherry wine. Rub four lumps of sugar on a lemon and orange, pound and mix it in, and grate nutmeg over the top.

CHRISTMAS MINCE-MEAT.

Boil six pounds of lean beef until tender; let it get cold, and then chop it very fine with your cleaver. Pick three pounds of beef suet and chop that fine. Stone four pounds of raisins, and cut them up. Wash two pounds of currants and dry them. Cut in bits one pound of citron, and chop one peck of peeled apples. Have two teaspoonfuls of fine cinnamon, one of allspice, one dozen cloves, one large nutmeg, one teaspoonful of black pepper and large spoonful of salt in separate papers, all nicely powdered, three pounds of nice brown sugar, and the syrup from the peel of two oranges preserved; chop the peel up *fine*. Put in your tray a layer of the beef, then suet, then salt and pepper, next sugar, apples, and the other fruit, then your spices and chopped orange peel.

When all are in, pour the syrup of peel over it with one quart of French (or some other good) brandy. Work it all up with the hands until well mixed. This will keep in stone jars until the spring and cannot be surpassed, if made strictly by directions. When you wish pies made of it, line your baking plates with a rich puff paste, and fill with the meat, then add sweet cider and a little wine to moisten the meat. Cover with a top crust and bake a pretty brown. Serve them hot. I tested this twenty-five years ago.

ANOTHER MINCE-MEAT.

Three pounds of tender lean beef, one and a half pounds of suet, two pounds of chopped apples, two of raisins, two of currants, one of citron, two of sugar, one gill of rose-water, the juice of four lemons and the peel preserved and chopped fine, one pint of brandy; have salt, mace, cloves, allspice, pepper, cinnamon, and ginger pulverized, and add to your taste. Never use much mace or cloves. Mix it thoroughly, as in above recipe, and bake in the same way. Cider added when they are baked, or wine, greatly improves them. Mince-pies are baked in quantities at the North, and kept for weeks in a dry, cool place, and when wanted they are steamed until hot through.

CAROLINA SWEET POTATO PUDDING.

Slice peeled sweet potatoes, put them in a saucepan with water enough to cover them. Season them with a little allspice in grains, wine, and brandy, with sugar to the taste; boil it up until the potato is soft. Make a nice puff or plain paste, line a deep dish with it, and pour all in. Cover a top paste and bake it.

MELISSA'S POTATO PUDDING.

One quarter of a pound of boiled sweet potatoes, same of sugar and butter, one wine-glass of mixed wine and brandy, half a gill of rose-water, one teaspoonful of mixed spice, cinnamon, and nutmeg, with three beaten eggs. Bake in puff paste without any top crust.

GRATED POTATO PUDDING.

Peel and grate four nice sweet potatoes, beat six eggs with half a pound of sugar and half a pound of melted butter; season it with nutmeg, a little allspice, and a pinch of salt. Stir the grated potato in, beat until well mixed, and bake it in paste. Cut the paste in slits around it, two inches wide, and turn them to a half square. All plate puddings look better with the paste cut and baked in forms.

POTATO CUSTARD.

Boil six sweet Carolinas, and strain them through a sieve. Beat eight eggs and one large cup of sugar, with one cup of milk and same of butter, a little nutmeg, essence of lemon, and a gill of wine or brandy. Mix the potato in and bake in pie plates covered with nice paste.

LEMON CUSTARD.

Beat five eggs with five cups of sugar, grate three lemons and squeeze the juice, mix it with three cups of new milk and one tablespoonful of corn starch, rice flour, or fine wheat flour, and bake it on crust. If you beat the eggs separately, stir the white in just as you put it to bake.

PENNSYLVANIA PUDDING.

One pint of milk, one tablespoonful of washed rice, half a cup of raisins, and same of sugar, a pinch of salt, and a little nutmeg. Mix it up and put it to bake. Stir it, after it has been skimmed four times, to keep the raisins and rice mixed. Let it bake until the rice is done, and serve it cold with cream and sugar.

SUET PUDDING. NO. 2.

Beat four eggs with one cup of sugar, add one pint of sweet milk and a cup of sour, teaspoonful of soda and two cups of chopped suet, tablespoonful of butter and flour enough to make a stiff batter. Add raisins, currants, or any dried fruit, and boil it three hours. Eat with sauce.

APPLE PUDDING.

Stew twelve large apples, and rub them while hot, through a sieve. Mix in them half a pound of butter, half a pound of sugar, and six well beaten eggs; put a paste in your pudding dish, and pour the mixture in and bake it.

THORPE'S LEMON PUDDING.

Cream six ounces of butter and one pound of sugar together. Beat the yelks of fifteen eggs and stir slowly in, then the juice of two lemons. Line three baking plates with a nice puff paste, pour the mixture in and bake them a light brown. Good when cold.

THORPE'S BOILED PLUM-PUDDING.

Beat twelve eggs, with half a pound of sugar, and half a pound of butter; stir in smoothly one pound of flour, and then one pound of stoned raisins, well floured; flavor with lemon and boil it in a tin shape, or pudding-bag, for one hour and a half. Eat it with cold sauce. Always dip your pudding-bag in boiling water and flour the inside, to make it turn out smoothly.

BREAD PUDDING.

Take the crumb of a small loaf of bread and pour two quarts of milk over it; when well soaked, beat it hard and add four eggs beaten with one large coffee cup of sugar and tablespoonful of butter, grease your pudding pan, pour it in and bake one hour. One nutmeg grated will improve it, though they are very good without.

A CHEAP PUDDING.

Mix four tablespoonfuls of flour into a quart of sweet milk, add the yelks of five eggs and stir well. Beat the whites of the eggs to a stiff froth and stir it in just as you put it in the pan to bake. Bake twenty minutes and eat with sauce.

PINE-APPLE PUDDING.

Grate a well peeled pine-apple, take its weight in fine white sugar and half the weight in butter, cream the butter and sugar together, and stir in the grated pine-apple, then five eggs well beaten, and a coffee cup of cream. Bake it with or without crust as you may prefer.

FANNIE'S LEMON PUDDING.

Beat eight eggs well and mix in eight ounces of white sugar; rub some lumps of sugar on two lemons, and, beat them in a mortar with the juice; cream six ounces of butter and mix all well together. Bake in a pie plate or pudding dish on paste.

FANNIE'S ALMOND PUDDING.

Blanch one half pound of almonds and pound to a paste with a little rose-water. Cream one pound of sugar and three quarters of a pound of butter together, and stir in eight well-beaten eggs, then the almonds, and one pint of cream. Put it in a deep dish with a rim of puff paste around the edge, and bake it fifteen minutes.

FANNIE'S PINE-APPLE PUDDING.

Peel a pine-apple, take its weight in sugar and same in butter; cream the butter and sugar, then add the *grated* pine-apple, with five beaten eggs and a cup of cream. Line the pudding dish with puff paste and bake.

FANNIE'S FAVORITE PUDDING.

The yelks of fifteen eggs, beat with one pound of sugar, six ounces of butter, and the juice and grated peel of one lemon. Line pie plates with pastry and bake ten minutes.

FANNIE'S COCOANUT PUDDING.

One cocoanut grated, three eggs beaten together, one and a half cups of milk. Sweeten to the taste, add juice and peel of two lemons, and bake it in pastry made with butter.

FANNIE'S LEMON PUDDING.

Beat three eggs with one cup of sugar, the juice and grated peel of one lemon, pour it in a saucepan and cook four minutes, stirring it all the time; take it off the fire and stir in the white of egg beat to a stiff froth; have a pastry baked in a pie plate, pour the mixture on it and bake it a few minutes.

FANNIE'S MOLASSES PUDDING.

Stir one teaspoonful of soda in one cup of molasses, add one cup of butter, same of milk, and flour enough to make it stiff. Boil it five hours, and eat it with a nice sauce.

FANNIE'S BREAD PUDDING.

Line a pudding dish with thin slices of bread, then fill the dish with grated bread crumbs, raisins, and bits of butter; beat up custard with milk, eggs, and sugar, and flavor it; pour it over it and bake, until done, in a quick oven. One quart of milk, eight eggs, and half a pound of sugar for the custard.

HINTON PUDDING.

Put slices of sponge cake in a pudding dish greased with butter, butter each slice and cover it with peach or other preserves; fill the dish with layers in the same way; make a custard with eight eggs, one quart of milk and half pound of sugar; let the milk boil and stir the eggs and sugar in it. Then add lemon extract to your taste, and pour it over the cake in the pudding dish; place the dish in your oven or stove, and bake it a light brown. Send it to the table warm, and you will have a delicious dessert.

BATH PUDDING.

Thicken one pint of milk with two tablespoonfuls of flour; when cold add six eggs and tablespoonful of butter; one ounce of blanched almonds, the juice of one lemon, with a little of the peel grated, and half pound of white sugar. Bake it in cups.

ORANGE PUDDING.

Grate three sponge biscuits in enough milk to make a paste; beat three eggs and stir them in with the juice of a lemon and half the peel grated. Put a teacup of orange juice and one of sugar, with half cup of melted butter in the mixture; stir it well, put it in a dish with puff paste around it, and bake slow one hour.

CINNAMON PUDDING.

Beat five eggs separately, add five large spoonfuls of sugar to the yelks; then the whites, and quarter of a pound of melted butter; mix it well and make it black with pulverized cinnamon. Bake it in a paste in pie plates.

CAKE PUDDING.

Beat five eggs with two cups of sugar, one cup of butter, and same of milk; sift one teaspoonful of soda in three and a half cups of flour and stir it in slowly; dissolve two teaspoonfuls of cream tartar, and stir it in just as you put it to bake. Flavor according to taste.

LAVINA'S SICILY PUDDING.

Take a large lump of loaf sugar and rub it over two lemons (always scrape off the lemon in a saucer as the sugar yellows), mix it with one pound of powdered loaf sugar. Beat the whites of eight eggs to a stiff froth and then in them the sugar; very slowly in this mixture stir in one tablespoonful of fine flour; put in the juice of one lemon and beat all well together. Butter a dish and bake it quickly, or line pans with puff paste, cook the paste partly done, and then fill them with the mixture and bake twenty minutes. If you substitute oranges, use the rind of one and juice of two. Sprinkle sugar over the top when cold.

APPLE PUDDING.

Beat five eggs, leaving out the whites of two; mix them with one quart of stewed apples that has been flavored with lemon and made sweet to the taste with sugar. Beat the whites of two eggs to a stiff froth, and stir in three tablespoonfuls of fine sugar with a little lemon to flavor. After the apples and eggs are poured in your pudding dish, pour the whites on and bake quickly.

COCOANUT PUDDING.

Beat the whites of ten eggs to a stiff froth, stir in half a pound of butter and the same of sugar that has been creamed together, and mix it alternately in the white of egg with a nicely grated cocoanut.

IRISH POTATO PUDDING.

One pound of mashed potato, twelve ounces of butter and same of sugar. Stir the butter and sugar well in the potatoes, then six eggs beaten light. Season with lemon-peel, orange-peel grated, or mace and cloves.

CITRON PUDDING.

Beat eight eggs, cream one pound of sugar and three quarters of a pound of butter together; flavor with lemon extract. Line a pie plate with puff paste, cover it with slices of citron and pour the mixture over. This will make three puddings.

SPONGE PUDDING.

Beat six eggs with two cups of sugar, add one cup of cream, one of butter, and one quart of flour, with one teaspoonful of soda sifted in it. Flavor with lemon and bake in a dish. Eat it hot with butter and peach preserves.

COCOANUT PUDDING.

Beat the yelks of four eggs with ten ounces of sugar and eight ounces of butter. Whip the whites of eight eggs to a froth and stir it in alternately with one grated cocoanut. Bake it in puff paste.

BOILED PLUM-PUDDING.

Stone and cut up one pound of raisins, beat twelve eggs with half a pound of sugar, stir in half a pound of butter with one pound of flour, add a gill of brandy and part of a nutmeg grated. Boil it two hours and eat it with wine sauce.

PLAIN BOILED-PUDDING.

Beat nine eggs with nine spoonfuls of flour and one quart of milk. Put a pinch of salt in it and boil it one hour.

PENELOPE'S COCOANUT PUDDING.

Cream one pound of butter and the same of white sugar together. Beat eight eggs very light, and stir them slowly in. Then add one pound of grated cocoanut with one gill of nice wine. Line pie plates with crust, fill them with the mixture, and bake slowly until a pretty light brown. Eat them cold.

ETTA'S PLUM-PUDDING.

Beat four eggs. Stir in them half a pound of flour and half a pint of new milk; add half a pound of beef suet chopped fine, half a pound stoned raisins well floured and a few currants, with a teaspoonful of salt. Boil this pudding four hours briskly, and serve with wine sauce.

SUSAN'S PLUM-PUDDING.

The day before you wish to have this pudding for dessert, stone and chop fine one pound of raisins, wash in warm water one pound of currants, pick and dry them, and chop half a pound of beef suet. Next morning soak a pound loaf of bread in a pint of warm, sweet milk; beat it fine, add to it the raisins, suet, and currants, with three eggs well beaten, a grated nutmeg, tablespoonful of sugar, and wine-glass of brandy. Put it in a floured bag or pudding mould, and boil it four hours. Serve with cold sauce, made of sugar and butter and flavored with wine and teaspoonful essence of lemon or vanilla.

FIG PUDDING.

Take one pound of nice dried figs and chop them fine; grate enough bread to weigh three quarters of a pound, six ounces of moist sugar, six ounces of beef suet chopped fine, a teacupful of milk, and a little nutmeg. Mix the bread and suet first, then the figs, sugar, and nutmeg, then one beaten egg and the milk. Boil it in a mould or pudding bag for four hours, and eat it with sugar and butter sauce.

SLICED BREAD PUDDING.

Cut some slices of light cold bread and butter them, then spread preserves of any kind over them, and repeat until you fill your pan or mould. Beat four eggs, pour over the bread in the pan one pint of boiling milk, then the eggs; place the mould in boiling water, cover it with a cloth, and let it boil twenty minutes. Serve with a nice sauce.

BOILED FRUIT PUDDING.

Make a paste crust and roll it thin, put some chopped apples or other fruit in it, roll it up, tie it in a cloth, and boil it for two hours. Serve with a nice sauce.

SPONGE PUDDING.

Beat six eggs and two cups of sugar together, put one teaspoonful of soda in a cup of cream, and add it with one cup of butter; season with lemon, stir in one quart of flour, and bake it in a slow oven.

CUSTARD PUDDING.

Beat twelve eggs light and stir gently in twelve spoonfuls of flour and one pint of milk. Bake it quickly and eat it with a nice sauce.

TAPIOCA PUDDING.

Soak four tablespoonfuls of tapioca in one quart of new milk. Stir it over a fire until it comes to a boil after it has soaked well; then add the grated rind of one lemon, half a pint of sweet cream and same of sugar; add the yelks of four eggs and stir well. Just before baking stir the whites in, after being well whipped, and bake five minutes in a hot oven.

BATTER PUDDING.

Beat five eggs very light, stir in one pint of sifted flour, and one quart of sweet milk. Bake it in a pan without a crust, and eat it with butter and sugar for sauce.

ARROWROOT PUDDING.

Dissolve four heaping tablespoonfuls of arrowroot in a little milk, and mix it with four well beaten eggs and two tablespoonfuls of white sugar. Boil one quart of milk and stir the mixture in it, boil three minutes, flavor with lemon, and eat it with cream and sugar.

LAURA'S BREAD PUDDING.

Beat the yelks of five eggs; add a pint of sweet milk and five tablespoonfuls of stale bread. Bake it a light brown and then put on a layer of preserves; beat the whites of the eggs very stiff and then beat in five tablespoonfuls of fine sugar; pour it over the top, return it to the oven, and bake a pretty light brown. If you like, add extract of lemon or vanilla to the white of egg, before putting it on.

MUSH PUDDING.

Take one teacup of sifted meal and mix with coffee cup of cold water, put it on the fire and stir until it boils; put in a pinch of salt, one cup of milk, one of sugar, and half cup of butter and three eggs; season to taste with an extract. Bake and eat it with butter.

DRIED PUMPKIN PIE.

Take one roll of pumpkin (as directed to dry it), put it in sweet milk, and let it soak two hours. Put in one egg, one tablespoonful of sugar, a teaspoonful of ginger, and one of allspice, and bake it in a crust.

GREEN APRICOT PIE.

Take the apricot before the stone is formed and stew it gently in sugar and water; when tender reduce and thicken the syrup. Line pie pans with crust, put them in, and cover it with an upper crust. Make grape pies the same way; always use sugar according to taste.

PRUNE TART.

Scald the prunes, take out the stones and break them, put the kernels in a little cranberry juice with the prunes and sugar, simmer them, and when cool make a tart of them on a crust in pie plate. Damsons, green plums, or any stone fruits are cooked in the same way.

TO STEW CRANBERRIES FOR TARTS.

Simmer them in moist sugar twenty minutes without breaking. One pint will require three ounces of sugar.

GREEN TOMATO PIE.

Wash the tomato and cut out the centre, put a piece of lemon in it, and stew it with three quarters of a pound of sugar to one of the tomato until it is well done; then put it in puff paste as other pies, and bake it.

PEACH PIE.

Peel and halve ripe peaches and stew them with sugar until cooked through; have enough water to make the juice. Make a rich paste, line baking pans, and fill them with the peach and plenty of syrup they were stewed in; put a top crust, stick it with a fork, and bake them.

CHERRY PIE.

Stone the cherries and stew them a short time with sugar and a very little water, put them in paste and bake as above.

DRIED PEACH PIES.

Stew the peaches until soft in water, then add some sugar with a little orange peel and stew again; bake in paste as above.

DRIED PEACH JACKS.

Stew the fruit as above, roll a round piece of paste, half fill it, turn the other half over and bake.

LIZZIE'S PASTE.

Sift one pound of flour and the same weight of butter, put one quarter of the butter and a little salt in the centre of the flour, with the yelks of two eggs; wet the salt, to dissolve it, and make the paste up with ice water to a pliant dough, then roll the paste out in a sheet, press all the water out and put it in the paste; double it over the butter, flour your rolling pin and board, and roll it gently until half an inch thick. Let it stand a short time doubled in four pieces, and then roll it again; double once more and roll it, and then roll out the size you wish for pie plates, or to bake as a crust for preserve puffs.

COCOANUT CUSTARD.

Beat six eggs with a large coffee cup of fine white sugar; after well beaten mix in one large tablespoonful of butter, add two tablespoonfuls of French brandy with one teaspoonful of lemon extract, stir in one cocoanut grated fine and one quart of milk, and bake it a light brown, in a deep pudding dish. Eat it cold.

MELISSA'S PUFF PASTE.

Work the water out of one pound of butter, and lay it in ice water; work a small piece in one pound of flour, and make it up with ice water; roll it out and butter it with some of the washed butter, sift a little flour over it, roll it up and then out again, and continue the same way until all the butter is well in. Bake it in a quick oven on pie plates for fruit pies, or in patty-pans for sweetmeats.

A NICE PASTE FOR PIES.

Rub a tablespoonful of nice lard in one quart of flour, with a little salt; work it up to a pliant dough, then roll it out and butter the sheet, sprinkle a little flour and roll it up, then out again and butter as before. After the second rolling, line plates or deep dishes with it, and fill with any mixture you have prepared for pies to bake in paste.

CHICKEN PIE PASTE.

Work the flour you wish to use, entirely up with sweet lard and a little salt; roll it out the size you wish, for the pie in a dish or plate, put in the chicken, cover it with a top paste, and bake it slowly until a light brown. Make this paste a little thicker than the above when you roll it out.

PUDDING SAUCE. NO. 1.

Stir to a cream one pint of sugar and one of butter; stir it for half an hour or more, then stir in half a pint of Madeira or Sherry wine, and flavor it with lemon or vanilla.

PUDDING SAUCE. NO. 2.

Take half a pint of butter and the same quantity of sugar; beat it to a thick cream. Mix a wine-glass of boiling water and the same of brandy, with the juice of a large lemon and half a nutmeg grated; stir all well, and put it in a sauce tureen.

PUDDING SAUCE. NO. 3.

Put one pint of sugar in a porcelain saucepan, and wet the sugar with water; put in a piece of dry orange peel, let it boil until a little thick, then add a large piece of butter. Pour it out in a tureen or bowl, and put half a pint of scuppernong in it, and grate nutmeg over the top.

PUDDING SAUCE. NO. 4.

Put a cup of sugar in a saucepan with a tablespoonful of butter and a cup of water; let it boil. Stir one teaspoonful of flour smooth with milk and put it in; stir it until it boils. Season it with brandy and nutmeg.

CREAM SAUCE.

Strain one pint of sweet cream and stir enough fine white sugar in it to make it thick; sweeten half a pint of wine, or less, according to taste, and put some extract in it; then slowly stir it in the cream and sugar; grate nutmeg over the top.

CINNAMON SAUCE.

Boil two nice sticks of cinnamon half an hour in one pint of water; stir in one pint of sugar, one tablespoonful of butter and a gill of brandy; boil it until it ropes. Very nice sauce for a plain molasses pudding.

A NICE COOKED SAUCE.

Dissolve half a pound of loaf sugar in three gills of Madeira or sherry wine over the fire; when it is boiling heat, stir in slowly the yelks of eight eggs well beaten. Beat it with an egg whip in the saucepan till it thickens, flavor it with a teaspoonful of lemon or vanilla extract, or a little fresh lemon and orange peel grated. Scuppernong or domestic grape and currant will do for common use.

COMMON SAUCE.

Boil one pint of water with pieces of dried orange peel and a pint of brown sugar; rub one teaspoonful of flour in three of butter, and stir it in when it has cooked to half a pint; boil and stir five minutes.

POOR MAN'S PUDDING.

One cup of raisins, one cup of suet, four of flour, two of milk, half a teacup of molasses, one teaspoonful of cream of tartar, one of salt, and half teaspoonful of soda. Boil it in a tin form two hours.

CREAM PUDDING.

Beat four eggs and two cups of loaf sugar, stir in one cup of cream and three of flour, with one teaspoonful of soda. Bake it like cake, and eat it with cream sauce and peach preserves.

Mrs. McMartin's Sweet Potato Pudding. S. C.

One pound of boiled potatoes, three fourths of a pound of sugar, half pound of butter, six eggs, and a wine-glass of brandy. Bake in a buttered pan and serve hot.

Clara's Cream Pudding. S. C.

One quart of rich milk, yelks of six eggs, two tablespoonfuls of butter, two of corn starch; sweeten and flavor it to taste. Bake it in a greased pan.

Uncle James's Flour Pudding. S. C.

One quart sweet milk, ten eggs well beaten, five spoonfuls of flour, and a pinch of salt. Either boil or bake. Serve hot with wine sauce.

Persimmon Pudding.

After the persimmons have been touched by the frost, gather them, and strain through a sieve enough to make one half gallon. Beat four eggs with four tablespoonfuls of sugar and same of flour and one pint of milk, with a large tablespoonful of butter or two of fine suet. Bake it in pans. Some use corn meal in preference to flour; it requires longer cooking.

Peach Dumplings.

Peel your peaches and halve them. Make up a paste and roll it out the size of a small tea plate. Fill it with peaches and put it in a baking pan. Make as many as you wish for the family, and fill the pan. Mix a little sugar with water and pour the pan half full and bake it in a stove or oven. Have sauce to eat with them, or add more sugar when you mix them, and eat with butter. If you make peach or apple dumplings to boil, always steam them done.

OXFORD DUMPLINGS.

Take two ounces of bread crumbs, four ounces of currants, same of beef suet, a tablespoonful of fine sugar, a little allspice, and rind of one lemon grated. Beat up two eggs and stir in a teacup of milk, and beat all together. Divide it in five dumplings, and fry them a light brown color in hot lard. Eat with wine sauce.

ORANGE TART.

Grate the peel of one orange, and squeeze the juice, and same way one lemon. Beat two eggs with a quarter of a pound of sugar, add two ounces of melted butter, and mix it well with the orange and lemon. Line a tart tin with puff paste, pour the mixture in and bake it a quarter of an hour.

APPLE FRITTERS.

Pare one dozen nice apples and cut them in slices, make a batter with four eggs, one quart of milk and one pint of flour, with a pinch of salt; stir the apples in, and fry them in hot lard. Eat with sauce.

PLAIN FRITTERS.

Take one quart of buttermilk or sour milk, a pint of sweet milk, three eggs, a teaspoonful of soda, stir in flour enough to make a thick batter. Have a large spoonful of lard boiling hot in a spider, drop them in with a spoon and fry a light brown. Serve them with liquid sauce or molasses.

CREAM FRITTERS.

Take a quart of sweet milk and a teacupful of cream, four eggs well beaten, half a nutmeg grated, teaspoonful of salt. Sift a teaspoonful of soda in one quart of flour and make it a nice batter; if too thin add a little more flour. Fry in hot lard and butter mixed, and eat with wine sauce.

Beat two eggs light, put in a teaspoonful of salt then thicken with flour. Roll it out as thin as a wafer, cut it in strips one inch wide and four inches long. Twist them around your finger and drop them in hot lard to fry.

TRANSPARENT PIE.

Beat eight eggs with half a pound of sugar, melt half a pound of butter and stir it in, beat them together a little while, flavor with lemon, and bake in puff paste.

PEACH PIE.

Take mellow, juicy peaches, cut them in quarters after peeling and taking out the stones. Line a deep plate with paste, put in a layer of peaches, a thick layer of sugar, a tablespoonful of water, and a sprinkle of flour. Cover with a crust and bake slowly one hour.

SWEET POTATO PIE.

One pint of mashed potato, one quart of milk, one cup of butter and two of sugar. Beat four eggs, add the butter, then the potato and the milk, flavor it with a little nutmeg, and bake it on paste in a pie plate.

ALMOND PIE.

Blanch one pound of almonds with a little white wine and one pound of sugar; mix it with one cup of bread crumbs, one of cream, and part of a nutmeg grated. Bake it in a slow oven, and cover it with citron or preserved orange peel after you take it out.

FANNIE'S SILVER PIE.

Peel and grate one large potato, add the juice and grated rind of one lemon, the white of one egg beaten, one teacup of cold water; line a pie plate with crust and pour the mixture in to bake. When done, beat the white of three eggs with half a cup of fine white sugar and a little rose-water, put it nicely over the pie, return it to the oven, and bake a light brown. Lay strips of jelly over the top when sent to the table.

FANNIE'S GOLDEN PIE.

Grate the peel of one lemon with the juice in a bowl, add one cup of sugar, one of new milk, the yelks of three eggs well beaten, and one teaspoonful of corn starch; line a dish with crust and bake it slowly. After it is done, beat the whites of the eggs with a tablespoonful of sugar, put it over it, and bake until the white is done.

GREEN APPLE PIE.

Peel tart apples and stew them nicely, strain them through a net strainer, season them while hot with butter or cream, flavor with nutmeg, and put them on a crust that has been baked in a pie plate. Always have sweet milk to drink with apple-pie.

THE BEST WAY TO BOIL DUMPLINGS (MRS. STEWART).

Make a rich, light pastry, and line a large bowl with it; fill with fruit,— blackberries, sliced apples, peaches, or raspberries, and cover with a thin layer of crust. Place a plate to fit the top of the bowl, tie the bowl up in a clean towel (or bag made for the purpose), and boil in a large kettle filled with water. This plan preserves the juice and obviates the need of thick crust, which is unwholesome as well as unpalatable. A dumpling made in this way and boiled well, eaten hot with butter and sugar sauce beat to a cream, is one of the most epicurean Southern desserts.

BLACKBERRY AND RASPBERRY DUMPLINGS, BAKED.

Make a rich pastry and roll it thin, cut it by a tea plate, fill it with berries, and put it in a large tin pan; do this until it is full. Put a little water in the pan and bake them slowly, until a light brown. Eat them with wine sauce or plain sugar and butter.

LIZZIE'S LEMON PIES. S. C.

Two lemons grated, two cups of sugar, one of sweet milk, two tablespoonfuls of corn-starch, the yelks of six eggs. Bake in pastry. Beat the whites of the eggs with eight spoonfuls of white sugar, and pour over the pies after they are baked. Set them in the oven or stove to dry for a few minutes.

CHARLESTON PUDDING.

Four cups of flour, sifted, with one teaspoonful of soda and two of cream tartar; beat six eggs with three cups of sugar, one cup of butter, and one of cream in them, and gently stir in the flour.

JENNIE'S PUDDING.

Beat five eggs and half a pound of sugar together; chop half a pound of suet and half a pound of apples together; stir it in the yelk of egg and sugar; then half a pound of flour, with half a pound of raisins, one gill of brandy, and one nutmeg. Mix all well and then stir in the whites of the eggs, beat to a stiff froth. Bake it two hours.

SWEET POTATO PUDDING.

Parboil some potatoes, grate them, and weigh one pound. Beat eight yelks of egg with three quarters of a pound of sugar, and stir in the same of butter, and put it in the potato, with one glass of wine or brandy, a nutmeg and lemon grated. Stir the whites of the eggs in when beaten stiff, and bake.

SWEETMEAT PUDDING.

Beat the yelks of twenty eggs with the whites of three; mix one pound of butter and one of sugar together, and stir in the eggs with one nutmeg grated in it. Line a pudding dish with rich paste and cover it with quince or peach preserves, pour the mixture over it and bake. When nearly done, beat the whites of eight of the eggs to a stiff froth, put two spoonfuls of fine sugar in it and a little lemon extract; take the pudding out, cover with the white of egg, and return it to the oven to cook a light brown.

LEMON PUDDING.

Beat four eggs, add half pound of butter and half pound of sugar that is beat to a cream, grate the peel of one lemon, and squeeze the juice; mix all well and bake in two pie plates lined with rich paste.

JEFFERSON PUDDING.

One pound of mashed potato made soft with milk, six eggs, half pound of white sugar, and some grated lemon; bake moderately forty minutes.

LEMON PUDDING.

Juice and rind of one lemon, one cup of sugar, yelks of two eggs, three tablespoons of flour, one pint of milk. Line a dish with paste; pour on the mixture and bake. Beat the whites of the eggs to a stiff froth and stir in four tablespoons of sugar; take it out of the oven or stove, pour the white of egg on lightly, return it and bake it a light brown.

AUGUSTA PUDDING.

Nine tablespoonfuls of flour, ten eggs, and one quart of milk. Boil the milk and pour over the flour, and let it stand till it is cold, and then put in the eggs after being beat separately and very light. Bake it in a tin mould or dish in a quick oven or heated stove. Serve with cream sauce.

CREAM PUDDING.

Beat six eggs well and stir them into a pint of flour with a pint of milk, a little salt, the grated rind of a lemon, and three tablespoonfuls of sugar; when ready to bake stir in the cream and bake in a buttered dish. Eat with thin wine sauce.

CORN MEAL PUDDING.

Boil one quart of milk, add two gills and a half of corn meal very smoothly, beat seven eggs with a gill of molasses, and tablespoonful of butter; mix all well and bake it in a greased pan two hours. Eat it with sugar and butter sauce.

BOILED CORN MEAL PUDDING.

At sunrise, put on a pot of water to boil this pudding. Mix three quarts of milk in one quart of corn meal, with three eggs and gill of molasses; put it in a bag or mould large enough to allow it to swell. Boil briskly, and serve it with wine sauce.

MUSH.

Put a dessert spoonful of butter in a quart of cold water with a little salt, and stir in fine corn meal until as thick as you wish it, and cook it until it tastes done. Eat it cold with milk and grated nutmeg, or with butter.

RICE PUDDING.

One cup of rice, one cup of sugar, and one of butter, one quart of milk, a little nutmeg or cinnamon. Beat all together, put it in a buttered dish, and bake it two hours.

PLAIN BAKED PUDDING.

Beat nine eggs, and sift in five tablespoonfuls of flour with one quart of milk in the yelks; then stir in the whites with a little salt and bake immediately. Eat with liquid sauce.

BREAD PUDDING.

Three quarters of a pound of grated bread, three pints of boiled milk poured over it, half a pound of sugar and quarter of a pound of butter stirred in the bread, and five eggs beaten and put in when cold. Bake it.

RICE PLUM-PUDDING.

Take one quart of new milk and sweeten it with half a pint of sugar; put in a little nutmeg or cinnamon, then a half pint of rice that is washed nicely, and quarter of a pound of picked raisins; bake it two hours or boil it in a tin mould.

PUMPKIN PUDDING.

To one small pumpkin, add one quart of milk, six eggs, ginger, cinnamon, and nutmeg to taste. Make it very sweet with sugar, and add a teacup of molasses and a little salt. Then bake it in deep plates.

APPLE PUDDING.

Beat six eggs and six spoonfuls of sugar together; add one spoonful of butter, and six large spoonfuls of stewed apples; flavor with any spice you prefer, or lemon, and bake it in a nice crust. This quantity will make two, in large sized soup plates.

COCOANUT PUDDING.

Cream half pound of sugar and half pound of butter together; add to it the whites of twelve eggs beaten to a stiff froth, with three quarters of a pound of grated cocoanut, and a wine-glass of wine and rose-water mixed. Put the mixture in a buttered dish. Lay puff paste around the sides, and bake half an hour in a moderate oven.

CUSTARD PUDDING.

Line a large dish with pieces of cake of any kind; then fill it with a nice boiled custard. Whip the whites of four eggs and beat a large spoonful of sugar in it as for icing; pour it over the top, and bake all a short time. Eat it cool.

A LEMON PUDDING PIE.

The grated rind and juice of one lemon, a teacup of sugar, one egg, a spoonful of flour, or one cracker grated, one wine-glass of wine, two large apples pared and grated, half a spoonful of butter, and a pint of milk. Boil the milk and butter together, and let it cool. Beat up the egg and sugar, and add them; add the wine and lemon just as you put it in the oven to bake.

A NICE SUET PUDDING.

Boil and mash five nice potatoes, and put one pound of chopped suet in them. Add one cup of molasses, one cup of sugar, one cup of milk, one cup of chopped raisins, one teaspoonful of soda, a little allspice, nutmeg, and cinnamon. Work in enough flour to make it like bread and boil it three hours in a tin boiler.

SOUTH CAROLINA PUDDING.

Stew enough apples to make a quart when mashed up. Season them with lemon and a spoonful of butter or teacup of rich cream. Boil a half pint of rice, put a pinch of salt in it and teaspoonful of sugar with some nutmeg grated. When both are cold, beat up six eggs with a tablespoonful or two of flour, stir all together, and boil it, or bake it in a moderate oven. Eat with sugar and butter sauce, flavored with Sherry or Madeira.

QUICK PUDDING.

Boil some rice; when done soft, break in three eggs, half cup of cream or milk, and some grated nutmeg. Give it one boil, send it to the table with bits of butter on the top.

MOLASSES PUDDING.

Beat three eggs with one cup of sugar, one of butter, one of milk, and half a cup of molasses; mix in one quart of flour; beat all well, then stir in one teaspoon of soda in a half cup of molasses, until it rises to the top of the cup, and stir it in well just as you put it in to bake. Eat hot with butter.

POTATO PUDDING.

Boil six potatoes soft and pass them through a coarse hair sieve. Cream one pound of sugar and the same of butter together; beat eight eggs and add them to the sugar and butter. Then put in a gill of wine, one of brandy, and half a gill of rose-water, with teaspoonful of allspice. Stir the mixture well in the potato, beat hard, and bake in a pan lined with paste or without, as you prefer.

TO COOK RICE.

Soak rice in cold water seven hours, then put it in boiling water and cook ten minutes.

ANOTHER WAY.

Put a teacup of well washed rice in a saucepan, and pour water enough to half fill the pan; put it on a hot fire and let it boil quickly. When the grain looks done, pour the water off, cover it over to steam a few minutes to make the grains separate, and put the saucepan inside the stove. The rice will brown in a short time. Run a knife around it, and turn it on a dish, and pour melted butter over it. Browning it gives it a pleasant flavor.

STILL ANOTHER.

Soak it three hours, mix part milk and water, let it boil up, then put the rice in and boil it fifteen minutes. Sweeten a cup of cream very sweet, grate nutmeg over it and pour it over the rice as soon as it is taken out of the saucepan, and placed in a covered dish.

RAISINS AND RICE.

Put one teacup of rice and half pound of raisins in a pudding-bag, drop it in a pot of boiling water, and frequently turn the bag. When done, slip the bag of and serve it hot on a dish to eat with nice sugar and butter sauce. Plain but good dessert.

RICE FRUMENTY.

Put a large coffee cup of rice on to boil, covered with water, and let it boil perfectly soft. Beat six eggs, stir in one cup of sugar, one quart of milk, salt-spoonful of salt, and stir it in the rice; give it one boil up, continuing to stir it until it tastes done (five minutes). Pour it in large bowls or covered dishes, put butter in bits all over the top, grate nutmeg over the butter, and let it cool.

PASQUOTANK WHEAT FRUMENTY.

The day before you wish to prepare it, have one quart of wheat picked, washed, and broken in a mortar perfectly dry. At four o'clock in the morning put the wheat in a clean pot with a cover, with one gallon of water. Keep this boiling steadily until ten o'clock, occasionally stirring it. If the water boils down, add a little more from the kettle. It must be very soft and well done. Beat twelve eggs, one pound of sugar, one tablespoonful of flour, and one of butter together. Put three quarts of the wheat from the pot in a warm porcelain kettle (be careful and not scrape the bottom of the pot), put the kettle on the fire and stir the eggs, sugar, and butter in with three quarts of milk. Let it have one boil, stirring all the time, to prevent its curdling; take it up in large bowls. Put butter over the top in bits, and sprinkle finely pulverized allspice on the butter. This was always made at wheat harvest, for white and colored families.

WHITE CUSTARD.

Take the whites of eight eggs, five tablespoons of white sugar, one pint of milk, and one pint of cream. Boil the milk and cream together, stir the sugar gently in the eggs; do not beat them or let them froth. Add the milk and cream slowly to the eggs and sugar, flavor it with lemon or vanilla extract, then pour it in cups, put the cups in a pan of boiling water, and set the pan in a cool oven. Add fire to it and bake them a light brown. Twenty minutes ought to be long enough to cook them right. This is very delicious and delicate for the sick.

BOILED CUSTARD.

Put one gallon of milk in a porcelain kettle over a hot fire; whilst heating through, beat thirty-two eggs and one and a quarter pounds of sugar together; when the milk comes to a full boil, stir the eggs and sugar slowly in it, stirring all the time; let it cook through for a few minutes, then turn it and stir until cool. Flavor with lemon or what you prefer.

BAKED CUSTARD.

Beat eight eggs together with eight spoonfuls of sugar, stir in one and a half quarts of milk, teaspoonful of lemon extract, and tablespoonful of butter; pour it in a pan or pudding mould and bake fifteen minutes. Nice to eat with sponge cake and preserves for dessert, and good for the sick.

BOILED CUSTARD No. 2.

Put half a gallon new milk, as fresh from the cow as you can get it, in a porcelain kettle to boil. Tie a vanilla bean in a thin piece of muslin and put it in the milk. Beat twelve eggs with half a pound of loaf sugar, and when the milk boils so as to puff up, pour one half on the eggs and sugar; then pour that over the remaining half in the kettle and boil for five minutes, stirring it hard all the time. Try it and if disposed to curdle, pour it off immediately, and set it in a pan of cold water, and stir until cool. If the bean is not convenient, use extracts.

BESSIE'S BUNKER HILL PUDDING.

Four cups of Indian meal, two of suet, two of molasses, one quart of milk, and a little salt; mix the meal and suet together with enough cold milk to moisten it, boil the milk, and put it in with the molasses. Put it in a tin mould, *hat* shaped, and set it in a kettle of water to come nearly to the top, but not over it; have the mould covered very tight and boil it five hours. This was given me by a Boston lady for this "Housewife."

FRENCH PUFF PUDDING.

Beat the whites of four eggs to a stiff froth, then the yelks with one cup of white sugar; mix them, flavor to taste, and bake twenty minutes in a quick oven.

JELLY ROLLS.

Beat three eggs with one cup of sugar, two tablespoonfuls sweet milk or water, one and a half cups of flour, with one teaspoonful of cream tartar and one and a half of soda sifted in it. Mix in a dough, spread it with jelly and roll it up, cut it in pieces an inch thick and bake, or bake it in one and then divide. Cream can be used instead of jelly for breakfast or tea.

DELIGHTFUL PUDDING.

One quart of boiled milk mixed with quarter of a pound of mashed Irish potato and same of flour, with an ounce or two of butter. When it is cold add three eggs well beaten, bake half an hour, and eat with wine sauce.

MRS. M.'S BAKED APPLE PUDDING.

Take one quarter of a pound of boiled apples and same of white sugar mixed; add two ounces of butter, the yelks of three eggs and whites of two, the rind and juice of one lemon. Mix well and bake it in puff paste one hour.

Mrs. K.'s Sliced Lemon Pudding.

Boil two lemons until perfectly soft, cut them in thin slices, taking out the seed; line a dish with puff paste, put a layer of lemon, one of sugar, and one of sliced apple alternately, until the dish is full, and bake it.

Boiled Molasses Pudding.

One cup of butter, one of molasses, one of milk, one of raisins, and three of flour; dissolve one teaspoonful of soda in the milk and sift two of cream tartar in the flour; put spice to taste, and a little salt if the butter is fresh. Boil four hours in a mould, and eat with sauce. The fruit and cream tartar can be left out if a plain pudding is wanted.

Plain Plum-Pudding.

Stir one pound of sugar and half pound of butter together and mix well with twelve eggs, then sift in one pound of flour and one of raisins. Boil it two hours and eat with sauce.

Anna's Pudding.

Beat eight eggs with eight ounces of sugar and eight ounces of butter and one grated nutmeg. Put it in a saucepan over the fire, and stir constantly until it thickens; pour it out to cool, and bake it on a rich paste in a moderate oven.

Granville Mince-Meat.

Boil hogs' feet very tender, chop two pounds; seed and chop two pounds of raisins, same of currants, of apples, sugar, citron, and one pound of fresh butter or suet, one tablespoonful of salt, mace, cloves, and cinnamon to the taste. Mix all with one quart of French brandy; add more apple if you like. Bake in rich puff paste.

POTATO PUDDING.

Boil six potatoes soft and pass them through a coarse hair sieve. Cream one pound of sugar and one pound of butter together, beat eight eggs, and add to the sugar and butter; then put in a wine-glass of brandy, the same of wine, and half a wine-glass of rose-water, with a teaspoonful of fine allspice. Stir the mixture well in the potatoes, beat hard, and bake in a pan without crust.

ANN'S PLUM-PUDDING.

Rub one pound of flour and one of beef suet well together, add a pound of stoned raisins, a cup of brown sugar, one grated nutmeg, a few cloves, and milk sufficient to make a stiff batter. Dip your pudding-bag in hot water, and flour the inside. Pour the mixture in it, and put it in a pot of boiling water. Boil briskly for six hours, occasionally turning the bag to prevent the fruit from settling.

POOR MAN'S PLUM PUDDING.

One pound of raisins, half a pound of currants, one and a quarter pounds of flour, one cup of molasses, one teaspoonful of saleratus in a cup of cold water; mix the dry ingredients, then the molasses, the saleratus and cup of water, put it in a bag, and boil it six hours.

CABINET PUDDING.

Line a pudding pan with slices of pound cake or sponge. Beat eight eggs with one pound of sugar, stir in one quart of rich milk, and flavor with essence of lemon. Pour it in the pan with the cake, set it in a kettle of water and cook it, and when cool turn it out on a dish.

LEMON CHEESE CAKE PUDDING.

Cut the rind off two lemons and boil them soft, then beat them into one pound of sugar. Beat the yelks of eight eggs, add to them half a pound of butter, and then the lemon and sugar, with two tablespoonfuls of flour, and bake it in puff paste.

MRS. L.'S LEMON PUDDING.

Line a pie plate with crust and bake it. Put in a saucepan three beaten yelks of eggs, one cup of sugar, the juice and grated peel of one lemon, and a tablespoonful of butter. Let it cook six minutes, stirring all the time; take it from the fire and stir the whites of the eggs, beaten to a stiff froth, immediately in, pour it over the baked paste, and bake it a few minutes. This makes a delicious pudding.

A DISH FOR SHROVE TUESDAY.

Pancakes.

Make a batter with one pound of flour, four eggs, a little salt, and one pint of sweet milk, with a dessert spoonful of butter. If not as thin as you wish, add more milk or a little water, grease a hot griddle, pour a small teacup half full of the batter on it, let it run thin, bake it quickly, and fold it with each side turned to meet in the middle. Set the plate over hot water to keep them hot as you bake them, and send to the table to eat with molasses or wine sauce. In olden times, 'tis said, the lower classes in Catholic countries would toss a pancake up the chimney on Shrove Tuesday, and if it came out whole, they were sure of good luck all the year.

A FRENCH LADY'S RECIPE FOR PANCAKES.

Make a paste with flour, eggs, butter or oil, with a little brandy, salt, milk, and water, and let it stand three hours. Then fry it in hot water in cakes the size of your frying-pan, browning both sides, and when hot, dust nutmeg and a thick coat of white sugar over it and fold it as above.

Lucy Howard Pudding.

Take one quart of milk and put it on to boil, then stir four spoonfuls of flour in cold milk, and when the quart has boiled, pour it over the flour, add half a cup of butter and one large cup of sugar; when it is well mixed, beat up six eggs, stir them in and bake. Very good for an invalid.

Dried Apple Pudding.

Beat four eggs and stir them in eight large spoonfuls of stewed dried apples; add one cup of milk and one spoonful of butter, season with lemon peel or extract, and bake in a pan.

Cottage Pudding.

Beat four eggs with two cups of sugar, one of butter, two of milk, and stir in four cups of flour with one teaspoonful of soda sifted in it. Bake in a pan and eat with sauce.

Transparent Pudding.

Beat eight eggs separately until very light, melt half a pound of butter, and stir half a pound of sugar in it; flavor with nutmeg and lemon, and bake it in puff paste.

Apple Pudding.

Slice some apples, and put them in a pan on the top of the stove to stew in a little water; make up a paste with lard rolled in flour that has been sifted with soda and cream tartar in it, make it in cake to fit in the pan, put it over the apples, cover it over, and let it cook until done.

Dauphine Pudding.

Line a pudding dish with paste and put in a layer of sweetmeats or marmalade. Boil one pint of milk and stir in it three well beaten eggs, two tablespoonfuls of sugar and one of flour; stir it over the fire until it thickens, and add a pinch of salt with some vanilla extract. Pour the mixture over the sweetmeat and bake it in a moderate oven. When it is done, cover it with a meringue made of the whites of four eggs and a teacup of sugar, return it to the oven, and slowly cook it until the meringue is a light brown.

QUEEN OF PUDDINGS.

Soak one pint of bread crumbs in one pint of milk, beat the yelks of eight eggs and whites of four with one cup of sugar, flavor with lemon, add one tablespoonful of butter, and bake it. Beat the four whites of egg that were left out with a cup of sugar, put it over the pudding as soon as baked and cook it until the meringue is a light brown.

APPLE PUDDING.

Six eggs, three quarters of a pound of sugar, half a pound of butter, one pint of stewed apples, one cup of bread crumbs, flavored with nutmeg and lemon, and baked in a pan.

META'S PUDDING.

Take the whites of four eggs and one pound of unbroken loaf sugar; rub the sugar on the rind of two lemons and then pound it fine. Beat the eggs to a stiff froth and stir in the sugar, and the juice of one lemon. Have pie plates lined with rich, light pastry, and bake it half done; cover it with the mixture and bake a few minutes; do not let it brown.

JULIA'S JELLY PUDDING.

Beat six eggs separately, put one cup of sugar in the yelks, one cup of melted butter drained off, one cup of jelly, and one of sweet cream; add all with the eggs and sugar, then stir in the whites, and bake in a rich, light pastry.

GYPSY PUDDING.

Spread sponge cake, cut in thin slices, with jelly or marmalade, and put them together like sandwiches, and lay them in a dish. Make a rich boiled custard, and while hot, pour it over the cake. Let it cool before you serve it.

NANNIE'S COCOANUT PUDDING.

The juice and grated peel of two lemons, one cocoanut grated, one pound of sugar, half a cup of butter, one pint of milk, and the yelks of four eggs.

RALEIGH PUDDING.

Cream one cup of flour and eleven ounces of butter together. Beat ten eggs with three cups of sugar. Mix all with four grated oranges and bake in paste.

SUFFOLK APPLE PIE.

Cover a pie plate with pastry. Pare and core apples, cut them in half and put them on the paste; on each half put one tablespoonful of sugar and a piece of butter the size of a hickory nut, cover it with wine and bake it.

SCOTLAND NECK APPLE PUDDING.

Take one pint of stewed apples and beat six ounces of butter and twelve of sugar in them; put the juice and grated peel of one lemon, half a nutmeg, one teacup of sponge cake crumbs, a few bitter almonds, and when the apples are cold, add six eggs well beaten.

SCOTLAND NECK PLUM-PUDDING.

One cup of molasses, same of butter and raisins, one cup of milk with teaspoonful of soda in it, flour enough to make a thick batter. Flavor with cinnamon and cloves. Boil it four hours and eat it with wine sauce.

FAYETTEVILLE ORANGE PUDDING.

Boil the peel of six oranges perfectly soft, change the water six or eight times while boiling, to prevent any bitter taste, and pound it in a marble mortar. Wash some fresh butter and after it has been well worked, weigh one half of a pound and mix it with half a pound of loaf sugar finely powdered, with the yelks of four eggs well beaten, and the pounded peel; then add the whites of the eggs that are whipped to a stiff froth, with the pulp and juice of two oranges. Line baking pans with puff paste, and bake quickly. When cold sprinkle sugar over the top.

FAYETTEVILLE LEMON PUDDING.

Beat separately seven eggs. Add three quarters of a pound of loaf sugar with the yelks, then add half a pint of rich cream, and quarter of a pound of fresh butter nicely washed, two large tablespoonfuls of flour, the rind of two lemons, and, at the last, the juice of one. Directly after stirring in the whites of the eggs beat to a stiff froth. Bake them in puff paste in pie plates and eat them cold. If you use a range, put them above for crust to bake and pudding to rise before it begins to brown.

FAYETTEVILLE CITRON PUDDING.

Beat the yelks of sixteen eggs and the whites of four, add one pound of white sugar to the yelks, and then one pound of fresh butter, and a dessert-spoonful of flour, with a gill of wine, and half a pound of citron cut in slices and stirred in lightly. After it has been flavored, add the whites of eggs, and bake it in puff paste in a moderate oven or stove.

MOCK COCOANUT PUDDING.

Beat the whites of twelve eggs with one pound of white sugar, stir in half a pound of butter and three tablespoonfuls of corn meal, season with lemon extract, and bake it in puff paste.

* * *

"Work" is the word for the times. Household occupation must not be looked upon as a drudgery or a disgrace. Work is a necessity, that we may realize the luxury of labor. Employment is happiness, and the means of success, in every condition of life. Heaven itself would scarcely be heaven if it only recalled the idea of the wearied old woman who thought "she would have a nice time doing nothing forever!" Activity in every duty, to your God, your parents, your husband, your neighbors, your servants, the poor around you, the sick and dying, and in every station in life, to which it hath pleased God to call you, is the true rest of soul and body. "'It is dreadful to *have* nothing to do,' it is worse, a great deal worse, to *do* nothing. It is the death of life, a living death."

Florence Nightingale in her letter on woman's work, says: "But to all women I would say, look upon your work, whether it be an accustomed or an unaccustomed work, as a trust confided to you, This will keep you alike from discouragement and from presumption, from idleness and from overtaxing yourself. Where God leads the way, He has bound Himself to help you go the way."

PICKLES AND SAUCES.

GREEN PICKLED CUCUMBERS. NO. 1.

Gather small cucumbers with a short stem. Put them in salt and water brine, strong enough to bear an egg, let them remain in the brine well covered for three days (always put a flannel rag on the top of the brine to take up the scum, and wash it off every morning), the third day pour your brine off in a clean brass kettle, and give it a boil up; pour it hot on the pickles. Do this for three mornings and stop three until you scald them nine times. Then, when cold, place them on dishes to drain, and in your porcelain kettle put sufficient vinegar to cover them, according to the size of your jar. Put in some allspice, cloves, cinnamon, few blades of mace, pod of green pepper, piece of horse-radish root, race ginger, few mustard seed, and spiced cucumbers (from the apothecary's), with one cup of sugar. Boil these up well, pour hot over the pickles, and tie closely. When perfectly cold, open, and if not under vinegar, add enough to fill the jar to the brim. They will keep good for two years, and you will find them number one.

SLICED CUCUMBER PICKLE.

Gather them full grown, before they begin to turn yellow, peel off the green rind, slice them tolerably thick, fill a large bowl with them and a few onions cut small. Sprinkle a little salt between each layer, let them stand six hours, then put all in a colander to drain. When the liquor has run off, put them in your jars with cayenne pepper between each layer, and cover well with strong cider vinegar. When full, put two tablespoonfuls of good sweet oil on the top and cover close. Two weeks after, pour this vinegar off and add fresh.

PEPPER VINEGAR PICKLE.

Boil one dozen pods of red pepper in two quarts of vinegar (always using porcelain kettles for boiling vinegar), soak cucumbers, tomatoes, or young cimblins that you have had in salt brine for two days, put them in a brass kettle with grape leaves on the sides and bottom, put a pint of vinegar and quart of water on them and let them slowly heat through. Drop them hot in the pepper vinegar, and if not enough, when cold, add vinegar to cover them.

ONION PICKLE.

Put your onions in a brine of salt and water and let them remain one week; then put them in fresh water, change it twice every day, and let it remain three days. Stick each onion with a clove, and pack them in a jar with pepper, mace, and allspice. Sprinkle between and cover them well with cold vinegar.

DAMSON AND CHERRY PICKLES.

Weigh the fruit. To five pounds of fruit, put three pounds of sugar, one quart of vinegar, two ounces, of cinnamon, same of cloves, half the quantity of mace. Put the fruit in a jar. Boil the vinegar, sugar, and spices, and pour them boiling hot on the fruit.

CABBAGE PICKLE.

Quarter cabbages and split the quarter, put them in a wooden tray, and sprinkle each piece with salt. Let it remain twenty-four hours, then drain them from the salt. After it is well drained, pack it in a jar with a layer of sugar, some onion chopped fine, and different kinds of spices. Boil sufficient vinegar to cover it, and pour on boiling hot; tie it up closely. For a two gallon jar, with cabbage in it, one gallon of vinegar will answer.

MARY'S SWEET PICKLED CUCUMBER.

Take two pounds of sugar, one ounce of cloves, one of cinnamon, and one pint of vinegar. Boil them and remove the scum. Take ripe cucumbers, scrape out the pulp, and cut them in strips one inch thick. Put them in cold water for five minutes, and then in the pickle to boil until you can put a quill easily through. Tie them up tightly in a jar, and keep in a cool place. Ripe cantelopes can be put up in the same way.

Sweet Pickled Water-Melon Rind.

Put the rind of water-melon in salt for three days, then soak it in clear water until fresh (two days may answer), then scald it in vinegar and water. Next day boil as much vinegar as it will require to cover the quantity you make, with a few cloves, some cinnamon, mace, allspice, ginger, and a little black pepper, with sugar to the taste, and pour it over the rind while hot.

Ripe Cucumber Mustard Pickle.

Peel ripe cucumbers and lay them in salt six hours. Drain them through a colander, get some good English mustard, put a layer of cucumber cut in slices, cover it with mustard, a little black pepper, and a little sugar. Fill the jar in this way and pour hot vinegar over it, with a few spices boiled in and strained out.

Pickle Peppers.

Gather large bell pepper, put it in a weak brine of salt and water, boiling hot; pour it off, and scald them with it three mornings. If green as you wish, take them out and put them in vinegar and water for a few days, with a bit of alum in it. If not green, boil the vinegar and water up, and pour it over them, and let it stand until cold, then drop them in strong, cold vinegar, and tie up closely.

Pepper Mangoes.

Prepare bell pepper by the above recipe, fill it with cabbage chopped fine, mustard seed, horseradish, *few* celery seed, and a little allspice. Tie them with wide strips of muslin and drop them in cold vinegar. Put cross sticks over the top of pickles to keep them from floating. They keep well if kept under the vinegar. If you wish the seed taken out of peppers, do it after they are scalded. Stick a knife in them when you first gather for pickling.

PICKLED EGGS.

Boil fresh eggs very hard, put them in cold water, and remove the shells. When cold, take a sharp knife and cut them open lengthways as smoothly as possible. Lay them carefully in wide mouth jars. Boil some vinegar, with whole pepper, allspice, ginger, and a few cloves of garlic in it, and pour it scalding hot on the eggs. Tie up closely and let them stand one month. They are then fit for use and very delicate.

PICKLED TOMATOES.

Select tomatoes not over ripe, and wipe them with a soft cloth. Put them in a jar with a few shallots and silver onions that have been pickled. Boil some vinegar with a few spices, and when perfectly cold, pour it over them and close the jar tight.

TO PICKLE PLUMS.

Gather green plums before they begin to turn; make a pickle of mustard seed, a little salt, and vinegar, boil it three mornings, and pour it hot over the plums. They resemble olives, and answer when you cannot get the olive to put in sauce.

PICKLED PEACHES.

Put large cling-stone peaches in a kettle lined with grape leaves, sprinkle a bit of saleratus among them, cover with salt and water, and simmer them over a slow fire until green. Boil vinegar enough to cover them, with whole pepper, allspice, and mustard seed, and scald them with it four mornings.

SWEET PICKLED PEACH.

Take two pounds of peaches cut in half. Boil one pound of sugar and one pint of vinegar with a little ginger and pour over them, pour it off, boil, and scald nine mornings.

A cool dark closet is the best place for pickles.

OLD VIRGINIA CHOW CHOW.

Three pecks of ripe tomatoes, three of green, five large heads of cabbages, one dozen green peppers, same of ripe, half a pound of celery; chop very fine, cover it with salt, and let it stand twenty-four hours. Then drain the brine off thoroughly; cover it with vinegar and three pounds of sugar. Scald it over an hour in a porcelain kettle, take it off, and add one cup of scraped horse-radish, one of mustard seed, ounce of cloves, two ounces of spice, same of ginger, and one of ground mustard. Tie it up close, and let it stand a month before using it.

PICKLED CHERRIES.

Boil one quart of vinegar with two pounds of sugar, few sticks of cinnamon, and whole cloves, and skim it nicely; when perfectly cold, drop ripe cherries in it and keep them under the pickle. They retain their flavor and keep well.

MELON MANGOES.

Take young cantelopes, large as a good sized orange, put them in a strong brine of salt and water, and let them remain twenty-four hours; then take them out and cut down one of the slices (only one cut; it will readily open after being in the brine, and is far better than cutting out the slice or plug); slip your finger in and clean the seeds out nicely, then put in cold water to rinse them. After all are cleaned, return them to the brine, and scald them several mornings, by pouring the brine off in a brass kettle and giving it a boil up (small bit of alum in the jar improves them). When green as you wish, scald them in part vinegar and water and let them remain in it three days; then prepare a stuffing of cabbage cut fine, mustard seed, few celery seed, pickled cucumber cut fine, onion if you like it, horse-radish scraped, allspice, cloves, pieces of cinnamon, teaspoonful of sugar to each melon, and few grains of pepper. Fill them with this mixture, putting in one at a time, and put them in a stone jar, and cover well with strong cider vinegar. Some persons like one teaspoonful of salad oil in every mango. Have strips of bleached cottons half an inch wide to tie around the melon and secure the stuffing. These are good two years old.

CUCUMBER MANGOES.

Prepare your cucumbers as for plain pickle; have large, full-grown ones for mangoes; make an incision length way of the cucumber; don't take anything out, but gently fill it with the same stuffing given for melons. You will be surprised to see how much you can put in it; secure it with strips wound around it, put it in a jar, and fill with cold vinegar, with pieces of horse-radish, ginger root, and allspice over them.

PEACH MANGOES.

Use the same stuffing and open them carefully to extract the seed, after being in salt and water two days. Boil the vinegar with a teacup of sugar and pour on them.

WATER-MELON SWEET PICKLE.

Cut ten pounds of water-melon rind in strips or any shape you choose (taking off the green part); put it in a porcelain kettle with water enough to cover it, and give it one good boil up; drain it in a colander and put it in a stone jar. Boil one quart of vinegar, two pounds of sugar, and one ounce of cinnamon together, and pour it hot on the rind in the jar, and repeat it three mornings. Then tie up the jar and use when you wish it.

PEACH SWEET PICKLE.

Peel peaches that are nearly ripe, weigh them, and put them in a porcelain kettle with half their quantity of sugar, half a pint of vinegar to each pound, some cloves, allspice, and cinnamon, and cook them until the syrup looks a little thick. To a peck of peaches, twelve cloves, tablespoonful of allspice, and one of cinnamon will be sufficient.

RIPE PEACHES PICKLE.

Peel them and drop them in vinegar that has been boiled with one teacup of sugar to one quart of vinegar.

SWEET PICKLE CANTELOPES.

Take ripe cantelopes, peel the rind off and cut in slices, clean the seeds out nicely and shave out the soft part (the eighth of an inch) next to the seed. After preparing as many as you wish to put up in this way, weigh them, and put them in stone jars. Have your porcelain kettle ready; and put one half the weight of the cantelope in sugar and half a pint of vinegar to one pound of sugar in it; add one ounce of stick cinnamon to every ten pounds, and one teaspoonful of allspice. Boil it all together and pour it hot over the cantelope in the jars; do this with the same poured off three mornings; the fourth morning put all in the kettle and cook until the cantelope is soft enough to put a straw in it.

SWEET PICKLE DAMSONS.

To one pound of damsons allow three quarters of a pound of brown sugar, six cloves, half a teaspoonful allspice, and three inch stick of cinnamon. Put the damsons in a jar. Boil the other ingredients, and pour over them, and repeat five mornings.

GREEN TOMATO SAUCE.

Slice four gallons of green tomatoes; put in three tablespoonfuls best English mustard, three gills of mustard seed, two spoonfuls of pepper, three of salt, one of allspice, one teaspoonful of cloves, pint of chopped onions, one quart of sugar, five pints of vinegar, one half teacup of celery seed. Boil it two hours.

SWEET PICKLE PEARS.

Weigh peeled pears and put them in a jar; to every pound allow three quarters of a pound of sugar and half a pint of vinegar. Put the sugar and vinegar in a porcelain kettle with some sticks of cinnamon and a few cloves. Boil it and pour it hot over the pears three mornings, then put all in the kettle, and give them one boil up.

CABBAGE PICKLE.

Quarter and half quarter of nice solid cabbage, cover it with salt, and let it stand twenty-four hours; drain and dry it. Put on as much vinegar as you wish in a porcelain kettle with mustard seed, allspice, cinnamon bark, and a little sugar; when it boils put the cabbage in and let it cook half an hour. This keeps better than any I ever put up.

PICKLED GHERKIN.

Cut the gherkins with a short stem, pack them in salt, and let them lie one week. Drain them nicely, and pack them in a jar with vine leaves, and keep them in the corner of the fire-place or near a stove, well covered with vinegar and water, with a small piece of alum in it for several days to green. When as green as you wish, cover them with vinegar and a few spices. If they do not heat in the jar, boil the vinegar up and pour over them.

TO PICKLE SWEET APPLES.

To one peck of apples make a syrup of four pounds of sugar and one quart of vinegar. Boil the apples in the syrup until tender, and then take them out and save that syrup for other sauce. Put the apples in a jar, boil five pounds of sugar and one quart of vinegar with some cinnamon and cloves twenty minutes, and pour it hot over the apples. This is a delicious pickle and keeps well.

RIPE CHERRIES PICKLED.

Drop them in cold vinegar with the stems on. Boil it one week after, let it cool, and return it to the cherries.

OYSTER CATCHUP.

Take one gallon of large oysters and wash them in their liquor. Put them in a marble mortar with a teaspoonful of salt, four blades of mace, and one ounce of cayenne pepper. Pound them up well and add half a pint of wine to each pint of liquor; give it a boil, and then strain it through a sieve or colander and boil it again. Skim it well, add a glass of brandy to the gallon, bottle it, and you can always have the oyster flavor with any sauce or meats.

CELERY VINEGAR.

Pound half a pint of celery seed and mix them in a quart of cider vinegar, with a few mustard seed and teaspoonful of sugar. Shake it often and strain it off in twenty days for use. This is healthy and decidedly agreeable.

THYME AND MINT VINEGAR.

Pick the leaves of mint or thyme and put one handful to a quart of vinegar. Strain it off every morning for three days, and put in fresh leaves. Never let it stand longer than twenty-four hours in the vinegar. The third day, strain and bottle it to be used for sauces, when the fresh leaf cannot be had.

CUCUMBER CATCHUP.

Chop up fine three dozen peeled cucumbers and eight peeled onions, sprinkle three quarters of a pint of fine table salt over them. Put it in a sieve or colander and let it drain twelve hours. Then mix one teacupful of mustard seed and half the quantity of ground black pepper. Put it in a stone jar, after you have mixed it well, and cover it with strong cider vinegar. Tie it up close. Good to use in three days, and keeps well.

CUCUMBER CATCHUP. NO. 2.

Peel two dozen cucumbers, put them in a flat dish and sprinkle salt over them; let them stand three hours, then drain and wipe them dry. Grate them with a coarse grater, season them with pepper, and put one quart of strong vinegar on them. Bottle the catchup in wide mouthed bottles, and use it in the winter. Bags of coarse cloth are good to put the grated cucumber in to drain. Onion must be put with it if liked.

RIPE TOMATO CATCHUP.

Peel a half bushel of tomatoes; add one quart of good vinegar, one pound of salt, half a pound of black pepper, two ounces of cayenne pepper, half a pound of allspice, one ounce of cloves, six large onions, and two pounds of brown sugar, and a few peach leaves. Boil it in a porcelain kettle, and strain it or not as you choose.

WALNUT CATCHUP.

Gather one peck of walnuts when you can easily put a knitting-needle through them; have them broken in small pieces with a mallet. Put them in a jar with one pound of salt and two quarts of cider vinegar. Let them remain three weeks, then strain them through a colander. Set the liquor aside; put one quart of vinegar on the pieces of walnut, and let it remain twenty-four hours. Then mash them in the vinegar and strain the liquor off through a cloth, carefully pressing it. Put all in the kettle, with an ounce of black pepper, quarter of an ounce of cloves, half an ounce of ginger, same of nutmeg, and a teacup of sugar. Boil it well for half an hour. Strain it, and when cold, bottle and seal it.

Tomato Catchup. No. 2.

Fill a large jar with peeled ripe tomatoes, put it in an oven of cold water, and let them cook for three hours, with a piece of dough over the top of the jar. Then strain it through a colander and put to every pint of the juice a half pint of cider vinegar, one small onion, one large spoonful of salt, same of pepper and sugar. Put all in a porcelain kettle and boil it until as thick as honey. This is very fine, and the tomato flavor well preserved.

Tomato Catchup. No. 3.

Put one peck of tomatoes, eight tablespoonfuls of salt, same of black pepper, one of allspice and cloves, twelve pods of red pepper, and six spoonfuls of mustard together. Boil it one hour and a half. Strain it through a sieve and when cold, bottle and seal it. Always make a sieve of netting over a hoop for catchups.

Tomato Catchup. No. 4.

Boil half a bushel button tomatoes (small round ones), wash them but not skin. Let them boil two hours. Then strain them through a sieve, and to every quart of juice add one tablespoonful of ground cinnamon bark, one of black pepper, one of mustard, half of cayenne and nutmeg, and two of salt. Boil all together three hours. Then put one quart of vinegar to half a gallon of juice and boil half an hour. Bottle when cold and seal it.

Randolph's Tomato Catchup.

Take one peck of fine red ripe tomatoes, wash them in cold water, and put them in a preserving kettle without any water. Sprinkle in three large spoonfuls of salt; let them boil steadily an hour, stirring them frequently; then press them through a colander, and then through a hair sieve. Wash out your kettle, return the liquid, put it on the fire, with one pint of chopped onions, half a quarter of an ounce of mace broke into small pieces, and tablespoonful of whole black pepper. Boil it down until consistency of thick honey, and just enough to fill two bottles. Dry weather in August is the best time to put tomato up in catchup or for soups. This recipe I have tested twenty years, and never knew it fail to keep well.

TOMATO CATCHUP WITH VINEGAR.

Put one peck of ripe tomatoes in a porcelain kettle, cut up in quarters; add one pint of cider vinegar, teacup of sugar, one gill of mustard seed, teaspoonful of black pepper, teaspoonful of salt, one blade of mace, one dozen grains of cloves, and two dozen of allspice. Boil all an hour and strain through a colander. Bottle when cold and cork tight.

HORSE-RADISH SAUCE.

Scrape or grate the root of horse-radish after the outer bark has been well cleaned. Spread it on a dish and sprinkle a little salt, cayenne pepper, sugar, celery seed, and as many mustard seeds as you choose. Boil some cider vinegar with a few cloves and grains of allspice, and when cold mix it with the ingredients in the dish, and put it in wide mouthed bottles.

GREEN TOMATO SOY, FROM MRS. GRANBERRY.

Put a layer of tomatoes, cut in slices, and onions in a jar, with salt sprinkled between each layer; let it stand thirty-six hours, then wash the salt out and drain them. To one gallon put half an ounce of mace, same of black pepper, allspice, celery seed, and cinnamon. Put them in three quarts of vinegar with one teacup of mixed mustard seed, and half a pound of brown sugar, and boil it up. Then pour in the tomato and onion and let it boil ten minutes. Put it in a jar hot and add a gill of sweet oil, if you like it.

HORSE-RADISH VINEGAR.

Scrape the root, and put a teaspoonful of sugar and a little black pepper with it in cold vinegar.

CHOW CHOW. NO. 2.

Cut up enough white cabbage to weigh eight pounds; weigh eight pounds of sugar; grate one teacup of horse-radish; cut fine four pods of green pepper. Put the cabbage in a large jar, layer of cabbage, then sugar, pepper, and horse-radish, with tablespoonful of salt, until the jar is filled. Put a small piece of alum in and cover it well with vinegar and one pound of mustard seed.

GREEN TOMATO PICKLE.

Cut up green tomatoes in slices, put a layer of tomatoes, a little salt, a layer of chopped onion, then sugar, mustard seed, some scraped horse-radish, and bits of ginger. When the jar is filled, cover it with strong cider vinegar.

COOKED GREEN TOMATO PICKLE.

Cut in slices one peck of tomatoes, salt them, and let them stand twenty-four hours; then drain them and let them dry. Put them in a porcelain kettle with half a pound mustard seed, half a pound of sugar, a few cloves and allspice. Cover them with vinegar and boil one hour, stirring them well.

WALNUT PICKLE.

Gather young walnuts when you can run a pin easily through them. Peel them to the kernel, put them in a strong brine of salt and water, and scald them nine days. Pour the brine off every morning; boil it up, and pour it back. After the ninth scald, soak them in part vinegar and water for three days. Then boil sufficient vinegar to cover them, with cloves, allspice, ginger, mustard seed, cinnamon, and horse-radish. Pour it boiling hot on the walnuts after they have been drained from the vinegar and water, and tie up tight. The pickles are nice, and the liquor one of the best catchups made.

PEACH PICKLE.

Put green peaches in a weak brine for two days, take them out, and wipe them dry. Put them in a jar with spices between each layer, and cover them well with cold vinegar.

ARTICHOKE PICKLE.

Wash them clean, put them in salt and water, and two days after, wipe dry, and put them in vinegar.

FANNIE'S VINEGAR SAUCE.

Take one gallon of vinegar, half an ounce of ground black pepper, two boxes of best mustard, half an ounce of red pepper, half an ounce of ground spice, one pound of sugar, half a pound of horse-radish grated. Mix it well and bottle it for meats.

FANNIE'S TOMATO CATCHUP.

Peel one gallon of tomatoes, put four tablespoonfuls of black pepper, same of salt, two of mustard, and one of allspice in them, and one quart of strong vinegar; add sugar to the taste (one half pound may do), put it in a kettle, and simmer it eight hours over a slow fire.

SOUR-KROUT.

Line a clean barrel with cabbage leaves on the bottom and short distance up the sides. Then put a layer of fine cut cabbage, three inches high, and sprinkle four tablespoonfuls of salt on it; press it tight with the hand. Put in four layers this way, and then pack hard with a wooden pounder. Four more layers and another pounding, and so on until the barrel is full. Cover with cabbage leaves, and put a board and weight on it, and set it away to ferment. At the end of three weeks, remove the scum, and if necessary, add water enough to cover the krout.

SAUCE FOR WINTER.

Cut up five pounds of white cabbage, five pounds of full grown green tomatoes, three pounds of onions, one pound of full grown green pepper. Mix them well with one ounce whole grains of black pepper, same of allspice and cloves, one ounce of mint leaves, and one and a half of salt. Pack it in a clean vessel, put a weight on the top, keep it in a cool place, and in two months it will be nice to use with meats.

NONA'S CHOW CHOW.

Chop three heads of cabbage; take half a pint white mustard seed, same of horse-radish scraped; put a layer of cabbage in a jar, then the seed and radish, and cover them with a sprinkle of salt. Do this until the jar is full, and cover with cider vinegar, and put in two ounces of sugar.

ANOTHER CHOW CHOW.

Three gallons of chopped cabbage, one teacupful of black and white mustard seed, six pods of red pepper chopped fine, two dozen cucumbers out of salt, eight onions, half a cup of ground allspice, pepper, cloves, ginger, and horse-radish, chop a little green celery, and mix it all in a jar. Boil enough vinegar to cover it, with two ounces of sugar to a quart.

MRS. BAKER'S PREMIUM MANGOES. VA.

Put small melons or cucumbers in strong brine of salt and water for two days; scald them three times by boiling the brine and pouring it back over them. Then mix half vinegar and water and scald them three days in that. For a three-gallon jar take one teacup of black pepper, same of allspice, one and a half of ginger, half an ounce of mace, same of cloves, and beat all together, but not fine. Chop one large head of cabbage and eight onions, scrape two teacups of horse-radish and mix one quart of white and black mustard seed. Weigh five pounds of sugar, put one teaspoonful in each mango, and mix part of the spices with three cups of it and add the cabbage and onion. Fill the mangoes, then take the balance of the sugar and spices and boil in sufficient vinegar to fill the jar; pour it boiling hot over them and tie up closely.

MUSHROOM CATCHUP.

Take one peck of mushroom flaps from the stem, wash, salt, and crush them. Boil them three hours, and strain them through a cloth; put the liquor on the fire with salt to taste, cloves and garlic the same, and boil until the quantity is reduced one half. A very few cloves of garlic and fourth of an ounce of cloves is quite enough for a peck.

MRS. STEWART'S CHOPPED PICKLE. S. C.

Two gallons of green tomatoes sliced, five tablespoons of ground mustard, three gills of white mustard seed, two tablespoonfuls of allspice, two of cloves, one gill of salt, one quart of chopped onions, one pound of sugar, one gallon of vinegar, two tablespoons of ground ginger. Put into a kettle and boil till it becomes thick and the tomatoes look clear.

MRS. STEWART'S GREEN TOMATO CATCHUP. S. C.

Stew sliced green tomatoes till they can run through a coarse sieve. Add some good strong vinegar, a little salt, sugar, black pepper, mustard, and onions chopped fine, and cook well. One gallon of tomato juice, half gallon of vinegar, two tablespoonfuls of salt, six of black pepper, three onions, half pint of mustard seed, and half pound of sugar, will be the right proportion.

OIL MANGOES.

Mix one quart of white and black mustard seed, add one ounce of mace, same of cloves, four ounces of horse-radish scraped, the same of ground ginger and garlic, with a little turmeric, celery seed, and sugar. Beat them together in a mortar and make into a paste with oil. If your mangoes have been greened and prepared in the usual way for pickles, fill them with this paste and cover them over with boiling hot vinegar and tie them up closely.

TURMERIC PICKLE.

Slice cucumbers and onions, equal parts, and put them in salt and water; change it every day for three days. Then scald them in vinegar. To three gallons put one cup of allspice, same of mustard and black pepper, two pounds of brown sugar, and enough turmeric to color it yellow. Put it in a jar with a dessert-spoonful of sweet oil and a layer of spice on each layer of cucumber and onion. Cover it with cold vinegar and stir frequently.

OXFORD SAUCE.

Half a gallon of vinegar, half a tablespoonful of cayenne pepper, half a teaspoonful of allspice, two spoonfuls scraped horse-radish, one gill of ground mustard, and a quarter of a pound of sugar. Mix all well together, and bottle it for fish or meats.

RED PEPPER CATCHUP.

Take four dozen pods of ripe or green peppers, two quarts of vinegar, one quart of water, three tablespoonfuls of grated horse-radish, five onions sliced, one handful of garlic, and boil it until the onion is soft. Then strain it, and when cold bottle it.

FRENCH PICKLE.

Chop one gallon of cabbage, quart of onions, half gallon green tomatoes, six pods of peppers, three tablespoonfuls of mustard, one of ginger, cloves, cinnamon, celery seed, horse-radish, two of salt, quarter of a pound of sugar, half a gallon of vinegar. Cover with salt one hour, and then add vinegar and spices, and boil until tender.

"STRENGTH AND HONOR ARE HER CLOTHING."

Strength is given to enable you to discharge faithfully the duties incumbent on, and necessarily intrusted to the head of the family, and strength of mind to administer to the daily wants of your household. The infant is to be taught and trained by you for the special service for which God created it. Teach it honesty and truthfulness from the mother's breast. Teach it to honor father and mother, and exemplify that command by your daily life. *Never* deceive the one you have chosen to be a companion. While he provides for the bodily wants of each, you should train his child to maintain the honor due unto his name. Let *all* your wants and cares be known to him; strengthen his love by honoring *his* word; strengthen his happiness by seeing you are happy; strengthen his hope of eternal life, by your Christian walk and conversation. Let him honor you as the mother of his child by the gentle influence of the necessary discipline it is your duty to exert; and you, strengthened by his smile of approval, may cause future generations to clothe your names with strength and honor.

CAKE.

REMARKS ON MAKING CAKE.

Before commencing operations for cake making, have placed on a table, first, your scales to weigh; second, plates and dishes to turn the different ingredients in; third, a large earthen bowl or tin pan that is commonly called a dish-pan; fourth, a large dish; fifth, a wooden bowl or tray with a sieve in it; sixth, a cup or glass tumbler; seventh, a wire egg whip; eighth, a large spoon or wire spoon; ninth, a nutmeg or large grater; tenth, a rolling-pin and biscuit board; eleventh, the pans you wish to bake in,—nicely greased with lard, and paper cut to fit evenly in the bottom. Weigh your flour and turn it in the sieve; then your sugar and put it in a plate; then your butter and put it in the flour (after sifting it in the tray). If your sugar is coarse or lumpy, place it on the biscuit board and roll it with the rolling-pin and then run it through the sieve; Cream the butter and flour together until smooth and white. Break your eggs, whites in the large flat dish, yelks in the wooden bowl or large tin pan that the whole is to be mixed in; beat them well and then add your sugar. Recollect it is of more importance to beat the yelks and sugar light than any other part of the cake. When light, put in a small piece of the flour and butter at the time, and mix it well in, occasionally adding some of the white of egg that has been beaten to a stiff froth; continue adding the whites until all are well stirred in. Have brandy in your cup or glass, and your nutmeg grated in it; mix it well, and pour it slowly in with any extract you may prefer. Give the whole one hard beat, and then fill your pans and follow directions for cake baking. Read over your directions, and see if you have not brought into requisition all the eleven articles named to be used, and after having them all nicely cleaned, return them to their respective places in closet or pantry, until cake-making day again requires their use. If you make small cakes you must roll them on your biscuit board, and then you will require tin cutters of different shapes or a glass tumbler. Flour your board well and roll the dough out in sheets, and cut them out; gather up the pieces around the shape, work it up, roll out again, or mix it with the next piece you break off; have your stove pans in readiness and fill them, or put them on the board and tray and send them to the Dutch oven, following directions for cooking small cakes. If you make jumbles and have not a mould to put your dough in, roll it out with the hand and sprinkle fine sugar on the board in place of the flour. If cake batter for small cakes, have the pans all greased, put them on a large waiter, and send them to be baked, and as soon as the first are done turn the cake out, put the pans in hot water, wash and wipe them dry, then grease again and fill as the first, always allowing room for them to rise; when done, let them cool before packing them away.

REMARKS ON BAKING.

To tell a quick oven, hold your hand in until you count twenty; slow one, count thirty. The lid of the oven must be heated until it browns flour, to do nice baking, and the degree of heat kept up by constantly adding fine embers on the lid and underneath. In baking cake in a Dutch oven, never let a large coal be on the lid or under, as it will bake a hole through the cake. Raise the lid as seldom as possible, turn the oven occasionally, and always put a ring of embers on the hearth, in front of the oven, to keep equal heat. When the cake begins to brown on the top, raise the lid, and cover the oven with paper, then put the lid on. The paper prevents its being too brown. Keep more fire under than on the top, as it rises better. When the cake leaves the sides of the pan, run a steel knife through it, and if it comes out clean it is done. Brush the fire from the oven and let it remain a few minutes; take it out, and wrap a towel around the pan a short time. If it does not come out easily, wet a cloth with cold water and put it on the bottom of the pan, and turn it over on a plate; knock the sides and it will come out smooth. Wheat bread is cooked (like cakes) in a slow oven; corn meal should have a quick oven. Never put a cake to bake in a hot stove; let it be cool, and raise the heat as the cake rises. Biscuit must be baked in a quick oven, hot enough to brown flour; crackers in a slow one; sugar tea cakes in a quick, and molasses in a slow oven. Graduate the heat of the stove for baking by the dampers.

BELLA'S FRUIT CAKE.

Prepare the day before it is wanted, one pound of currants, well washed and dried, stone two pounds of raisins, and cut in shreds half a pound of citron. Next morning beat twelve eggs separately, stir one pound of sugar in the yelks, cream one pound of flour and one of butter together, and mix it well with the eggs and sugar; flour your fruit well and slowly stir it in; layer of raisins, then currants and citron until all are in; then stir in a glass of brandy (half gill), one tablespoonful of ground cloves, one of cinnamon, and one of mace. When well mixed, pour it in a pound and a half tin pan or mould, place it in a warm oven or stove, and bake slowly for three hours.

BROWN SUGAR CAKE.

Two quarts of flour, sift and rub quarter of a pound of butter in it; beat together ten eggs, and one and a half pounds of sugar; stir in it a wine-glass of brandy, with a nutmeg and some orange peel grated in it; then work the flour and butter up with it, roll it out, and bake in a stove pan or oven, in cakes cut out with a shape.

JULIA'S GINGERBREAD.

Stir half a pound of brown sugar, and half a pound of butter together; add one pint of molasses, large teaspoonful of cinnamon, one of allspice, and one of cloves, with four tablespoonfuls of ginger; then alternately, five beaten eggs and one pound and a half of flour; stir it well, and at the last put in half a teaspoonful of pearlash or cooking soda well dissolved, and bake in a pan.

COMMON GINGERBREAD.

Rub one pound of butter and two and a half pounds of flour together; put in half a pound of brown sugar, three tablespoonfuls of ginger, and teaspoonful of pearlash dissolved. Make it in a stiff dough with one pint of milk and half a pint of molasses; roll out in thin cakes, cut them with cake cutters, and bake.

LUCY'S THIN GINGER CAKES.

Sift four large tablespoonfuls of ginger with two quarts of flour; rub in half a pound of butter or lard, and make it in a dough with molasses, thick enough to roll out, and cut with shapes or a tumbler; roll them thin, and bake in stove pans or oven.

GINGER CAKES.

Beat three eggs well, add half a pint of cream, then put it in a saucepan over the fire, and stir until warm. Put in one pound of butter, one and a half pounds of white sugar, two and a half pounds of ginger; stir it carefully over the fire until the butter is melted. Then pour it on two pounds of flour, form a paste, break it as you do biscuit, roll it out, and cut it with thin shapes. Bake in a warm oven.

GINGERBREAD NUTS.

Rub one quarter of a pound of butter in one pound of flour, half a pound of sugar, ounce of ginger, peel of one lemon, and three eggs. Work it well and bake in small thin cakes, rolled out.

KNOX GINGER-CAKES.

Five cups of flour, four eggs, one cup of sugar, one of butter, one of sour milk, half cup of molasses, one tablespoonful of ginger, teaspoonful of soda. Roll out and bake.

LOUISIANA GINGER-CAKE.

Heat one pint of molasses; put in a cup of butter, melted, three eggs beat together, teaspoonful of soda, and one pound of flour with tablespoonful of ginger. Bake it in a pan and eat with butter.

JOHNSON TEA-CAKE.

One and a quarter pounds of flour, four eggs, one pint of milk, one pound of sugar, four teaspoonfuls of yeast powder or one tablespoonful of yeast. Beat sugar and eggs together, then the milk and yeast, and then the flour. Let it rise two hours in a warm place and bake in a quick oven.

SPANKMEDOWN.

Five cups of flour, two of molasses, two of butter, two of sugar, one of milk, half a pound of raisins, two large spoonfuls of ginger, one grated nutmeg, and two teaspoonfuls of saleratus. Throw all the ingredients in a tray. Work all well together, and bake in one large pan or small ones, as you prefer.

WHITE CUP-CAKE.

Four pounds of flour, two pounds of sugar, and one of butter. Beat five eggs with the sugar; put one teaspoonful of soda in a cup of sour milk; grate one nutmeg and put in it, with one teaspoonful of cinnamon. Then cream the butter and flour together, add the eggs and sugar, with the other ingredients, stir it well, and bake in a tin mould.

LOAF-CAKE.

Three pints of flour, five eggs beat with two cups of sugar and two of butter, one cup of molasses stirred in, and then the flour, one teaspoonful of allspice, and at the last, one of soda and two of cream of tartar, dissolved in sweet milk and well stirred in. Bake in a large pan.

MEASURE CAKE.

One pint of flour, one teacup of butter, two of sugar, a grated nutmeg, and four eggs.

ALMOND CAKE. NO. 1.

Blanch one pound of almonds and beat them to a paste with rose-water; cream one pound of sugar and the same of butter together. Beat the whites of sixteen eggs to a stiff froth, and sift one pound of flour; add two tablespoonfuls of flour and two of eggs to the butter and sugar, alternately, until all are in. Then add the almonds and bake immediately.

ALMOND CAKE. NO. 2.

Cream one pound of butter and the same of sugar together. Beat ten eggs well, add the sugar and butter to the yelks and then the whites, stir in slowly one pound of flour, two pounds of stoned raisins, one pound of citron cut small, one grated nutmeg, and one pound of blanched almonds that have been well beat in a marble mortar; grease your cake mould, line the bottom with paper to fit nicely, and bake slowly two hours.

THORPE WHITE CAKE.

Cream one pound of sugar and half a pound of butter well together; stir in slowly one pound of flour and the whites of fifteen eggs beaten to a stiff froth, and a wine-glass of white brandy. Bake in a quick oven.

SPONGE-CAKE.

Beat ten eggs separately, put in their weight of sugar and the weight of seven in flour; beat sugar and yelks together, then add the whites, and sprinkle the flour slowly in.

CORN STARCH CAKE.

Stir to a froth three quarters of a pound of butter and one pound of fine white sugar, add one half cup of sweet cream and the whites of nine eggs beaten very light. Take from a pound package of corn starch two tablespoonfuls and replace it with same quantity of flour; then sift it and stir it in. Flavor with lemon.

CORN POUND-CAKE.

One pound of sugar, half pound of butter, one pound of corn meal, five eggs well beaten, one teacup of milk or cream, with a teaspoonful of saleratus. Take out a teacup of meal and put one of flour in place of it. Flavor to your taste.

SPONGE-CAKE.

Take the yelks of five eggs, the white of one, and beat with half a pound of sugar and a teacupful of water until thick as pound-cake; then add slowly six ounces of flour.

WHITE CAKE.

Beat the whites of four eggs to a stiff froth, then add half a cup of sour cream, same of butter, one and a half cups of sugar, three of flour, and teaspoonful of soda and lemon.

GINGER POUND-CAKE.

Beat six eggs, add two cups of sugar, two of molasses, two of butter, two tablespoonfuls of powdered ginger, one of cinnamon, one nutmeg grated, one teaspoonful of saleratus, one of lemon extract; beat all well together and stir in six cups of flour. Bake in two pans.

SOFT GINGERBREAD.

Beat three cups of flour, one of butter and one of sugar together; add one cup of molasses and one of sour cream, with a little of the flour. Beat separately four eggs, add the yelks with more of the flour; put one tablespoonful of ginger, same of cinnamon, one teaspoonful of ground cloves, and one of soda; stir in two cups of fruit, the whites of the eggs and the remainder of the flour. Bake in tin pans well greased.

Cup Sponge-Cake.

Three cups of sugar, same of flour, nine eggs, three tablespoonfuls of cold water. Flavor to the taste.

Saratoga Springs Cake.

Mix four cups of sugar and two of butter together; dissolve two teaspoonfuls of saleratus in two cups of milk, beat six eggs, add them alternately with the milk, and eight cups of flour, to the sugar and butter; grate a nutmeg, and put a little mace with it, stir it in and bake in two cakes.

Cream Cake.

Beat five eggs with three cups of sugar, add one cup of butter, one of cream, and four of flour, one teaspoonful of saleratus, dissolved and put in at the last.

White Mountain Cake.

Stir one cup of butter and three of sugar together; dissolve one teaspoonful of cream tartar and half the quantity of soda in half a cup of sweet milk; then the whites of ten eggs beaten to a stiff froth and three and a half cups of flour slowly stirred in. Bake this in three cakes. Ice each cake, pile them in layers, and ice the top and sides.

Jelly Cake.

Beat three eggs and two cups of sugar, add one of milk and half cup of butter, half a teaspoonful of soda and one of cream tartar sifted in three and a half cups of flour; bake it in tin plates, cover with jelly and so on four or six times.

FANNIE'S SUGAR CAKES.

Work one quarter of a pound of butter in two quarts of flour; beat ten eggs with one and a half pounds of sugar, put a gill of brandy and one nutmeg grated in the eggs, and work the flour in it to a stiff dough. Roll them out and cut with shapes.

FANNIE'S HASTY CAKE.

Beat four eggs and four cups of sugar together, add one cup of butter, sift one teaspoonful of soda in six cups of flour, and stir it in with two tumblers of buttermilk. Bake quick.

FANNIE'S JUMBLES.

Two quarts of flour, two pounds of sugar, ten eggs, three quarters of a pound of butter; work it up in one mass, roll it thin, and glaze them with white of egg put on with a feather, and bake them a light brown.

HETTIE'S DELICATE CAKE.

Cream seven ounces of butter and beat the whites of eight eggs to a stiff froth. Mix in slowly one pound of white sugar, then stir in one pound of flour with the butter, put in half a nutmeg grated fine, and flavor with extract of lemon, almonds, or a little rose-water. Bake it in a buttered pan with white paper over the butter, cut to fit in the bottom smoothly.

FANNIE'S SPONGE-CAKE.

Weigh ten eggs and put their weight in sugar in twelve yelks. Beat the ten whites to a stiff froth, put it in the yelks with the juice and grated peel of one lemon. Then *slowly* stir in the weight of six eggs in flour, and bake immediately. Sponge-cake must not have much grease in the pan.

One Pound Fruit-Cake.

One pound of flour and same of butter creamed together, one of sugar, and twelve eggs beaten. Add the flour and butter, gill of brandy with a teaspoonful powdered mace and cinnamon in it. Beat well, and then add one pound of stoned raisins well floured, same of citron out fine, and one pound of almonds blanched in rose-water. Bake in a quick oven.

Fannie's White Cake.

Beat to a stiff froth the whites of twelve eggs; cream twelve ounces of sugar with ten ounces of butter, season with lemon extract, and stir in fourteen ounces of flour, and bake at once in a quick oven.

Fannie's Gold Cake.

One cup of butter, two of sugar, four of flour, one of milk, four eggs, one teaspoonful of soda, and two of cream tartar. Beat eggs and sugar, then flour and butter. Mix the cream tartar and soda in the milk, and stir it in just as you put it in to bake.

Nona's Delicate Cake.

Stir to a cream one pound of white sugar and one pound of fresh butter, with the salt washed out. Put one teaspoonful of lemon extract and one of vanilla in it, then the beaten whites of twenty eggs, beaten to a stiff froth, then one pound of flour slowly stirred in. Bake immediately in a quick oven.

Nona's Corn-Starch Cake.

One cup of butter, two of sugar, one cup of sweet milk, two of flour, one of corn-starch, one teaspoonful of soda, and two of cream tartar, and the beaten whites of five eggs.

NONA'S WHITE CAKE.

Three cups of sifted flour, one and a half of sugar, one cup of sweet milk, one egg, two tablespoonfuls of butter, two teaspoonfuls cream tartar, one of soda, and one of essence of lemon. Beat the butter and sugar to a cream, dissolve the soda in the milk, and put that into the egg and essence and two cups of flour. At the last, sift the cream tartar in the other cup of flour and stir it lightly in.

BLACKBERRY CAKE.

Beat four eggs with two cups of sugar, one cup of butter, three and a half of flour, with one teaspoonful of soda sifted in it; add one cup of sour milk. If your milk is sweet, put one teaspoonful of vinegar in it. Stir it well, and then stir in one cup of preserved blackberries; flavor it with lemon. It is a nice dessert with wine sauce.

LAURA'S CUP CAKE.

One cup of cream, one of sugar, two of flour, two eggs, half a teaspoonful of soda, and one of cream tartar. Bake in shapes.

LAURA'S COCOANUT CAKE.

Four cups of flour, three cups of white sugar, one cup of milk, half a cup of butter, three eggs, one teaspoonful of cream tartar, and one nearly full of soda. Mix well and add one cocoanut nicely grated.

LAURA'S DROP CAKES.

Beat three eggs and six ounces of sugar, add three ounces of butter and eight ounces of flour. Drop it from the spoon in a warm oven and bake quickly.

SIS SUBMIT'S MOLASSES CUP CAKE.

Two cups of molasses, same of butter, one of milk, two eggs, one teaspoonful of soda, a nutmeg or lemon extract to flavor it. Mix all together, and stir flour in until so stiff the spoon will not easily move, and bake in a pan.

PLAIN MOLASSES CAKES.

Take three quarts of flour and sift it with two large spoonfuls of ginger. Work one tablespoonful of lard and one of butter in it, then work it to a stiff dough with molasses. Roll them thin on a biscuit board and bake them in a moderate oven.

FANNIE'S GINGERBREAD.

Beat six eggs with two cups of sugar and two of molasses. Add one cup of butter, one teaspoonful of ginger, same of soda, and work it in ten cups of flour.

FANNIE'S BUTTERMILK CAKE.

One pound of flour, one of sugar, half a pound of butter. Beat six eggs light with the sugar, add the butter, then the flour, with a teaspoonful of soda in buttermilk enough to make it as pound-cake batter.

MATTIE'S WHITE CAKE.

Beat the whites of fifteen eggs to a stiff froth. Cream one pound of fine white sugar, and half a pound of nice fresh butter together. Mix the eggs with it and slowly sprinkle in one pound of fine flour. Season with one gill of white brandy and two teaspoonfuls lemon extract.

FANNIE'S COCOANUT CAKE.

Beat twelve eggs separately; cream half a pound of butter in one pound of flour, beat the yelk of egg and one pound of sugar together. Then add two pounds of almonds that have been blanched and beat smooth in rose-water, and two grated cocoanuts; grease your pan, line the bottom smoothly with white paper, grease that, and bake the cake in a quick oven.

FANNIE'S BLACK CAKE.

Beat twenty eggs, one pound and a half of sugar with the yelks; cream one pound of butter with one and a half pounds of flour and stir it in the yelk and sugar, then put in two wine-glasses of brandy with one of wine, with two teaspoonfuls of cinnamon, four grated nutmegs, teaspoonful of mace stirred in the brandy. Flour three and half pounds of raisins, three of currants, one and a half of citron and put it slowly in, with half pound of blanched almonds.

MAPY'S PLAIN CAKE. S. C.

Two cups of flour, two eggs, one cup of sugar, half cup of butter, the same of sweet milk, half teaspoonful of soda. Flavor with nutmeg and a little brandy. Drop on buttered tins and bake.

MRS. HOPSON'S GINGER CAKE. S. C.

One cup of sugar, one cup of butter, one of molasses, four eggs well beaten, four cups of flour, three fourths of a cup of sweet milk, with one teaspoonful of soda dissolved in it. Ginger and spice to your taste. Bake in buttered tins.

MAGGIE'S CUP CAKE. S. C.

One cup of butter, two of sugar, three of flour, four eggs, one teaspoonful of soda; if too stiff add a little cream. Flavor to the taste and buttered tins.

MRS. FRAZER'S JUMBLES. S. C.

Five eggs, three cups of sugar, one and a half of butter, one teaspoonful of soda; flour to make stiff enough to roll. Flavor to the taste with spices or essence.

WAFER CAKES.

Beat six eggs very light. Put half a pound of sugar in the yelks, and a quarter of a pound of butter. Mix the eggs and stir in enough flour to make a stiff batter. Season with lemon extract and nutmeg. Heat wafer irons and grease them, put two large spoonfuls of the batter in and cook. Turn them as you take them from the irons. Have a nice round smooth stick to roll them on. Fill the hollow with whipped cream and put preserved strawberries in each end. Plain pound-cake batter makes them very nice. One teaspoonful will do to put in the irons.

FEATHER CAKE.

Beat four eggs, with four cups of sugar, one cup of butter, and one of milk. Sift one teaspoonful of soda and two of cream tartar in six cups of flour, stir it in and flavor with lemon.

TIPTOP CAKE.

Five eggs well beaten, with four cups of sugar, one cup of butter, two of milk, and six cups of flour piled up, with one teaspoonful of soda, same of cream tartar sifted in it, and slowly stirred in the eggs and milk. Flavor with one teaspoonful essence of almonds.

DOVER CAKE.

Two eggs beat with one cup of sugar, one half cup of butter and same of milk beat in it, two cups of flour, with half teaspoonful soda and one teaspoonful cream tartar sifted in it. Stir all well together and flavor with nutmeg.

COFFEE CAKE.

One cup of cold coffee strained, one cup of sour cream, two large cups of brown sugar, five eggs, one cup of currants, one of raisins, one teaspoonful of cloves, allspice, cinnamon, one grated nutmeg, and a teaspoonful of saleratus, with flour enough to make it stiff.

WHITE CAKE.

Take one pound of pounded sugar, the same of flour, and half pound of butter. Beat the whites of nine eggs, cream the sugar and butter together, add the eggs and then the flour, after it has been sifted, with one teaspoonful of soda and two of cream tartar in it. Bake it in jelly cake pans.

LEMON CAKE.

Beat five eggs with two cups of sugar, one of butter and four of flour, the juice and grated peel of one lemon, and a cup not quite full of milk. If it is sour, put enough soda in it to sweeten it. Beat all hard and bake in patty-pans.

LOAF CAKE.

One cup of molasses, warmed, with half a cup of butter in it; two eggs stirred in when cold, two cups of flour, and one of currants or dried cherries, chopped fine; half a cup of sugar beat in, with a teaspoonful of soda touched with vinegar. Flavor with any extract or spice.

QUEEN CAKES.

Wash and dry one pound of currants, and mix them with the same weight of flour and fine sugar; wash one pound of butter in rose-water, then mix with it eight well beaten eggs, and gradually the flour, sugar, and currants; beat it an hour. Grease little tin shapes or cups, fill half full, sprinkle a little sugar over the top, and bake them in a moderate oven.

MAY QUEEN CAKE.

Beat two pounds of butter to a cream with two tablespoonfuls of essence of lemon or rose-water; then add two pounds of flour, two pounds of white sugar, and ten eggs well beaten; add half a pound of blanched almonds, and half a pound of citron cut fine. Beat it all well together, put it in tin shapes well greased, and bake them a light brown.

DROP SUGAR CAKES.

Beat eight eggs very light, add one pound of sugar, same of flour and teaspoonful of essence of lemon; drop them from the spoon in the oven, and bake.

ALMOND CAKE.

Blanch a half pound of sweet and an ounce of bitter almonds, put them in a marble mortar with a few drops of cold water and beat them to a paste. Then add to them ten eggs; beat light and slowly one pound of fine white sugar and half a pound melted butter; beat all well together and then add the rind of a lemon grated fine; put it in a cake mould greased with lard, and bake it one hour and a half. Excellent.

CARAWAY-SEED CAKE.

Cream one pound of butter and one of sugar together, beat the yelks of eighteen eggs and the whites of ten separately, mix in the whites first and then the yelks and beat for ten minutes. Add two grated nutmegs, and sprinkle in one pound and a half of sifted flour; then beat in three ounces of picked caraway seeds, and put it immediately in your oven and bake an hour.

SWEET POTATO CAKE.

Take some fine old Currituck yams, slightly parboil them, and grate one pound. Beat twelve eggs with two pounds of sugar, and one pound of butter mixed in with the yelks and sugar; add two tablespoonfuls of flour with half a teaspoonful of soda in it and one of cream tartar; slowly sprinkle in the potato and white of egg, give it one beat, and bake it in three square shallow pans. You can flavor it if you wish, but it is not needed.

Bettie's Mountain Cake.

One pound of flour, one of sugar, half pound of butter, six eggs, one teaspoonful of soda dissolved in a cup of milk, two of cream tartar sifted in the flour; season to the taste with lemon and nutmeg.

Chess Cake.

The yelks of sixteen eggs, half a pound of butter and one pound of sugar. Beat the whole very light and flavor with lemon extract. Bake in shapes lined with puff paste.

Mrs. Hoyt's White Cake.

Cream one pound of flour and three fourths of a pound of butter together, beat the whites of eighteen eggs to a stiff froth and stir one pound of fine sugar slowly in. Stir a little of the flour and butter in at the time, till all are well mixed. Flavor with one teaspoonful of almond extract and bake it in a quick oven.

Mrs. Hart's Cream Puffs.

Beat the whites of two eggs to a stiff froth and mix it in one cup of sweet cream and a dessert-spoonful of butter; make it into a paste with flour and roll it out as thin as a wafer; cut it by a saucer and drop it in hot lard to fry a light brown (it will require but a few moments to cook). When done take them out with a skimmer and sprinkle sugar over them, while hot, through a piece of coarse muslin.

Cocoanut Puffs.

Put grated cocoanut in piles on a flat dish with a dessert-spoonful to each; put some jelly in small pieces over the top, and pile whipped cream on them, as for syllabub; cut pieces of paper and put the cocoanut on, if you want to move it, to decorate with.

COCOANUT ON SPONGE-CAKE.

Fill a large pan with sponge-cake batter, quarter of an inch thick. Beat up sugar and egg as for icing, stir the cocoanut in thick, and flavor with lemon extract. When the cake is nearly done take the pan out, out it across with a knife, three inches square, cover it with the cocoanut and egg, return it to the stove or oven, and let it cook a light brown. When preparing wedding cake for parties, this is easily done with extra icing.

NEW ORLEANS JUMBLES.

Take a clean tray, and put in it one pound of flour, one pound of sugar, one pound of butter, two grated nutmegs, the rind of two oranges and of two lemons grated; work it all up in a mass. Then break two eggs on the dough and work them in. Sugar the biscuit board with fine white sugar, as you would with flour; roll a small piece of the dough in it with your hands; join the ends as a ring, and bake them in a clean stove pan, or Dutch oven, washing it out clean every time you put fresh ones in; take them out very carefully, after cooking a few minutes, on a knife blade, and put them on dishes to cool before packing away. They are very rich, and taste as fresh as an orange.

LEMON CAKES.

Beat six eggs separately, add six ounces of white sugar, put in slowly six ounces of flour, then the whites of eggs and juice of the lemon. When well beaten, sprinkle in the grated rind of the lemon, put it in tin shapes, and bake in a warm oven.

MARTIN JUMBLES.

Sift one teaspoonful of soda in two pounds of flour in a wooden tray. Throw in one and a half pounds of brown sugar, three quarters of a pound of butter, two tablespoonfuls of cinnamon, eight eggs, leaving out the whites of four, and a wine-glass of brandy; work all up in a mass, sprinkle some fine sugar on your biscuit board; roll a piece of the dough in your hand, then in the sugar, and make it in form of a ring, by joining the ends together; place them, not very close, in a stove pan, or Dutch oven, and bake a light brown; let them cool a little, and take them out carefully with a knife run under them; wipe the pan or oven out clean every time you put in a fresh lot to bake, and never grease or flour it. They are very nice and keep well.

DOVER CAKE.

Half pound of butter, one pound of flour, one pound of loaf sugar, half pint of milk, six eggs, wine-glass of brandy, half glass of rose-water, one nutmeg, teaspoonful of cinnamon, teaspoonful of saleratus dissolved in lemon juice or a little vinegar. Stir the sugar and butter together; add the spice and liquor, eggs and flour alternately, and gradually the milk. If you choose you can add one pound of fruit, slowly putting it in. Bake in a greased mould.

BRADFORD CUP CAKE.

Eight cups of flour, with one teaspoonful of soda sifted in it; work in it two cups of butter or lard; beat six eggs with two cups of sugar, two of molasses, and one cup of sour milk, with spice to taste; beat all together, and bake in a tin pan well greased. If you use lard, put in a little salt.

PLAIN TEA CAKES.

Six eggs with coffee cup of sugar beat together, tablespoonful of lard or butter; work well; roll out and cut small with tin shapes.

INDIAN POUND-CAKE.

The weight of eight eggs in sugar, and six in meal; stir half a pound of butter and the sugar together; beat eight eggs very light, and stir it in alternately with the meal; add one nutmeg, grated, and bake in a tin pan well greased.

DOUGHNUTS.

Three pounds of flour; work three quarters of a pound of butter in it; beat four eggs with one pound of sugar, put in a teacup of hop yeast, and one pint and a half of milk; flavor with teaspoonful each of cinnamon and nutmeg, with tablespoonful of rose-water; work the flour up with the mixture; roll it in a sheet, and cut with a small cutter, and fry in boiling lard.

CRULLERS.

Two pounds of flour, half pound of butter worked in it; beat seven eggs with three quarters of a pound of sugar; flavor with spice of any kind; work all together, roll them out and cut with shape, and fry in lard.

FANNIE'S BISCUED GLACEE.

Rub off the yellow rind of four oranges or lemons with lumps of loaf sugar; then pulverize and mix it with one saucerful of fine sugar; mix the juice of the orange or lemon in, and stir all in two and a half pints of cream; add more sugar if not sweet enough. Beat six eggs separately, and then mix them before stirring them in the cream; grate enough sponge-cake to make a thick batter, and beat it all together, free of lumps. Put it in a porcelain kettle on the fire, stir it all the time, and give it one boil. When cool, freeze it as you do ice-cream.

FANNIE'S CHARLOTTE RUSSE.

Sweeten one quart of cream and flavor with vanilla; churn it with syllabub churn. Dissolve one ounce of gelatine in half a pint of milk; scald but do not boil it; pour it over the yelks of three eggs well beaten, and add it to the cream. When cold, put it in a glass dish with sponge-cake on the sides, or in the centre of a sponge-cake cut out for that purpose.

FANNIE'S CREAM.

Put one fourth of a box of gelatine in one pint of sweet milk, and set it over the fire until it dissolves, stirring it all the time to prevent the gelatine from sticking; sweeten one quart of cream to the taste and add the milk to it when cold; churn it with a syllabub churn until it is very thick; put it on ice to cool and eat it with sweet cream.

FANNIE'S MERINGUE.

Line a deep dish with puff paste, and cover it with sweetmeats; put it on to bake; when the paste is done, beat four eggs to a stiff froth, with one pound of sugar, the juice of one lemon, and the rind rubbed with lumps of sugar. Spread it over the sweetmeat, and bake a pretty light brown.

FANNIE'S A LA CREAM.

Boil ten eggs hard, slice them; line a dish thin with bread crumbs, then a layer of eggs, bread crumbs, butter, pepper, and salt; melt four ounces of butter, and stir it in one quart of cream with one tablespoonful of flour; pour it over the egg and bread, and bake it brown in a hot oven.

GINGER SPONGE-CAKE.

One cup of molasses, two of sugar, one of butter, one of milk, four eggs, four cups of flour, with one tablespoonful of ginger.

JUMBLES.

Four eggs, half a pound of sugar, same of butter, two quarts of flour, teaspoonful of soda; work all up together, add spice to your taste, and bake them in rings.

NAPLES BISCUIT.

Beat twelve eggs separately; stir one pound of sugar with the yelks, then add the whites and one pound of flour; bake it in long pans one inch thick, cut in strips, two inches wide, as soon as done, and ice them all over.

DOUGHNUTS.

Take two pounds of flour, half a pound of sugar, two large spoonfuls of yeast, and sufficient new milk to make it like bread. Make it up at night; next day work in half a pound of butter, and fry it in cakes size of a half dollar (in specie times) in boiling lard. Take them out with a perforated ladle.

MRS. H.'S MOLASSES FRUIT-CAKE.

Beat five eggs, stir in three cupfuls of molasses, sift one spoonful of soda and one of cinnamon in five cupfuls of flour, and stir it in; grate one nutmeg, and beat a tablespoonful of cloves to season it. Cut fine one pound of half done dried apples, one pound of figs, and stir them in with three cups of butter. This is very nice, and very much like fruit cake made with raisins and citron.

ALMOND MACAROONS.

Blanch one pound and a quarter of sweet and four ounces of bitter almonds, in boiling water. As soon as the skins slip off nicely, drop them in a marble mortar and pound them to a paste with a few drops of white of egg. Mix two pounds of sugar with a little grated lemon, and mix the almond paste in it with the whites of four eggs. Take up pieces the size of a wine-glass; make it in balls; mix the yelks of two eggs in a gill of water and glaze the tops of each ball; flatten them one fourth of an inch thick, and bake in a slow oven from ten to fifteen minutes, and you will have Laurede's nice fresh macaroons.

BOSTON KISSES.

Beat twelve eggs to a stiff froth, and slowly sprinkle one pound of fine sugar in it while beating; do not stir it; as soon as the sugar is in, stop beating. Have a tin tube and put it on paper about three inches long and bake in a quick oven. As soon as dry, press the centre down, fill with thick cream, seasoned to taste, pile it high in the centre and turn one piece on the other, to form an egg shape.

FANNIE'S ALMOND DROPS.

Blanch one pound of almonds, and beat them in a marble mortar to a paste with rose-water; beat three eggs to a stiff froth, and stir in half a pound of sugar; mix the almond paste in and drop-it on tin sheets or buttered baking pans, in piles sift sugar over them, and bake brown in a slow oven.

MRS. E.'S PUFFS.

Boil one quart of milk with one pound of butter, and one pound of sugar. After it has boiled up, stir slowly in one pound and a half of flour, and stir it until it thickens; let it cool, and then add the yelks of eighteen eggs; grease tin baking cups; beat the whites of the eggs to a stiff froth, and stir in last; then half fill the cups and bake. You can add a little cinnamon or extract if you like.

A WEDDING SUPPER.

In small towns ladies assist their friends to prepare for the wedding supper or parties, and I here append a synopsis of one I superintended for one of North Carolina's fair daughters in the fall of 1868. One hundred guests were expected. The table for meats was spread in one room, for sweets in another. At the head of the meat table a turkey weighing twenty-five pounds, cooked early in the morning, and a fine roast pig at the foot, both properly garnished; on the right of each a plain and richly stuffed ham; midway a fine boned turkey resting in jelly, with a large pair of ducks opposite; chicken salad from ten chickens, between head and centre, centre and foot on both sides, in salad stands; a saddle of mutton half way from head to centre, and a round of spiced beef from foot to centre, on opposite side; dishes of beef tongue neatly sliced, baked chickens, and a fine boiled turkey covered with hard boiled eggs, between salad and mutton, with pickled oysters, cold slaw, and pickles of various kinds interspersed; celery in six glass stands flanked by castors, with sauces, catchups, and salad oil. Four piles of plates, with napkins between each plate; on each side, bread and crackers within reach of all; a spoon on every salad stand; carving knife and fork with every dish of meat; pickle knife, fork, and spoon on each dish of pickle, and piles of soup-plates with a spoon in each, on the corners, in which to serve ten gallons of hot stewed oysters. Large vases of flowers through the centre of the table to add to its pleasing effect. This supper was served at twelve o'clock, the gentlemen waiting on the ladies, and servants dispensed with while discussing the viands and partaking of social enjoyment. (Champagne used to flow in olden times—that we will not dwell upon). One hour after the meats were served, the bridal pair precede their guests to the other apartment where the cake table was spread, with the glitter of silver, glass, and china, bearing the iced cakes, frosted fruits, quivering jelly, snowy syllabub, golden custards, blancmange, trifle, typsey cakes, floating islands, and fruits. Flowers in large bouquets, flooded with brilliant lights to impress a pleasing picture on the mind long after their beauty had faded and gone. For the bride's cake, a box three feet square and six inches high was placed in the centre of the table, covered with damask, pure and white; around the edges and sides a small wreath of flowers and evergreens, with a tasty bouquet in the *centre* on *each* side. From each corner of the box, pillars five feet high and four inches around, inclining a little *in* at the top, were wreathed with white curled paper with flowers and evergreens fixed prettily in. On the top of each pillar, round pieces of tin were tacked to hold candles, and then covered by large roses and japonicas in clusters. A beautiful hanging basket, embossed with silver, was suspended by four cords, one from each post (that was fastened before the posts were dressed) and hung little more than half way; small grape leaves were sewed on the cords, and tiny bunches of grapes hung under the leaves as a grape-vine. Frosted evergreen sprays were placed in the basket, and on it nestled lemons, crystallized pears, peaches, nectarines, apples, and plums, with long clusters of Malaga grapes hanging across and over the sides. Under this basket, in the centre of the box, was placed the bride's cake, weighing eight pounds, and iced in beautiful forms with thick Florida icing, and exquisite French candies on the side, with a pure white bouquet of roses, lilies of the valley and small flowers, emblematic of youth, innocence and *love*, in the centre. Inside of each post on the corner of the box, oblong wire baskets were made to fit, and filled with French candies in small sprigs of evergreen and flowers lined with prettily cut paper, and sugar fruits placed between. On each side (through the centre of the table) was a large glass bowl filled with amber jelly, next a bowl of syllabub, piled high and decorated with strips of fruit jelly. Then tall pyramids of oranges, with bunches of purple grapes over the tops, and bunches of raisins around the bottom; silver baskets with macaronis and kisses, bowls of tipsey cake, trifle, and floating island, moulds of blancmange and Charlotte Russe on glass dishes, and eight dozen glasses of syllabub and colored jellies interspersed. On each end of the table a large fruit cake on a glass salver beautifully ornamented, vases of flowers between the bride's cake and each end, with china dishes of sliced fruitcake, plain pound-cake, delicate cake, marble cake, white cake, citron cake, jelly cake, cocoanut cake, sponge-cake, chess cake, jumbles, snow-balls, candies, apples, and nuts tastefully disposed. Saucers and spoons, with small china plates and napkins, on each side of the table, with silver ladles to serve the syllabub and jelly. Ice cream pyramids are only used in warm weather, and were not added, as snow was plentiful, and Southern houses not heated by furnaces. This is written as a guide. Follow the directions, and see if its *simple* elegance and utility will not compare favorably with the dazzling supper prepared by skilled and artistic confectioners.

GENERAL LEE FRUIT CAKE.

Break fourteen eggs and beat them separately, then add one pound of sugar to the yelks. Stir to a cream one pound of flour and one and a half pounds of butter, and slowly mix it in the yelks and sugar. Then add the whites with one gill of French brandy and same of Madeira wine, one tablespoonful of cinnamon pulverized, same of allspice, two nutmegs grated fine, one teaspoonful of mace and cloves mixed. Stir all well together and slowly add alternately three pounds of stoned raisins pulled apart, three pounds of dried, well washed currants, two pounds of citron cut in thin pieces, and two pounds of almonds, that have been blanched and coarsely pounded in a marble mortar with a little rose-water. Grease a tin cake mould, put paper in the bottom, and bake it in a moderate oven four hours. Put the icing on in fifteen minutes after it taken out of the oven or stove. Use recipe for Florida icing.

GINGER SNAPS.

Three quarts of flour, three quarters of a pound of sugar, same of lard, three tablespoonfuls of ground ginger, one of cloves, one of cinnamon, one of salt, one teaspoonful of soda, and molasses enough to make it in a dough. Roll thin, cut round and small, and bake quickly. Cakes will be crisp and sweet.

MERCHANT'S CAKE FOR A PICNIC.

Four pounds of flour, four of sugar, four and a half of butter, four dozen eggs, four pounds of currants, four of citron, eight pounds of seeded raisins, three spoonfuls of cloves, same of mace, three nutmegs, three gills of brandy, and same of wine. Sift one teaspoonful of soda and two of cream tartar in the flour and make as other fruit cakes. This is nice for a wedding cake.

MRS. B.'S SPONGE CAKE.

Break sixteen eggs in a large wooden bowl, put the weight of twelve in crushed sugar and six in flour in the eggs, with the rind and juice of one lemon. Beat it until all the sugar is dissolved, and the dough looks as if it were filled with flour. This is the best sponge-cake I ever saw, and always light. Nothing beat separately.

PORTLAND CAKE.

One cup of milk, two of sugar, three of flour, one of butter, four eggs, half teaspoonful of saleratus, one of cream tartar, and the rind of a lemon grated.

CONCORD CAKE.

Three cups of white sugar, one of butter, one of sour milk, five eggs, one lemon, and five cups of flour, with one teaspoonful of saleratus.

WATER SPONGE-CAKE.

Six eggs, four cups of sugar, four of flour, one of cold water, two teaspoonfuls of cream tartar, and one of saleratus.

CRULLERS.

Mix one pint of milk, one cup of melted butter, one cup of yeast together, and make it into a stiff dough with flour. Set it to rise. Next morning add two cups of sugar, four eggs, one nutmeg grated, and a teaspoonful of cinnamon. Make it out in cakes like lady fingers, and fry in boiling lard until a light brown. Take them out of the lard with a perforated skimmer and spread them to cool. Sprinkle fine sugar over them while hot.

FRENCH LOAF-CAKE.

Beat four eggs with three cups of sugar, one of butter, and one of milk. Sift one teaspoonful of soda and two of cream tartar in five cups of flour, add one lemon with the peel grated and two cups of grated cocoanut. Bake in round loaves like bread and slice it.

COOKIES.

One cup of butter, two of sugar, one of sour milk, one teaspoonful of soda, two of cream tartar, a few caraway seeds, and flour enough to roll them out.

MRS. M.'S CUP CAKE.

Beat to a cream two cups of sugar, one of butter, and one of sour milk. Sift one teaspoonful of soda and two of cream tartar in three cups of flour, and stir it in. After all are mixed break in five eggs, beat hard and bake it quickly.

MOCK LOBSTER CAKE.

One cup of white sugar and same of flour, mixed in three eggs, third of a teaspoonful of saleratus dissolved in one spoonful of milk, and stirred in. Bake it half an inch thick, and when done place it on a board. Cover it with preserves and roll it round while hot.

LADY-FINGERS.

One cup of butter, two of sugar, three of flour, four eggs. Mix the sugar and butter, then the eggs and flour. Roll it out in fine sugar in pieces three inches long and one wide, give it a curl, and bake it.

GINGER SNAPS.

One cup of molasses, half a cup of sugar, and half of butter, same of warm water, two large spoonfuls of ginger, one teaspoonful saleratus. Mix and make a stiff dough with flour and roll out thin.

TENNESSEE CAKE.

The whites of sixteen eggs, three quarters of a pound of butter, same of flour, and one pound of sugar. Flavor to taste.

COCOANUT CAKE.

Two cocoanuts grated, one pound of sugar, same of flour, and butter, with the whites of fourteen eggs.

LADY CAKE.

The whites of twelve eggs, one pound of sugar, three quarters of flour, and half a pound of butter, two ounces of sweet almonds and one of bitter, and one glass of rose-water.

WHORTLEBERRY CAKE.

Beat two eggs with one cup of sugar; stir in half the quantity of butter and one cup of milk. Sift one teaspoonful of soda in four cups of flour, add a pinch of salt, and one pint of fresh whortleberries. Eat it warm with butter for dessert.

GOSHEN CAKE.

Mix quarter of a pound of fresh butter with one pint of molasses over the fire; when the butter is soft, stir it well, and add one teaspoonful of cinnamon. Beat three eggs and stir them slowly in, with enough flour to make it the consistency of pound-cake batter; add one teaspoonful of soda dissolved in hot water.

CAKE WITHOUT EGGS.

Stir two cups of sugar and one of butter together, dissolve one teaspoonful of soda in one cup of sour milk; stir it in with flour enough to make a stiff batter. Flavor it with one gill of brandy, half a nutmeg, and one teaspoonful extract of lemon, and bake quickly.

CITRON CAKE.

Beat four eggs and add one pound and a quarter of sugar, three quarters of a pound of butter, one pound and, a half of flour. Dissolve one teaspoonful of soda in a pint of milk, and stir it in with one teaspoonful of lemon extract and half a nutmeg. Then add half a pound of citron, cut in thin pieces, and bake quickly.

SCOTLAND NECK CITRON CAKE.

Twelve eggs, one pound of flour, half a pound of butter, one and a half pounds of citron, two pounds of almonds, two pounds of cocoanut, one gill of wine, same of brandy, and one teaspoonful of mace.

BUTTER SPONGE-CAKE.

Fifteen-eggs, the weight of ten in sugar, eight in flour, six in butter; cream the butter and part of the sugar together; beat the yelks and balance of the sugar light. Then stir in the butter and sugar creamed together, the whites of the eggs well beaten, and the flour slowly stirred in; season with lemon, and bake in a quick oven.

SCOTLAND NECK CHEESE-CAKE.

Beat the yelks of eight eggs; cream one pound of sugar and half a pound of butter together, and mix in the eggs. Boil the rind of two lemons perfectly soft, mash them and beat them in with two tablespoonfuls of flour, and bake them in patty-pans lined with pastry.

GINGERBREAD.

Mix together one pound of sugar, one of butter, three of flour; add one pint of molasses, quarter of a pint of cream, two ounces of ginger, and one tablespoonful of soda, and bake it in small cakes cut with tin shapes.

VIRGINIA TEA-CAKES.

One and a half pounds of sugar, one cup of butter, one of lard, one of milk, two teaspoonfuls of soda dissolved in the milk, three eggs, and four pints of flour. Make it in a stiff dough, and roll it out to cut with cake-cutters.

* * *

If cares disturb you, wear the star of hope. "The time has come when the will of woman, the taste and skill of woman, the love and energy of woman must be seen and felt. There is a power as well as charm in the working gifts and graces of woman. To plant, to beautify, to bless with patient toil and complete success with which every wise woman buildeth her house, is to build up the fortunes and fame of her country, and to make the desert rejoice and blossom as the rose."

"Woman's invention will often solve man's difficulty sooner than all his logic."

PRESERVES.

To Preserve Peaches.

Peel clear stone peaches, and cut them in halves; weigh them and take their weight in sugar; put your sugar in a porcelain kettle, and cover it well with cold water; add the beaten whites of two eggs to every ten pounds; stir it well, and put it over the fire; boil and skim it until perfectly clear; then put in the peaches and cook slowly until the syrup is as thick as honey, carefully removing the scum that rises on the top. Put them in your jars warm, dip a piece of white paper in brandy, and place on the peaches; tie them up nicely, and keep in a dry place.

Cling-Stone Peaches.

To every pound of peaches, allow three quarters of a pound of sugar; peel them, and throw into cold water until all are peeled; then pour that water in the kettle you are to preserve in, and add your sugar with beaten whites of two eggs; skim it well and put in a few pieces of lemon peel, then the peaches; let them boil up, then take them out and let them cool; return them and boil in the syrup until easily penetrated with a straw.

To Preserve Water-Melon Rinds.

Cut off all the green, thick rind and take the white part and cut it in shapes or strips; boil in clear water until tender, with a teaspoonful of soda and a dozen peach leaves to every half gallon; then take out the rinds, and soak them in alum water one hour; afterward boil gently in ginger tea one hour; make a syrup of equal weight of the sugar and rinds. Put it in a porcelain kettle, with sufficient water to cover the sugar; put in it whilst cold, the beaten white of an egg to clarify it; let it boil and remove the scum that rises (a good plan is to strain the syrup); rinse the kettle out and return it to boil up; put the rinds in and some ginger root tied in muslin; let it boil up; take the pieces out on flat dishes to cool, and when cold, put it in the syrup again to cook until soft. Keep it in a large earthen bowl two days, then pour off the syrup and the juice of a lemon or tablespoonful of extract; boil it up and pour hot over the rind. Then put it in your jars.

APPLE MARMALADE.

Pare nice tart apples, and core them; boil them in clear water until soft enough to mash up; strain the water from them, and to every pint put one pound of sugar; let the syrup boil; skim it, and then put the apple in it and cook until it is thick. This is very nice for children, and keeps well.

APPLES PRESERVED LIKE GINGER.

Peel and cut in quarters enough apples to weigh six pounds; weigh them and take the weight in sugar with half a pound of race ginger; pack the apples in a jar, a layer of apples, then sugar and ginger until all are put in. Next day bruise an ounce of ginger and infuse it in half a pint of boiling water, closely covered. Next day, put the apples, sugar, and ginger, with the water from the bruised ginger, in a preserving kettle, and boil it for one hour or until the apple looks clear and syrup rich, adding some lemon peel cut very thin, just before done. This tastes like West India ginger, when nicely done.

SIBERIAN CRAB APPLE.

Weigh them, and to every pound allow the same of sugar; make a syrup with the sugar, and when boiled, drop the apples in and let them cook, but not break; take them out, and when cool put them in a jar, and for three days boil the syrup and pour over them.

APPLE JELLY.

Pare, core, and halve nice sour apples, without bruise; weigh them, and put their weight of sugar in a porcelain kettle with just enough water to dissolve it;

let the water and sugar boil, and skim it; then lay the apples in carefully without crowding them, and let them cook until tender enough to eat; with a silver spoon place each piece on a shallow dish, and let it cool; add one more pound of sugar to the syrup; boil and skim it; when the apples are perfectly cold, pour the syrup over, and let them remain in the jelly. It will keep for weeks, and is not only delectable with sweet cream, but an ornament to the dessert table or tea.

APPLE JELLY. NO. 2.

Cut apples up without peeling them; put them in a porcelain kettle, and cover them well with cold water; let them boil one hour, then strain them through a coarse bag, and to every pint of the juice add one pound of white sugar; return it to the kettle, put a stick of cinnamon and the peel of a lemon in, boil it until it congeals in the spoon when cooled, and put it in common tumblers, with a piece of paper pasted over the top.

To Dry Cherries or Damsons.

Pick them from the stem and weigh them; to every four pounds allow one pound of brown sugar. Put the sugar in a kettle and wet it with water enough to dissolve it; let it boil and skim it, then put in the fruit and give them one boil up. Remove the scum carefully from the top, pour them in a jar, and three days after boil the syrup and pour it hot over the fruit. Three days after, take them out of the jar and dry them in the hot sun, or put them in a moderate oven and stir them occasionally. When dry, put them in paper bags, and keep them in a dry place for pies in winter.

To Dry Peaches.

Peel them nicely, take out the seeds and spread them thin on pieces of boards and put them in the hot sun every morning. If damp and cloudy, let them have air, but do not put them out. Turn them every day. When dried sufficiently, put them in bags with sassafras chips occasionally put in to keep the worms from eating them. Hang them in a dry place.

DRIED APPLES.

Peel your apples and cut slices off of the core; spread them on boards and expose them to the hot sun four or five days, turning them often. Then put them in cotton bags, with sassafras chips (as for peaches), and hang them in a dry place, and hang the bags in the hot sun every day or two for a month. Every family should have an apple peeler, with the corer and slicer attached; as they can now be had.

DRIED APPLES SLICED.

Cut your apples in thin cross slices without peeling them, fourth of an inch thick, as you do to fry; dry them carefully, and keep them as in above receipt. These are put up to fry in winter, and have to be slightly parboiled before frying them for breakfast or dinner.

GREEN APPLE DRIED.

Peel the apple and stew it done, with one pound of sugar to five of fruit; spread it thin on dishes and dry in the sun, then put into paper bags, and keep for Brown Betsey.

RIPE CANTELOPES PRESERVED.

Peel the rind off and take out the soft part of the cantelope near the seed; cut it in slices and put it in a bowl; sprinkle a little alum over it, and let it stand twelve hours well covered with boiling water. Drain it and scald it with weak ginger tea; drain it again and put it in a preserving kettle with one pound of sugar to every pound of cantelope, and boil it an hour.

WATER-MELON RIND.

Cut the rind in all sorts of fanciful shapes with a sharp penknife; weigh it and to every pound allow one and a half pounds of loaf sugar. Put it in weak alum water for three days, then soak it in clear water twenty-four hours, put it then in a kettle lined with grape leaves and a layer between each layer of melon, cover it with water and simmer it two hours, then spread it out on dishes to cool. Put the sugar in the kettle with a pint of water to every pound and a half of sugar, and the whites of two eggs beaten; let it boil, skim off the egg, and strain the syrup; wipe out the kettle and return the syrup. When it boils, put the rind in and cook it two hours; take the rind out, boil the syrup again and pour it over the rind. Next day pour it off, boil the juice of a lemon to every quart of syrup, and when it looks thick in the spoon pour it on again and tie it up.

GLASS MELONS AND CITRONS.

Gather the citron and glass melon when nearly ripe, peel them thin and scrape out all the seeds; cut baskets or edge the halves with a scallop or point; put them in a preserving kettle with water to cover them, half a dozen peach leaves and a piece of alum half the size of a shell-bark nut; boil them one hour in this, then let them cool and boil them half an hour in clear water. Make a syrup of one pound and a quarter of sugar and one pint of water to a pound of fruit; boil it, and put the melons in to cook until clear. Take them out and put lemon peel with a small bit of ginger in the syrup, and when thick pour it over the melon. The glass melon looks like West India preserves, and is very nice. May-tops may be preserved by the same process, not peeling them but taking out the seed with the stem.

QUINCE PRESERVERS.

Peel the quince and cut it in nice round pieces; (save all the good peel and cores for jelly) put the pieces in a porcelain kettle and cover them with cold water; let them boil until soft enough to put a straw through; take them out, and put on a syrup, equal weight in sugar covered with water, with the white of an egg. Skim and strain it as soon as it boils, then put the quince with it and cook it until the syrup looks thick. Save the water it was boiled in for jelly.

STEWED PEARS.

Peel your pears and put them in a porcelain kettle; cover them with water, and let them cook half an hour after the water boils; then add as much sugar as you wish, with pieces of lemon peel, and stew until they are soft, but not broken. These are preferable to baked, when nicely done, to eat with cream or milk.

PEAR PRESERVERS.

Peel and quarter large pears and allow one pound of sugar to a pound of fruit; stick one clove to a pear in the pieces. Boil the sugar with half pint of water to the pound; put in some bits of lemon peel, and when the syrup has boiled up clear, put the pear in and let it cook to heat through; take it out, let it cool, and put it back to cook until it is soft, but not broken. Small ones can be put up whole, with a clove in the end.

PEAR MARMALADE.

Take ripe, juicy pears, cut them in small pieces, and stew them with their weight in sugar; let them stand half an hour, then mash them fine with a pestle, and cook them one hour. Pear is hard to keep in preserves, and always requires equal weight in sugar.

PEACH JELLY.

Take very ripe peaches, strain them through a coarse bag; allow a pound of sugar to one pint of juice and a few kernels of the stone. Boil it twenty minutes.

PEACHES A LA STRAWBERRY.

Cut ripe peaches in small pieces, with soft, mild, eating apples; allow three peaches to one apple, mix them with sugar, and let it stand three hours. Makes excellent mock strawberries.

PEACHES FOR TEA.

Cut ripe peaches in small pieces, sugar them, and serve with rich cream. Nothing better.

QUINCES BAKED.

Peel the quince and cut off nice pieces, put them in a pan with sugar and water, and bake them. Eat with cream or milk.

PEACHES BAKED.

Peel the peach, cover it with sugar in a pan half full of water, and bake soft. These are nice for a dessert or tea with cream.

BAKED PEARS.

Pears are good baked with or without the peel in sugar and water. Bake them slowly.

BLACKBERRY JAM.

Gather the blackberries in dry weather, weigh them, and put one pound of sugar to one and a quarter of fruit. Mash them well together and cook perfectly done, free of any syrup.

RASPBERRY JAM.

Weigh one pound of sugar for every pound of fruit, then put in one pound of the fruit extra, mash them well with a marble mortar, and cook them until nearly all the syrup is taken up. The great art in keeping fruits is cooking them done.

Gooseberry Jam.

Pick the stems off, and scald them in hot water; let them stand until the water is cold, then scald again. Put one pound and a quarter of sugar to every pound of fruit, put it in your kettle with enough water to dissolve it. When it boils and the scum is removed, put in the fruit that has been drained from the water it was scalded in; you can use that to boil more in for a jelly, and put a pound and a quarter of sugar to pint of water. Some recommended soda in the water they are parboiled in, but it gives an unpleasant taste to the preserve. This jam, in baked puff paste, makes a pleasant dessert with a glass of milk and sponge-cake.

Quince Jelly.

Take the shavings from the preserved quince with the perfect cores, and put them in the water the pieces were parboiled in; boil them until perfectly soft, then strain through a coarse bag, and to every pint, put one pound of sugar; boil it exactly twenty minutes. Put it hot in half pint tumblers, cut a piece of white paper a little larger than the glass, mix flour and water, and put it nicely around the edge of the paper, and press it on tightly; wash the glasses off with a wet rag and put them away for use. Always wash jars and tumblers perfectly clean after being filled, and you will have no food for ants.

Strawberries Preserved.

Weigh them and put the same weight in loaf sugar; let them stand two hours; boil them twenty minutes, and put them up in small glasses.

Strawberry Jelly.

Mash the fruit and squeeze the juice through a bag; to every pint put three quarters of a pound of sugar, and boil it twenty minutes briskly. This keeps better than the preserve. All small fruits must be cooked until the seed looks done.

STRAWBERRY JAM.

Mash the fruit with equal weight of sugar and cook done.

PINE-APPLE JELLY.

Pare and grate pine-apples, weigh them, and to every pound put one pound of white sugar; stir it until it is well mixed and thickens; then strain it in jars, and put paper dipped in brandy over the top, as soon as it congeals. Tie it up tightly.

ORANGE JELLY.

Take six large juicy oranges and one lemon, one pound of loaf sugar, and half an ounce of gelatine; dissolve the sugar in half a pint of water, pour half a pint of boiling water over the gelatine; when dissolved, strain it, put the sugar and water on the fire; when it boils, add the gelatine, the juice of the oranges and lemon, with a little of the peel, and let it boil up, and then strain it in moulds to cool.

TO MAKE GOOD JELLY.

Press the juice from any fruit you like; put one pound of sugar to every pint of juice, and stir it until the sugar is all dissolved and well mixed, and in twenty-four hours after you put it in glasses or a stone jar (if the sugar has been well mixed in), it will make a nice jelly, keep well, and save all the trouble of boiling.

* * *

Be systematic in all your household duties. Have regular hours and require your servants to be punctual in keeping them. Always have a kitchen clock, and if the meals are on the table at the regular hour and you are not ready, do not scold them for not waiting. It may not be so palatable, yet there will be no disarrangement, as will be the case whenever the business of one hour is put off and crowded into that of another.

Business men can be prompt in their engagements, their tempers kept mild, and their lives made happier, by never having to wait for their meals to be prepared when they have to go in haste to eat them. The gentle smile of the wife and the call of the little ones for papa to come to dinner, as his footsteps cross the threshold of his door, will be as sweet music to his ear, soothing all the cares and vexations of the busy mart he has just left behind him.

If there is a care on his brow, ask no questions—meet him with a smile, and let *that care* be lightened by the happy face of "God's best gift to man."

"The systematic housekeeper will do the work of a family without hurry or confusion, the unskillful one worries herself into illness."

ICE-CREAM.

Frozen Custard.

Break thirty-two eggs in a deep bowl, then put on the fire, in a porcelain kettle, one gallon of sweet milk; when it is warm put in one pound and a quarter best white sugar, and stir it until the sugar is dissolved. Let it come to a full boil and when rising to the top, stir slowly in the eggs that have been beaten while the milk was boiling. Stir all the time until it begins to thicken and tastes done, being very careful not to let it curdle. Then pour it in the large bowl or a deep tin bucket, and set the bucket in cold water, continuing to stir until the water feels warm; change the water, and let it stand until ready to freeze. Place the freezer in the tub that holds the ice and salt, and always have salt under the bottom of the freezer. Put ice half way and then salt, then ice well covered over the top of it with salt. Pour the custard in the freezer, and flavor it with any extract you prefer. Stir it in with a long spoon, cover it tight, and let it stand a short time tightly packed. Then keep it turning until hard, occasionally cutting it from the sides as it freezes. Always wipe the top off before opening it.

Nannie's Sherbet.

Rub the yellow rind of three lemons with lumps of sugar. Squeeze the juice of six and carefully take out the seeds. Put the sugar and juice with one pound of nice white sugar in half a gallon of water. Beat to a stiff froth the whites of five eggs, and stir two tablespoonfuls of fine sugar in them. Then slowly stir it in the lemonade, and put it immediately in a patent freezer, with salt and ice around the freezer and turn it until frozen as hard as you wish it. This is very delicate, and resembles a dish of snow. Plain freezers will not do for this, as it must be constantly stirred to keep it well mixed.

PLAIN SHERBET.

Make a rich lemonade, use twice the quantity of sugar you would for the drink. Pour boiling water over a little of the thin yellow rind and when nearly cool, add it to the lemonade. Strain it in a freezer, and freeze as you wish.

Oranges can be prepared as above. Use less sugar.

VANILLA CREAM.

Boil one quart of milk with a vanilla bean (in a muslin bag) until the milk is flavored with it. Beat the yelks of ten eggs and one pound of sugar together; add the vanilla milk to three pints of rich cream, set it over the fire, and gradually stir in the eggs. Let it come to a boil, stirring it all the time. Strain it in a freezer and freeze it very hard. Always use salt plentiful if you want it hard. If these creams are wanted in the form of the mould, place the mould suddenly in hot water, then in cold, and turn it out.

NORTH CAROLINA CREAM.

Take one gallon of pure sweet cream and strain it through a net sieve. Rub lumps of sugar on two lemon rinds and mix it with one pound of loaf sugar. Add one pint of Madeira wine, and half a glass of water on the sugar to make it mix with the cream; stir it all together. Take a syllabub churn and pump it light and thick, then stir it and put it at once in the freezer and freeze it hard. Nice to eat with strawberries.

CREAM WITH FRUITS.

Sweeten any small fruits, and mix with one half sweet milk and cream and freeze. Peaches are delicious prepared in this way.

BROOKLYN PISTACHIO CREAM.

Scald one pound of pistachio nuts and take off the skins; pound them a few at a time in a glass or marble mortar, adding rose-water, as you do for almond paste. Take half a gallon of sweet cream, and put one pound of loaf sugar in it, then gradually mix the pistachio paste. Put it in a porcelain saucepan and let it have one boil over the fire. Put it in a freezer, flavor it with almond extract, and freeze it.

ALMOND CREAM.

Prepare a pound of almonds as you do the pistachio nut. Mix it with half a pint of sweet milk to a smooth paste. Then stir it in three pints of sweet cream with half a pound of loaf sugar. Boil it up in a porcelain kettle; when cold put in a little almond extract, and if not very sweet, stir in a little more sugar and freeze it. It is O. K.

COCOANUT CREAM.

Grate a cocoanut and sprinkle quarter of a pound of sugar in it. Put on the fire three pints of cream and two of sweet milk. When it boils up, stir the cocoanut in it, and as much sugar as you like; add a gill of rose-water when cold and freeze it.

SYLLABUB.

Put one pint of wine in a deep bowl, with the juice of one lemon and half a pound of fine white sugar; stir in it one quart of sweet cream. Churn it with a tin churn made for the purpose, and skim the froth as it rises. Fill glass bowls with it or put a piece of jelly in small glasses and fill with the froth. Always churn for ten minutes before skimming, as it thickens and is better.

CAROLINA SYLLABUB.

Sweeten half gallon of rich cream *very sweet* to taste; put in half a pint of Madeira wine and same of brandy; let it stand half an hour, then pump it with the tin churn and skim the froth. Have a sieve made of netting; put it over something deep and pile the froth on the sieve; fill the bowls with the froth from the sieve. This will stand twenty-four hours; the drip can be returned and pumped over. If it does not rise well, put in a teacupful of cold water and churn hard.

PLAIN SYLLABUB.

One pint of cream and one of milk, teacup of sugar wet with wine-glass of water, half a pint of mixed wine and apple brandy; churn as above.

TIPSY CAKE.

Put a sponge-cake in a glass bowl, pour one pint of wine over it (Madeira, sherry, or any nice light wine), then stick the top full of blanched almonds cut in two. Have ready a nice rich boiled custard, flavored as you like, and pour it warm over the cake until the bowl is full. Then put balance in a glass pitcher to serve with the cake, as the bowl seldom holds enough to cover all the slices. You may split the cake if you choose before putting it in, and spread jelly of some kind on it.

TRIFLE.

Fill a large glass bowl with slices of sponge cake and saturate them with wine. Fill the bowl with a rich boiled custard (made with eight eggs to the quart of milk and quarter of a pound of sugar), flavor the custard with lemon. Whip up syllabub after the recipe, and pile it up high on the custard, then cut very thin slices of jelly and lay it over the whipt cream. The custard for this must be very cold and thick.

APPLE FOOL.

Stew ten apples with sugar enough to make them *very* sweet, beat the whites of ten eggs to a stiff froth, and mix them nicely together and set them on ice.

HOG'S FEET JELLY.

Have the feet nicely cleaned and soaked two days in cold water, changing twice or three times. Put them on to boil in a large pot of water; when the feet are done take them out with a long skimmer while the liquor is hot. Set the pot aside and let it remain still until the next day, then skim off all the grease that is on the top (and put it aside to try for oil); take a clean spoon and scrape the jelly off clean, then press blotting paper over it. Take it out in large pieces without disturbing the bottom where the pieces of bone have settled. Put it in a porcelain kettle with a quart measure; to every quart put two pounds of white sugar, one quart of Madeira or sherry wine, a few pieces of cinnamon, the juice of two lemons with a little of the peel, and the whites of two eggs strained with the shell washed and crushed. Boil this hard for twenty minutes, without stirring it after it commences to boil. When the scum has accumulated at one side, take it off and dash one teacup of cold water in it and let it stand ten minutes; take off the thick scum very carefully. Have two bleached cotton bags, pour it through one in a large bowl and through the other in moulds while it is hot. It is no more trouble than a pudding if managed rightly, and will keep good in small glass jars two months, in a cool place, and always good with sweet cream over it.

MARION'S JELLY.

To a package of gelatine add a pint of cold water, the juice of three lemons, and the rind of one. Let it stand one hour, then add three pints of boiling water, one pint of sherry wine, a wine-glass of French brandy, two sticks of cinnamon, a few cloves; let it stand until it tastes of the cinnamon, and then strain it through a thin bag in moulds, and put it in a cool place. This was given me in Vicksburg, Miss.

ANOTHER.

Cover a package of gelatine with one pint of cold water and let it stand fifteen minutes. Have some boiling water and pour three pints on the rind of one lemon and one orange cut off as thin as possible, four sticks of cinnamon and two pounds of sugar. Mix the gelatine in this, and keep it over a hot water kettle to keep hot by steam. When it is all nicely mixed and gelatine dissolved, stir in the juice of two lemons and two oranges with one quart of sherry wine and mix well. Strain it through a cotton bag, and you will find my way of making jelly improves the flavor and is very palatable.

CHARLOTTE RUSSE

Soak one ounce of gelatine half an hour in cold water enough to cover it; when soft put it in a pint of sweet cream; if you wish vanilla flavor, break up a bean and tie it in thin muslin, and put it in the cream. Put the cream in a porcelain saucepan, and boil it over a slow fire until the gelatine is dissolved, stirring it well from the bottom. Beat the yelks of eight eggs, and stir in one pound of fine white sugar; then strain through a muslin strainer, the cream in the yelks and sugar, stirring them all the time. Put it again in the saucepan or kettle, and let it simmer over a slow fire until very thick; be careful not to boil it long enough to curdle. When perfectly cold, add the beaten whites of four eggs with four tablespoonfuls of fine sugar stirred in, and a glass of nice wine, sherry, Madeira, scuppernong, or California, and teaspoonful of extract of vanilla, if not strong enough of the bean; mix all well. Line moulds with thin slices of sponge-cake, fill them up with the mixture, and set them on ice, until the charlotte is wanted. Then turn them out in glass dishes or china plates to fit the mould. You may use any other flavor with this recipe; if lemon or orange, rub some loaf or crushed sugar on the rind, and add them to the yelks and cream, and reserve the juice to beat in the whites, as you do for icing. If with extracts, add it to the white of egg, before mixing it with the yelk.

CHOCOLATE CHARLOTTE RUSSE.

Cover an ounce of isinglass or gelatine with cold water, shave three ounces of Baker's prepared cocoa, and mix it with one pint of sweet cream, and the gelatine or isinglass. Put it in a porcelain kettle over a slow fire, and stir it until it boils, and is well mixed. Beat the yelks of eight eggs and whites of four together until very light; then stir them in the mixture, with half a pound of white sugar; simmer it over the fire, but do not let it boil; pour it in a bowl, and whip it to a strong froth. Having lined your pans or moulds with sponge-cake, fill them with the mixture, and set them on ice.

PIZZINI'S ICE-CREAM.

Make a custard with one gallon of milk, ten eggs, leaving out the whites of four, one and a quarter pounds of sugar, and four spoonfuls of arrowroot. After the cream has commenced freezing, beat the whites of eggs left out, and stir them in.

GERMAN CHARLOTTE RUSSE.

Dissolve one ounce of gelatine in one half pint of milk; when well dissolved, add a cupful of white sugar, and stir until the sugar is dissolved, then flavor it with lemon or vanilla extract, and strain it; let it cool; then take one quart of cream that has been cooled on ice, and whip it with a syllabub churn until it is a stiff froth. When the gelatine is about blood heat, stir the cream gradually into it. Line moulds with sponge-cake, and fill with mixture, and set the mould on ice.

MRS. E.'S FLOATING ISLAND.

Beat six eggs to a stiff froth; put in a tin saucepan one pint of milk and one ounce of sugar. Set it over the fire, and as soon as it rises, put lumps of the whites in it, with a skimmer, and turn them in half a minute; let them cook only one minute, then take them out with the skimmer, and drain them on a sieve. Mix two ounces of sugar with the yelks, strain the milk from the saucepan over them, set it on the fire, and give one boil up; flavor with extract to taste, turn it on a dish, place the lumps of cooked whites gently on the liquor, and you have a simple floating island. Serve cold.

LOUISIANA CREAM CHEESE.

Have a nice white cotton bag to pour a large bowl of clabber in; hang it and let it drip two hours; then fill perforated cheese moulds, the shape of a star, flowers, or heart; let it remain in this until wanted for tea; carefully turn it on a plate, and have a pitcher of rich, sweet cream, with sugar in it, and grated nutmeg. Serve the cheese in saucers, and cover it with the cream and sugar. The first I ever ate was in Darlington Parish, La.

ALMOND OR WALNUT CREAM.

Blanch the nut, pound it in a marble mortar to a paste, and mix it with cream. Use one pound of almonds to a quart of cream or three quarters of a pound of picked walnuts. Sweeten it to your taste, and freeze it.

FLOATING ISLAND.

Fill a large glass bowl nearly full with whipt cream (as for syllabub). Beat up four eggs with marmalade, put a round light sponge-cake in the centre of the whipt cream, and tastefully pile the marmalade and eggs mixed, on the top of the cake.

GOOSEBERRY FOOL.

Stew two quarts of gooseberries with their weight in sugar and a little water; when done strain them through a sieve, stir them in a rich boiled custard in a large glass bowl, and pile whipt cream high over the top, with strips of currant jelly, cut thin, and laid on the cream.

FLORIDA ICING.

Take the whites of ten eggs and one pound of white sugar. Put them in an earthen baking dish; do not stir them at all until you put it on hot coals. Then stir all the time until it is boiling heat, so hot you cannot bear your finger in it. Take it up and beat it in the same dish. When nearly cold put in a large pinch of tartaric acid, and beat it until as thick and smooth as white lead. This icing will dry immediately if brought to the proper heat in boiling. I give this as the original recipe and add my improvement. I find that loaf or crushed sugar makes the icing smoother and better every way. I now put the lumps in a pan and touch them with boiling water from the kettle just enough to mash the lump. Then I break the eggs on and cook as above. I can ice a cake at night, shut it up in a close cupboard, and have it beautifully white and dry the next morning. This quantity will ice two large cakes.

BOILED ICING.

Put one pound of sugar and half a pint of water on to boil. When it ropes, stir in slowly the whites of three eggs that are beaten to a stiff froth. Beat it till it is smooth and thick, and add lemon juice to the taste. This will ice one cake and a few small ones.

MRS. H.'S ICING FOR CAKE.

Put three tablespoonfuls of sugar finely powdered to the white of each egg, and mix it well before you beat it. Then beat it and flavor with lemon juice. It must be beat until it is very thick and white. Put it on with a knife, occasionally putting the blade in cold water to have it smooth. To put in fancifully, put it in a paper folded like a cornucopia, and form flowers by pressing it through the small end. Coarse lace cut in leaves and flowers, with wire to support them, can be covered with this or Florida icing, and the cake beautifully ornamented. Each leaf must dry well before the flowers are put together.

PLAIN ICING.

Beat the whites of four eggs very stiff, slowly stir in one pound of fine sugar and flavor it with lemon extract. You can add one tablespoonful of corn starch to this to dry it quickly, if you wish.

MRS. S.'S ICING.

Boil one pound of sugar and one pint of water till it is a thick syrup. When nearly cold, stir in the whites of two eggs that are beaten to a stiff froth, and beat it until white. Then stir in the juice of one lemon and a spoonful of corn starch.

ANOTHER BOILED ICING.

Cook one and a half pounds of sugar with one pint of water until it ropes. When milk warm, slowly stir in the whites of seven eggs well beaten, and beat it hard one hour. This will ice five pounds.

ITALIAN CREAM.

Put two pints of cream into two bowls. Into one bowl put six ounces of sugar, the juice of two lemons, and two glasses of wine. Add the cream from the other bowl and stir hard. Boil two ounces of isinglass with four cups of water till reduced to half. When it is lukewarm, stir it in the cream and put into a mould.

MRS. B.'S CHARLOTTE RUSSE.

Dissolve half a paper of gelatine in cold milk, then put it on the fire to warm until well mixed. Beat the whites of ten eggs to a stiff froth, and stir them in one pint of cream with half a pound of sugar in it; flavor with vanilla. Mix the gelatine and milk in and let it stand until congealed. Cut off the top of a sponge-cake, take out the crumb in the middle, and fill it with the mixture after it is congealed. Replace the top of the cake, and stick it full of blanched almonds, with fruit jelly between in small pieces, so each slice may be covered with almonds and jelly, and you will have a nice and pretty dish.

* * *

God made woman a help-meet for man. He made her for work and not for an expensive luxury. He made her to lighten the toils and cares of man, and with the meek and quiet spirit of a Christian's *silent influence*, to draw the unbelieving husband to Him. When woman is properly aroused to a sense of her duty, the laborers in God's vineyard will not be so hard to procure, and the holy places consecrated to His service remain closed, as many are, in our land of plenty, for want of spiritual teachers and the systematic management of their means of support.

The gentle teachings to the jewels He has intrusted to woman's care, to be trained for His service, can be impressed with good or evil, and their tender hearts made as pliant as wax to receive the impressions of the mould. While she is dependent on man for the only *true* happiness realized in this world, where a love known only to the pure in heart, with a union of kindred spirits, lightens the heat and burden of the day, yet the entire happiness of her home circle, and the future of the "little ones," for weal or for woe, are totally dependent on her management.

Drunkards have been heard to say that their taste for drink was excited by the brandied fruits, wines, and cordials which were set before them in their mother's house, and by her hand; and this taste, *thus engendered*, often leads children to break God's eighth commandment in order to procure what their appetites have been cultivated to demand, while the parent little thinks that the sin of which her servant is accused was really committed by her child. Where does the fault lie? Certainly with the mother, for she can instill truth and honesty into the mind of a two-year-old child,—I say *she can do it*, because I speak from experience,—and she may, by example, precept, and watchful care make such a man of him as her heart desires.

The children of many mothers are too often left to the care and guidance, and at the mercy of the nurse—for what?—that the mother may indulge in the pleasures of the giddy world.

She must appear, at a certain time, in her costly array, decked as a butterfly, to meet certain friends, and leaving her little ones—with a piteous sob, perhaps—to be soothed by one whose only interest is in the amount and payment of her wages, and who often makes use of drugs to rid herself of their charge, or locks them up, with a threat of revenge if a hint of it is given mamma. Meanwhile, the time is passing away in which the good seed should be sown, which the genial showers of a mother's love causes to spring forth, bearing, "first the blade, then the corn, and then the full corn in the ear;" and finally the reeling footstep and frenzied brain of her child, as he approaches her door with an oath upon his lips, makes her exclaim in the agony of her soul, "My son, my son, would that I had died ere I gave thee birth!"

"Avoid alcoholic drinks; in no case are they needed by those in health. The indulgence awakens a longing that leads to every vice and levels human beings with brutes."

FRUITS AND CORDIALS.

BRANDY PEACHES.

Peel fine large peaches that are nearly ripe, weigh them, and allow half a pound of best white sugar to every pound of fruit. Put the sugar in a preserving kettle and cover it with water. Boil it fifteen minutes after it gets hot through, and carefully remove the scum. Then drop one dozen peaches in at a time, until you get all cooked enough to put a straw in. Take them out carefully with a skimmer and put them to cool on flat dishes. When perfectly cold, put them in a jar, let the syrup cook thick, and when that is cold, mix half syrup and half French or apple brandy, and cover the peaches well with it. Keep them well covered.

BRANDY PEACHES. NO. 2.

Peel your peaches and weigh them; to every pound allow half a pound of sugar. Pack the peaches and sugar in a large stone jar, and fill it two thirds full of apple or peach brandy. Cover the top of the jar with a thick dough made of flour and water, set it in a large dinner pot of cold water, put on the fire, and boil it two or three hours. These never spoil and the cordial is delicious.

BRANDY PEACHES. NO. 3.

Peel large fine peaches nearly ripe, in the evening put them in a bowl with their weight in loaf sugar, and let them stand until the next day. Then pour off the syrup in a kettle and let it boil; drop the peaches in, a few at a time, until they are enough cooked to permit a straw to run in easily. Put them on flat dishes to cool, boil the syrup a little longer, and let that cool. Then put as much brandy as you have syrup and cover the peaches with it. These keep a long time.

BRANDY PEACHES. NO. 4.

Dip peaches in nice clear lye and rub them hard with a coarse towel until the down is all off; slightly parboil them in hot water and rub them again. Allow half a pound of sugar to one pound of fruit, and put it on the fire with half a pint of water to every pound. Put some allspice, a few cloves, and some lemon rind in the syrup. Boil it and remove the scum, drop the peaches in and give them a good boil up, and when cold, put them in a jar. Mix the brandy and syrup half and half when hot, and pour it over, and cork tight. Always clarify your syrup for peaches and other preserves with white of egg put in when the water is cold.

NORTH CAROLINA EGG-NOG.

To make a gallon of egg-nog, take one dozen eggs, break them, and beat the whites and yelks so separately. After the yelks have been beaten fifteen minutes, put twelve tablespoonfuls of fine white sugar in them and beat them until they rise and are thick. The great secret of having it nice is to beat the yelks thick. Whip the whites to a stiff froth, put half a pint of brandy in the yelks and sugar, and when well mixed, stir the whites slowly in. Have milk in a glass pitcher, to be added if preferred.

BETTIE'S EGG-NOG.

Take the yelks of sixteen eggs and twelve tablespoonfuls of pulverized sugar, and beat them to the consistency of cream. Add two thirds of a nutmeg, grated, and beat well together. Then add half a pint of brandy, and two gills of Madeira wine. Have ready the whites of the eggs beat to a stiff froth and stir it in the mixture; stir in slowly three pints of rich milk. Egg-nog is a great drink for Christmas holidays, and is a good nourishment for sick persons that require a stimulant.

TURNIP WINE.

Put sliced turnips in a cider press and press out all the juice; to every gallon, put three pounds of sugar and half a pint of brandy; keep it with something thin over it until it stops working, and then stop it close for three months. Change it then into another cask, and you will have a good, healthy wine.

PEACH WINE.

Take fruit nearly ripe, stone it, and bruise it to a pulp, put one quart of water to eight pounds of pulp and let it stand twenty-four hours. Then strain out the juice, and to every gallon add two pounds of sugar. Put it in a cask and when fermented and becomes perfectly clear, cork it tightly in bottles and seal it.

MRS. STEWART'S BLACKBERRY WINE.

Measure the berries and bruise them. For every gallon one quart of boiling water. Let the mixture stand twenty-four hours, stirring it occasionally. Then strain off the liquor into a cask. For every gallon add two pounds of sugar. Cork tight and let it stand till the following October.

TO MAKE RED GRAPE WINE.

Put forty pounds of black or red grapes in five gallons of cold water. Mix nine gallons of cider, twenty pounds of sugar, three handfuls of barberry leaves, two pounds of beet-root sliced, four ounces of red tartar; add four pounds of sassafras chips and one gallon of brandy, and you will have eighteen gallons of as nice wine as can be made in any part of our country.

CIDER WHITE WINE.

Take nine gallons of honey, two quarts of spring water, ten gallons of cider, two ounces of white tartar. Mix two ounces of cloves, same of cinnamon and mace, and add to the liquid, then stir in half a gallon of mm or brandy. This will make ten gallons.

AMIS'S GRAPE WINE.

To two gallons of pure juice, put one gallon of water and two pounds of sugar. Put it in a cask and in three months it will be a nice wine.

CHERRY BOUNCE.

Put Morella and wild cherries in a cask or demijohn, and cover them with brandy; let it remain three months closely stopped. Make a rich syrup of fine sugar and water, boil it thick, and when cold mix half syrup and half brandy from the cherries. This is delicious, and I have seen it thirty years old. Raspberry bounce is made the same way.

RASPBERRY WINE.

Make it like blackberries or with six gallons of water, four of cider, six of raspberries, twenty pounds of sugar, three ounces of red tartar, three quarts of brandy, with dry orange peel two ounces. Another way is to steam the berries. Boil the juice and to every gallon allow one pound and a half of sugar. Put it in a cask when cold, with a little nice yeast, and when it has ceased to ferment, add half pint of brandy to each gallon and cork it.

TO MAKE NECTAR.

Put one pound of loaf sugar into a large bowl, add one quart of cold water, stir until the sugar is all dissolved, pour over it one bottle of Madeira and one of hock, mix them well, grate half a nutmeg, with teaspoonful of lemon extract, and freeze it.

PUNCH.

Make a rich lemonade, press the peel with a muddler on hard sugar, pour some hot water over the pulp and a little of the peel and strain it in when cold. Mix a little brandy and rum together, and make the punch pleasant to the taste; set it on ice to cool or freeze it. Very nice slightly frozen.

PERRY.

This is a pleasant drink made from pears, exactly as cider is made from apples.

GOOSEBERRY WINE.

Take four gallons and a half of water, and five gallons of gooseberries. Mix six pounds of sugar, four pounds of honey, one ounce of white tartar, one ounce of dry orange and lemon peel, or two ounces fresh, add half a gallon of light brandy, and you will have nine gallons of nice wine. Currant wine may be made the same way. It is good in six months.

STRAWBERRY WINE.

Ten gallons of strawberries, eleven of water, twenty-five pounds of sugar, three ounces of red tartar, two lemons and two (oranges peel and juice), one gallon of brandy. This is delicious and keeps well. These were sent me by a friend.

FINCASTLE CURRANT WINE.

Gather full ripe currants on a dry day, pick them from the stalks and weigh them; crush them well with the hands, leaving none whole. To every two pounds of currants put one quart of water; stir it well and let it stand three hours; then strain it through a sieve, and add one pound of sugar to every three pounds of currants; stir it well, put it on to boil and skim as long as any scum rises; pour it off in a clean cask after it has stood sixteen hours to cool, and stop it close. If you make ten gallons, let it stand three weeks; if twenty or thirty gallons, one month. When it is perfectly clear, put a lump of loaf sugar in your bottles, bottle it, and cork tight, and keep it in a cool place. If well made, it tastes like pale Sherry.

SPRUCE BEER.

Boil one handful of hops and two of sassafras-root in ten gallons of water, with two tops of young spruce pine, and while hot add one gallon of molasses, two spoonfuls of ginger, and one of allspice; when cool, add half a pint of good yeast, stir it well, put it in a cask and cover close. When fermented and clear, put it in bottles and cork tight.

GINGER BEER FOR SUMMER.

To one gallon of boiling water, put one pound of loaf sugar, one ounce of best ginger-root bruised, one of cream tartar or a sliced lemon; stir it all until the sugar is dissolved, let it stand until milk warm, then add one tablespoonful of good hop yeast, poured over a slice of cold loaf bread, and allow it to float on the surface, and stand twenty-four hours well covered; then strain it and fill clean bottles three fourths full; cork with good corks and tie over. It will be fit for use in two days, and is a refreshing, healthy drink.

GINGER WINE.

Three gallons of water, three pounds of sugar, four ounces of race ginger washed in four waters, boil all well for one hour; strain it through a sieve in a cask with three lemons cut up and two gills of beer yeast; shake it well, and cover the cask tight, let it stand to ferment until clear enough to bottle. It will be fit to drink in ten days after it is bottled.

BLACKBERRY CORDIAL.

One quart of blackberry juice, one pound of white sugar, one tablespoonful of cloves, same of allspice and cinnamon; one pint of brandy, one nutmeg; boil it well fifteen minutes, and bottle it hot.

BLACKBERRY WINE.

Pour one gallon of boiling water over one gallon of blackberries, beat them with a pestle in the water and strain them when cold; put three pounds of loaf sugar to each gallon and simmer it one half hour on the fire, then put it in bottles with thin muslin or laces tied over the top (without any stopper) and let it stand until October, and you will have a good imitation of Port wine.

BLACKBERRY WINE. NO. 2.

Mash any quantity you may have with a wooden pestle, and strain them; to every gallon of juice put two quarts of water and three pounds of brown sugar; put it in a jar and stir it well, cover it with thin muslin and remove the scum that rises on the top every morning for one week, stir it every time, let it stand three weeks in the jar, then put it in jugs with muslin tied over until wine is made (about two months). Bottle and cork tight.

FANNIE'S BLACKBERRY WINE.

Boil and mash blackberries in a preserving kettle, when cold strain them through a cloth; to every quart of the juice, add half a pound of loaf sugar, quarter of an ounce of nutmeg, same of allspice, cloves, and cinnamon; boil it fifteen minutes, when cold, add one pint of French or apple brandy, and bottle it, sealing it up tight with wax.

MRS. JONES'S BLACKBERRY WINE.

Wash and pick the blackberries and mash them of an evening, strain them the next morning through thin muslin; to one pint of juice add nearly two pints of water, to one gallon (after all the water is put in), add three pounds of sugar; put it in a jug, tie it over with muslin, and let it stand a fortnight to ferment; then strain it off, and cork tight.

This country is famed for fine blackberries, and the recipes given have been well tried.

SCUPPERNAUG WINE.

Wash and mash scuppernaug grapes, and to every gallon add a pint of boiling water. Next morning strain them through a coarse cloth and to every gallon of juice put three pounds of crushed sugar. After it is well dissolved put it in a demijohn, tie a cloth over the top and put it where it will not be disturbed for six weeks; never let it be shaken. Bottle it and cork as soon as the wine is ready. If good in five weeks, bottle it. This is a recipe for home-made scuppernaug. On Roanoke Island where the grape is in its native soil, it is made of the pure juice with a little burnt sugar to color it and sometimes brandy is added by particular request.

SPRUCE BEER.

Boil one handful of hops and two of sassafras root in ten gallons of water, strain it, and while hot pour in one gallon of molasses with two large spoonfuls of essence of spruce, same of ginger, and one of allspice; when *cold* put it in a cask with half a pint of good yeast, stir it well, stop it close, and when fermented and clear, bottle it and cork tight.

PEACH CORDIAL.

Gather white heath or any nice cling-stone peaches, cut them to the stone in several places and fill jars or a cask. Cover them with peach brandy and let them remain eight weeks. Then to every gallon allow two pounds of sugar and half a pint of water. Make a syrup by boiling the sugar and water, and when it is cold, mix half syrup and half brandy; bottle it or keep it in the cask.

MOLASSES BEER.

Boil five quarts of hops and five of wheat bran in fifteen gallons of water, four hours, and strain it. Put it in a cask with one head out, and add five quarts of molasses, stir it and cover it with a cloth. When lukewarm stir in one quart of yeast, cover it with a cloth and board to fit close, and when it has fermented and looks clear, draw it off and put it in bottles that are well cleaned; soak the corks and cork tightly.

LEMON CORDIAL.

Cut six fresh lemons and put into three pints of milk, boil them until the whey is very clear, then pass it through a sieve. Put to the whey three pints of French brandy and three pounds of clarified sugar; stir it until the sugar is dissolved. Let it stand to refine, then put some chips of lemon peel, cut thin, in bottles, and fill with the cordial. This keeps well and is very nice.

RASPBERRY VINEGAR.

The best I ever made was one quart of vinegar with one quart of fresh raspberries, put in every morning for three days, straining it before adding the fresh ones. The fourth day press the juice in straining it. Put one pound of loaf sugar to every pint of juice and stir it until it is well dissolved. Put it in pint bottles and cork tight. This is a fine beverage with ice in summer and very agreeable to the sick.

ANOTHER RASPBERRY VINEGAR.

Put two pounds of the fruit and one of sugar in a porcelain kettle, and mash them well together. Cook it like a jam for twenty minutes, then stir in half a pint of cider vinegar to every pound. Give it one boil up and strain it. When cold, bottle and cork it. This keeps well but does not have the exquisite flavor of the fresh fruit the other has. I have tested both for years.

STRAWBERRY VINEGAR.

Make strawberry vinegar exactly like raspberry.

STRAWBERRY CORDIAL.

Stew ripe strawberries twenty minutes and squeeze them through a linen bag. To each quart of juice put one pound of sugar and one pint of white brandy. Put it in a demijohn to stand two weeks, then filter it through a coarse muslin or a fine sieve and bottle it.

RHUBARB WINE.

Grate the stalks of rhubarb on a coarse grater, strain the juice, and to each quart add three quarts of water and three pounds of brown sugar. Fill a demijohn to the brim with it and keep some to fill it as it works over. When it has done fermenting, put a little isinglass in to clarify it and bottle it. It will be good for use in two months, and the flavor resembles champagne.

* * *

"Cleanliness is next to Godliness."

Teach your children to value and love the use of soap. Teach them to save their pennies to buy a nice cake of sweet soap, instead of the poisonous confections that seriously injure their health. Make them understand that cleanliness is essential to respectability, and that they cannot be cleanly without the use of soap. It not only purifies, but preserves the skin, and keeps the pores (which would otherwise be clogged, and constantly subjected to skin diseases,) open, and free to exercise their healthful functions.

Use soap for the toilet, soap for the dishes, soap for the kitchen utensils, soap for the churn, soap for the pantry shelves, soap in the dairy room, soap on the windows, soap on the paint, soap on the floors, soap on the clothes, and soap on the slats of the bedstead,—ants, bugs, and roaches will never stay where soap has cleared the filth away.

MISCELLANEOUS.

MOLASSES CANDY.

To boil one gallon of molasses, have a kettle or large iron pot that will hold three gallons. Put it over a *hot* fire and do not stir it. Let it boil for ten minutes and then try it, by dropping a little in cold water. If it ropes, stir it, but let it remain on the fire until you try it again. If thick, pour it out as quickly as possible in buttered dishes and let it get nearly cool before you take it out to pull. Work it until white, then pull it out and hang it in the cold air to crisp. I have frequently boiled a gallon in ten minutes and a quart in five, by the same rule. Allowing it room to swell and never stirring it to admit the air and make it boil over. If you wish to flavor it, grate orange-peel or chip it fine, and put in just before it thickens.

KNOW-NOTHING BALLS.

Pop corn nicely popped and rolled in boiled molasses, the size of a large walnut, makes a nice ball for a change and children are fond of it.

WALNUT CANDY.

Boil the molasses as above, and stir in the kernel of walnuts just as it thickens. If you wish to pull it, put it on large buttered dishes. If not to be pulled, spread it thin on tin sheets. Let it cool and then break it up in small square pieces. Hickory-nut candy may be made the same way.

BOILED SUGAR.

Take three pounds of nice clarified sugar, put it in a porcelain kettle and wet it well with water, put in one tablespoonful of fresh butter and set it over a hot fire. Let it boil five minutes after it commences, then throw in half a tumbler glass of strong vinegar or the juice of two lemons. Stir it well and let it boil until it ropes. Try it in a spoon and if it cools quick and thickens it is done. Take it from the fire and stir in lemon or vanilla extract to the taste. Pour it out on buttered dishes and pull it as warm as you can bear it in the hand. This is a nice candy and preferred to the confectioner's. The rind of the lemon can be boiled in it.

ENGLISH WALNUT AND PECAN-NUT CANDY.

Boil sugar as above, crack the nuts and put them, in halves, on buttered tins, and pour the boiled sugar on each piece, while hot, with a large teaspoon.

COCOANUT CANDY.

Boil two pounds of sugar wet with water until it is very thick, and easily pulled. Then stir in the sugar as much grated cocoanut as you wish and spread it thin on sheets of tin. It does not require any butter, and is hard to pull, but very nice.

TO KEEP EGGS.

Put four quarts of air-slacked lime in four quarts of water, two tablespoonfuls cream tartar, and two of salt. Put nine dozen fresh eggs in a jar, and pour this mixture over them. Keep them in a cool place. If the water settles away, add more to keep them under. They will keep for months.

TO KEEP CRANBERRIES.

Pick them nicely, not leaving any that are not good and sound. Put them in a large wooden tub in a cellar and keep them in clear water an inch above the fruit. They are better kept this way, to stew them fresh when wanted.

To Bottle Gooseberries.

Pick them when full grown, before they ripen, take off the stems and fill dry bottles with them nearly to the top, then cover them with cold water that has been boiled. Dig a hole in the ground and bury the bottles two feet deep. Keep perfect all winter.

To Keep Tomatoes.

Just before the first frosts in the fall of the year, pull the tomato vine up with the green ones on it, and hang them under a shelter by the root. They will ripen and taste good until Christmas.

To Keep Onions.

Dry them in the shade and string them in long bunches one above the other, and hang them in a dry place. Cut the tops off, leaving two inches to tie by. Take a small bundle of dry straw and tie them one by one on it. Largest at the bottom and so on, with a loop left at the top to hang them up.

To Keep Irish Tomatoes.

Dig them in dry weather, and put them in the shade to dry as soon as dug. Never let them be exposed to the hot sun. Turn them about carefully every day or two for the first week, and then keep them in a dry place with straw sprinkled between, and when very cold cover them with straw. Never keep potatoes near salt in a damp climate. Charcoal sprinkled between them, keeps them very nice.

Drying Pumpkins.

Cut the pumpkin up and stew it until soft and dry, pound and strain them through a colander; then grease pie pans, and spread it on a quarter of an inch thick, and dry it roll it up after it is dry, and keep it in a tight box or bag from the insects. Each one will make a pie.

TO CAN CORN.

Boil it fifteen minutes on the ear, then dry the grains in pans an hour in the sunshine; salt it just as you would for the table; fill tin cans, leaving an inch of space; put one gill of water in each can, and have an aperture size of a pin in the cover for the gas to escape; then place the tins in a kettle of water within an inch of the top of the can, and boil moderately forty-five minutes. This will keep sweet all winter.

ANOTHER WAY TO CAN CORN.

Boil green corn until half done, cut it from the cob and pack it in stone jars, layer of corn, and layer of salt; when wanted for use, soak it all night and put it in fresh water next morning until you want to cook it.

TO PRESERVE CORN.

Cut the grain of young green corn lengthways, and scrape it from the cob with a knife, then cook it thoroughly with salt and a little sugar, as you would for the table. Heat your cans, put it in hot from the kettle, and seal instantly. When you wish to use it, heat it and serve with butter or cream.

TO KEEP LEMONS.

Cover lemons with milk or buttermilk, and they will keep moist and unhurt for weeks.

TO KEEP LEMONS FOR LEMONADE.

Slice them through when perfectly fresh, and pack the slices in glass jars with a thick layer of fine white sugar between, and they will keep good one year.

To Brown Flour.

Take a dry clean spider or pan, put flour in it, set it over the fire and carefully stir and scrape the bottom of the pan to keep it from scorching; when it is a dark brown, spread it on a dish or paper to cool. Keep it in a paper bag or jar to thicken gravies or soups.

To Keep Flies from Windows.

Boil garlic in the water you wash them with.

To Bottle Fruits.

Every housekeeper has accumulated bottles; always have them cleaned before putting them away; save the wide-mouth ones for fruits that are stoned, and the long neck for catchup and tomatoes to preserve for pottage. Make a wax of one pound of rosin, two ounces of beeswax, and two of Spanish brown, slowly melted together. When you wish to put up fruit, put the bottles *nicely cleaned* in a kettle of *cold* water and set it over the fire; have corks the right size soaking in water. Peel your peaches and put them in a preserving kettle without any water, and warm them briskly, stirring from the bottom to prevent their burning before the juice is made from the heat; while the bottles are hot in the kettle, fill them with the peaches that have been *heated through*, cover the peach with the liquor up to the cork, put the cork in, dip it in the hot wax, and then in cold water or ice, and smooth it with a knife. This is an easy and sure way of keeping fruits for the winter if the directions are carefully followed. Raspberries, blackberries, and strawberries must not boil but ten minutes. Gooseberries, currants, and pie-plant must be well cooked before they are put in, tomatoes must be sliced and boiled twenty minutes, then strained through a colander, to remove the skins, returned to the kettle and boiled up again, and the bottles filled when hot, corked and sealed as the fruits. Keep them in a cool, dry place. If you use tin cans, place them in cold water as soon as filled; have a wide mouth funnel, perforated ladle, sound fruit, and seal up *in stoutly* while the fruit is boiling hot, and you will never lose it.

To Can Peaches with Sugar.

Place your cans in a kettle of boiling water, peel and halve your peaches, sweeten to taste as you would for the table; put them in your preserving kettle without any water, and heat them through. Fill the cans with the hot peaches and see that every crevice is filled with syrup; close the can immediately; fill the grooves with wax; put a piece of ice or some cool water instantly on it, and smooth it with a knife. Work with dispatch in putting up fruits or vegetables, see that they are fresh and free from any decayed spots, and seal while boiling hot, and you have the whole mystery of potting. Always place tin cans in cold water as soon as they are sealed.

Hard Soap.

Pour four gallons of boiling water over six of sal-soda and three pounds of unslacked lime, stir it well and let it settle until perfectly clear; let it stand all night. When clear, strain the water off and put six pounds of nice grease with it and boil for two hours, stirring it most of the time. If it does not seem thin enough pour another gallon of water over the lime, stir it and drain it off, and add a little at the time it is wanted, to the boiling mixture. Try it by putting a little on a plate to cool, and if thick as you wish stir in a handful of salt just before taking it from the fire. Have a large tub well soaked to keep the soap from sticking. Let it remain until solid and you will have forty pounds of nice white soap.

Soft Soap.

Put ten pounds of potash in a half barrel, next day add twelve pounds grease, stir it well and then add one gallon of boiling water. Add the same quantity boiling hot every day until the barrel is full, stirring it all the time. If you wish to make less, use three pounds of grease and two and a half pounds of potash.

Common Soap.

Save your kitchen grease, melt and strain it, put it in a large iron pot and slowly add the lye from good wood ashes (oak or hickory is the best), cook it until it ropes, stirring often with a wooden paddle. If you wish it thick, add a handful of salt just as you take it from the fire and stir it well in.

SOAP WITH POTASH.

One pound of white rock potash makes fifteen pounds of white hard soap or a half barrel of soft. Dissolve one pound of the potash in one gallon of boiling water; add five pounds of hot, melted, clean grease, stirring it quickly until it is smooth and clear, then pour it in a box mould. Another way is to dissolve one pound of the potash in three and a half gallons of boiling water, and add five pounds of grease, boiling and stirring until the grease and lye are combined (nearly ten hours), add a little salt and it will bring all the soap to the top. Then dip it out in a mould or box and cut it in bars when cold. In boiling it may be necessary to add water as it is evaporated. New grease requires longer boiling than old.

To make yellow soap, dissolve two pounds of resin in the grease before adding the lye, and put rosemary, sassafras, or Bergamot to scent it.

TO PREPARE WASHING FLUID.

Boil one pound of sal-soda and half a pound of unslacked lime in a gallon of water twenty minutes. When cool, drain it off and put it in a jug. Soak your clothes overnight, then wring them out and rub on plenty of soap; cover them with water in your wash-kettle, add a cupful of fluid, boil half an hour, rinse, and hang out. This is an invaluable recipe. Try it.

One tablespoonful compound spirits of ammonia, in a basin of water, removes the unpleasant odor from perspiration.

Fresh meat must be put in boiling water, with one tablespoonful of salt to a gallon of water. Salt meat must be in cold water, boiled slowly and kept constantly boiling and well skimmed.

Cooking can be improved by a judicious use of sugar and molasses. All rye and coarse wheat bread should have a little molasses in it.

We are born to trouble, as the sparks fly upward.

Trouble? In what? in every calling. This world's charms would unfit us for the necessary preparation for the rest of the soul, if troubles were not wisely interwoven. As they are sent for good, let us take them by submitting to whatever falls to our lot. Compare them to a bundle of fagots, far too large for us to lift. He who sends them, does not require us to carry all at once. Ask Him mercifully to untie the bundle and give us one stick we are to carry to-day, and another to-morrow, and so on. We can learn to surmount *all* troubles, if we will only take the burden appointed for each day; but if we choose to increase by taking the stick from the bundle that was allotted to yesterday, and carrying it with to-day's, ever making the morrow's burden heavier before required to bear it, we can never learn to say,

"Thy will, O God, be done."

CARE OF THE SICK.

NURSING THE SICK.

All physicians admit that good nursing is a great help to their skill. Was there ever *one* known to object to a female administering to the wants of his patients? The noiseless step, the patient, watchful care, the gentle voice, the tender raising from the hot pillow, the steady breeze of wind from the fan to cool the fevered brain, the arrangement of the hair, smoothing the coverlid, bathing the temples, mixing the medicines, and last but not least, preparing necessary nourishment for the sick, all come under the immediate head of one of God's designs, when He created woman as an help-meet for man. Cultivate a love for these duties; no station in life is exempt from them. Sickness and death are the consequences of Adam's fall, and both rich and poor have to yield to the attacks of one and obey the summons of the other. The soothing voice of woman has been known to quiet and lull to sleep the unfortunate victim whose reason has been dethroned. The earnest, heartfelt prayer of the woman of Canaan, with her faith so beautifully exemplified in her appeal, moved her compassionate Lord, and His reply was, "Be it unto thee even as thou wilt." In the dead hour of night, when stillness reigns; in the morn, noon, and eventide, offer a prayer to Him, to bless the means used for the recovery of those intrusted to your care. The Holy Spirit may bless your efforts and impress Heaven's image on the heart. If the dread summons should be feared, gently prepare their mind to receive it, looking upon their passage through the valley and shadow of death, as a pleasant journey made easy by the presence of Him who sent it. How many souls that are precious in His sight might be assisted in their preparation for the "world to come," by the influence of their nurse, for which labor of love females are peculiarly fitted, and I urge them to encourage a love for it.

FOR THE SICK.

NUTRITIOUS COMPOSITION.

Mix equal quantities of sage and cocoa, put one tablespoonful in a pint of sweet milk, add half a pint of boiling water, and boil it a few minutes. Stir it all the time; add sugar and nutmeg to the taste.

CHICKEN WATER.

Boil a young chicken or piece of an old one to make one quart of chicken water. Boil it until the meat leaves the bone, and put nothing in it but a pinch of fine salt.

CHICKEN JELLY.

Pound a nicely cleaned young chicken, bones and all, and put it on to boil in one gallon of water with a little salt. Tie up a tablespoonful of rice and drop in it until it is soft; then take the rice out and boil it down to one pint. Strain the jelly from the chicken and let it cool. One tablespoonful of this is as nourishing as a soup-plate of soup would be, and more delicate.

WINE WHEY.

Put one pint of new milk in a porcelain saucepan and let it boil up. When puffed up to the top, dash one gill of Madeira or Sherry wine in; let it boil up again, then strain it from the curd; and sweeten it with loaf sugar to the taste.

TOAST WATER.

Toast slowly until a pretty brown two slices of loaf bread (home made), put it in a pint of cold water, and let it stand one hour before using it.

GRUEL.

Put on a pint of water to boil and slowly stir in two tablespoonfuls of fine corn meal. Cook it until it tastes done. Season it with a little salt and very little sugar, and grate nutmeg over the top.

CORN BREAD WATER.

Make a simple bread of meal and water, and bake it thin and hard, but not too brown, and use for delicate persons as loaf bread toast water.

BUTTERMILK.

Sweeten fresh buttermilk from the churn, put a few drops of lemon extract in it, and envelop the glass or tin cup in ice, until nearly frozen, or put it in a pint tin bucket and freeze it, as for ice-cream.

BUTTERMILK. NO. 2.

Boil one quart of fresh buttermilk, and when hot, stir in one tablespoonful of corn meal, sifted through coarse muslin and rubbed smooth with cold water, put a pinch of salt in, boil and stir it fifteen minutes, sweeten it, and dust a little cinnamon over the top.

MILK THICKENED.

Boil one quart of milk, wet three tablespoonfuls of flour (finely sifted), roll it up in a soft, smooth paste, and when the milk boils up stir it in, and continue to stir and boil for ten minutes. Put a pinch of salt in the milk, and when done, sweeten it to taste and grate nutmeg over it.

BOILED CUSTARD.

Boil one pint of milk with two tablespoonfuls of sugar in it, beat two eggs, and when the milk puffs, stir it in. This is sufficiently rich for the sick.

Irish Moss.

Wash and pick two tablespoonfuls of Irish moss and pour one pint of boiling water over it. Set it over the fire, and stir until all is dissolved, and when cool sweeten it, and grate nutmeg over the top. Use milk if you prefer it. I have found it an excellent nourishment for a sick infant, with milk.

Arrow-Root.

Put one pint of water on to boil in a saucepan with a pinch of salt; rub one teaspoonful best Bermuda arrow-root smooth with water, and when the water boils, stir it slowly in and cook it until it has no raw taste. Sweeten it with loaf sugar. The finest child I ever saw was raised on this quantity per day by the advice of a physician, with a delicate mother's milk.

Arrow-Root Blancmange.

Boil one quart of milk, rub an ounce of arrow-root smooth with cold milk, and a little salt. Stir it in when the milk is hot and cook it four minutes; pour it off through muslin, sweeten, and flavor to taste. If the sick prefer cinnamon or vanilla bean, always boil it in the milk.

Mulled Cider and Wine.

Put a teacupful of either, with same of water, on the fire to boil with a little allspice. Beat three eggs and mix with half a pint cider or wine, and stir it in when it boils; sweeten to taste, and nutmeg grated.

Beef, Veal, and Chicken Tea.

Cut slices of beef, veal, or chicken. and put them in a covered dish. Set it over a steam-kettle and pour boiling water over it; one pint is generally enough. Let it stand one hour. Then pour it off and season with a pinch of salt. This is very good for delicate persons, when but little nourishment is required.

RICE JELLY.

Boil one teacup of nicely washed rice in two quarts of water until perfectly soft. Strain it and season with a little salt, or sugar and butter, with nutmeg grated over the top. Very nutritious, and preferable to the grains of rice.

MILK PORRIDGE.

Rub a tablespoonful of flour smooth with cold water or milk and a little salt. Boil one quart of milk, and when it comes up, stir the flour in and boil it five minutes. Sweeten it with loaf sugar, and grate nutmeg over the top.

APPLE WATER.

Wrap paper around apples and nicely roast them. Pour boiling hot water over them, and set it in water to cool or on ice.

BAKED APPLES.

Peel and core them, fill the space with sugar, put them in a pan with a little water, and slowly bake them.

PANADA.

Put a half pint of water on the fire in a porcelain saucepan, add a wine-glass of wine and dessert spoonful of sugar; grate some nice cold bread, wet it with some of the water from the stew-pan, and stir it in at once. Two tablespoonfuls will be enough for this quantity.

PANADA. NO. 2.

Toast some bread and cut it in small pieces. Make a wine sangaree and pour it over the bread. Grate nutmeg over the top.

CHICKEN PANADA.

Boil a chicken nearly done. Take the white meat from the bone and let it cool. Save some of the water it was boiled in. Pound the chicken to a paste, and boil it in the water you saved until it jellies. Season it with salt, nutmeg, and a little lemon.

CHICKEN TEA.

Take the chicken left from the panada and boil it with a little mace, slice of onion, and five grains of pepper.

BATH-ROOM.

Every house should have a bath-room. What luxury can compare to a good bath, immersing the body, showering it, or throwing the water with the hand. It refines and elevates both soul and body. Not only cleanses the outer surface, but purifies all within and produces a happy feeling in discharging our *first duty* to self. It reanimates and brings into vigorous action, physically and mentally, the organs of the body, each dependent on the other to sustain life and the strength required for work. A surf bath in the ocean lulls to sleep, and gives a foretaste of Paradise in its soothing, peaceful effect. When aroused, the feeling is like "a giant refreshed with wine."

"Go and wash in the Pool of Siloam;" cleanse the heart by its spiritual effect, so the body by its visible, before it can be healed. "Wash and be clean, and thy sins shall be done away, the filth of the soul cleansed by the *spirit*, while the" body is purified by the element, given by the *Creator*, so necessary to all the wants of man. See how the beasts seek water and love to stand in it— fowls and birds of the air. Even the little canary in *his* cage will flutter in the water, and sing sweet notes after its bath. The ducks quack with delight, and the pea-fowl struts and fans out his beautiful feathers, sounding shrill notes of joy at the prospect of a nice wash from a shower. Should man, made after God's image (though subjected to the filth of the flesh), leave such wisdom, given to him as a reasonable being, to be exercised by brutes that perish, to elevate them above his moral nature. No, such was not intended. Though man was made to be the *head* and *king supreme* over his family, yet woman's daily habits are not only imitated by him, but those she has to lead in the pure way. Then as a Scripture injunction, teach them to purge the filth of the flesh by bathing the body, as typical of the cleansing of the soul before it can appear before its Maker, as well as the washing of the body before we appear before our families.

The parlor is not noticed last, from its conducing to no good end. The dining-room and chamber, more strictly suited to comfort and convenience claimed the first. Parlors are expected to be always in readiness to receive guests, where no business will interfere while entertaining them. The present fashion of keeping them dark, even in our small towns, is very good for negligent housekeepers, who give but one dusting a week. My idea is, that children should be accustomed to the bright parlor, decorated with sweet flowers and works of art, from their earliest childhood, and not taught to shun it as they do all dark places. How frequently the mother leads a stray child out in sobs, when receiving morning calls, because it wanted to see the pictures on the walls or curiosities on the *étagère*. If they were allowed the use of the closed room, their manners, when matured, would be free from the awkwardness so many young people display that have not had boarding-school advantages. Daily admit the pure air and light of heaven in the room selected to preserve the features of those whose place you are filling. Let the soft light from the painter's touch of that once bright, sparkling eye, beaming as it were from a guardian angel, inspire *all* to imitate the noble example, with the good name, so far above riches; and the vices ever frowned on by that noble brow, will find no resting place with those whose blood emanates from the same source. Entering the parlor with ease and grace, speaks volumes in the mother's praise. Shying off to a corner shows the parlor was too good for their child's, and only for stranger's enjoyment. Let them learn the use without abuse of everything; that nothing is too good for them you enjoy, and parlor amusements are to refine, and form habits in early life, that will not need a polish as burnished steel, when age entitles them to fill your place, entering a President's mansion or the social hall.